THE BREAKUP
OF YUGOSLAVIA
AND ITS
AFTERMATH

THE BREAKUP OF YUGOSLAVIA AND ITS AFTERMATH

Revised Edition

Carole Rogel

GREENWOOD PRESS
Westport, Connecticut • London

Library of Congress Cataloging-in-Publication Data

Rogel, Carole.
    The breakup of Yugoslavia and its aftermath / Carole Rogel.—Rev. ed.
        p. cm.
    Revised edition of: The breakup of Yugoslavia and the war in Bosnia.
    Includes bibliographical references and index.
    ISBN 0–313–32357–7 (alk. paper)
    1. Yugoslavia—Politics and government—1980–1992. 2. Yugoslavia—Politics and
government—1982–2003. 3. Yugoslav War, 1991–1995. I. Rogel, Carole. Breakup
of Yugoslavia and the war in Bosnia. II. Title. III. Series.
    DR1309.R64 2004
    949.703—dc22   2003061814

British Library Cataloguing in Publication Data is available.

Library of Congress Catalog Card Number: 2003061814
ISBN: 0–313–32357–7

First published in 2004

Greenwood Press, 88 Post Road West, Westport, CT 06881
An imprint of Greenwood Publishing Group, Inc.
www.greenwood.com

Printed in the United States of America

The paper used in this book complies with the
Permanent Paper Standard issued by the National
Information Standards Organization (Z39.48–1984).

10   9   8   7   6   5   4   3   2   1

Copyright Acknowledgments

The author and publisher gratefully acknowledge permission to reprint the following material:

Chapter 6 appears in a slightly different form in *International Journal of Politics, Culture, and Society* 17 (1): 167–82, fall 2003.

Excerpts from "Memorandum of the Serbian Academy of Sciences and Arts," translated by Dennison Rusinow, in Peter Sugar, ed., *Eastern European Nationalism in the Twentieth Century*. Lanham, MD: American University Press, 1995.

Excerpts from *Origins of Catastrophe* by Warren Zimmerman, copyright © 1996 by Warren Zimmerman. Used by permission of Times Books, a division of Random House, Inc.

Excerpts from an interview with Sonja Karadzic in *Duga* (Belgrade), September 12–26, 1992. Translated by Ann Clymer Bigelow.

Excerpts from Bogdan Bogandovic, "Murder of the City," translated by Michael Henry Heim, *The New York Review of Books,* May 27, 1993. Reprinted with permission from *The New York Review of Books*. Copyright © 1993 Nyrev, Inc.

"What the West Must Do in Bosnia" by Margaret Thatcher. Reprinted with the permission of *The Wall Street Journal* © 1993 Dow Jones & Company, Inc. All rights reserved.

Excerpts from Franjo Tudjman, *Nationalism in Contemporary Europe*. Boulder, CO: East European Monographs, 1981.

Tadeusz Mazowiecki, "A Letter of Resignation," *The New York Review of Books,* September 21, 1995. Reprinted with permission from *The New York Review of Books.* Copyright © 1995 Nyrev, Inc.

Excerpts from Francis A. Boyle, *The Bosnian People Charge Genocide*. Amherst, MA: Aletheia Press, 1996.

"Instead of Tears of Joy, Croatian Writer Expresses Fear and Worry About Peace" by Slavenka Drakulic. Reprinted by permission of the author.

Excerpts from Hashim Thaqi, "Kosovo," in William Joseph Buckley, ed., *Kosovo: Contending Voices on Balkan Interventions*. Cambridge, UK: William B. Eerdmans Publishing Company, 2000.

Excerpts from Veton Surroi, "Victims of the Victims," *The New York Review of Books,* October 7, 1999. Reprinted with permission from *The New York Review of Books.* Copyright © 1999 Nyrev, Inc.

Contents

A photographic essay follows page 102.

Preface

Yugoslavia's breakup in 1991 and the wars that followed are recent history for the student of the twentieth century. Some of the tale continues as current events, and it is difficult to foresee a final outcome. Decades may pass before the area stabilizes. Many of the reasons for the original crisis continue to exist; other problems have been created by the war and the Dayton Accords, the peace treaty that ended hostilities in 1995. It is a complicated story, for there are many players, often with names totally foreign to the general reader. There also are seemingly complicated emotional elements that need to be discussed but that are difficult to describe and assess. Yet there are fundamental political motives that are very real, quantifiable, and basic to the Yugoslavia story. I have focused on these political factors as they relate to persons in the former Yugoslavia and to the representatives of the international community who played major roles in the events. I believe that politics is at the root of what happened to Yugoslavia and cannot be underestimated as a primary factor in its collapse.

This book is intended as an introduction to the subject. Chapter 1 gives a brief overview of the history of Yugoslavia and the Yugoslav national groups, who were united for the first time in one state in 1918. It looks at their cultural and political pasts and examines how their integration into one "Yugoslav" nation was not achieved in either the first or the second Yugoslavia. It also points out that Tito's Yugoslavia was the darling of the communist states, the one most likely to succeed, and the one to fall the hardest after communism collapsed in eastern Europe in 1989.

Chapter 2 examines the collapse of Tito's Yugoslavia. It looks at how communism came to the country during World War II, how Yugoslavia under Tito became a dissident communist state—courted by both East and West—and how, in spite of its successes at modernization, the state would succumb to latent weaknesses. It harbored internal political enemies, and, once the Cold War ended, it found itself without international patrons.

Chapter 3 takes a chronological look at the course of the war in Bosnia-Hercegovina, which began in April 1992. It asks why Bosnia became the political battleground between Serbs and Croats, and how Muslims got in the way. It also asks why and in what way the international community responded to the first real war in Europe since World War II, which ended in 1945, nearly a half-century earlier. Chapter 4 looks at the emotional side of the Yugoslavia story. It surveys the ethnic, religious, and cultural aspects of what some have portrayed as deeply rooted divisions among the south Slavic peoples. It also discusses how political interests exploited popular feelings—especially fear—to serve selfish political ends.

Chapter 5 deals with international responses to the war in the former Yugoslavia. It examines how the major powers (mostly Western)—elated following the fall of communism, the end of the Cold War, and the success of the Persian Gulf War (1991)—found themselves in disarray when war broke out in southeastern Europe. It records their bumblings, their lack of resolve and moral principles, and, finally, their realization that asserting themselves as an international body could end their collective embarrassment. The result was the Dayton peace agreement, concluded in November 1995 and formalized in Paris the following month.

Chapter 6 focuses on Kosovo, a province nested within Serbia, a republic of the former Yugoslavia. It was where troubles had erupted already in 1981 between Serbs and Albanians and simmered throughout the 1980s and early 1990s. The chapter describes how Kosovo's Albanians, disappointed that the Dayton peace made no provisions for their wants and rights, turned to the militant Kosovo Liberation Army (KLA) for leadership. It shows how Serb police and army retaliation against the Albanians captured the attention of the Western powers, whose military response in spring 1999 further defined the changing role of the powers, especially the United States, in the postcommunist world.

The book's final chapter considers Yugoslavia's agonizing, drawn-out collapse and the wars that were a part of it. Yet no more than an attempt at explanation is possible with so little distance from the events and with the story still unfolding. The chapter looks at the work of the war crimes tribunal at The Hague, the UN-sponsored body that has only recently begun prosecuting the major suspects, and it tracks the continuing refugee problem. The chapter also gives a brief assessment of the current condition of Yugoslavia's successor states, two of which—Bosnia and Serbia—continue to have serious problems. There, crime and corruption contribute to instability, as does the involvement of the Western powers. Post-Dayton Bosnia, an artificial international creation, is the site of a nation-building experiment of the UN, NATO, and the OSCE; meanwhile, Serbia, continually pressed by the powers to reform and to extradite its war criminals, cannot erase a political culture that continues to see Serbs as victims.

The biographical sketches and the glossary are meant to aid the reader with auxiliary information. The biographies of Yugoslav leaders and Western diplomats give a personal dimension to the overall story. In politics, especially Balkan politics, such personages are often extremely important. The glossary defines terms, acronyms, and organizations that may be unfamiliar to the reader.

Primary documents on the breakup of Yugoslavia and the ensuing conflict are presented in a separate section. Each document is preceded by an introduction. Excerpts from the Memorandum of the Serbian Academy of Sciences and from Franjo Tudjman's book on European nationalism offer representative Serb and Croat nationalist views, respectively, from the 1980s. Warren Zimmermann's last cable reveals the farewell sentiments of the U.S. ambassador before leaving Yugoslavia after its disintegration. Selected UN resolutions are followed by writings of prominent persons responding to the war in Bosnia: Sonja Karadzic, daughter of the Bosnian Serb political leader; Bogdan Bogdanovic, a former Serb mayor of Belgrade; Margaret Thatcher, the former Conservative prime minister of Great Britain; and Tadeusz Mazowiecki, a former Polish prime minister who was appointed to head a human rights commission in Bosnia-Hercegovina. Also included are the testimonies of two Bosnian Muslim women who had suffered rape and torture during the war, and reflections on the Dayton Accords by President Bill Clinton and by Slavenka Drakulic, a Croatian writer. The final two documents are writings of Kosovo Albanians: Hashim Thaci, the head of the KLA, who explains why the organization was founded, and Veton Surroi, a journalist, who appeals to Albanians to honor the rights of their Serbian neighbors.

There are literally hundreds of publications on the former Yugoslavia and the states that have succeeded it, a fact that made selecting the best for this work a difficult task. This book's bibliography includes some works that cover early history and developments leading up to the breakup in 1991. The bulk of the selections, however, deal with the 1990s and with the wars in Bosnia-Hercegovina and in Kosovo. Included are a good number of excellent works by journalists who covered the events, but unlike the first edition of this book, this edition includes a larger selection of the superb books by professional scholars that have been published in the last five or six years and that have started to put the Yugoslav story into a larger context. Time and access to archives will, of course, allow future coverage of the subject to acquire greater depth and historical perspective. The bibliography also has a list of films, documentaries, Web sites, and special materials.

Acknowledgments

I would like to thank Randall M. Miller of St. Joseph's University, series editor of The Greenwood Guides to Historic Events of the Twentieth Century, in which the original edition of this book appeared, for his valuable editorial comments and encouragement on both the first and second editions of this book. Many thanks also to Kevin Ohe, Executive Editor for the Broad Reference Program at Greenwood Press, for his help in directing this project. I would also like to express my gratitude to Stjepan Vlahovich, who read and commented on most of this book in manuscript form, and to Ann Clymer Bigelow, who excerpted and translated the interview with Sonja Karadzic originally published in *Duga*.

Chronology of Events

500s and 600s	Southern Slavs settle in Balkans
Late 1100s	Bosnian state established
1389	Battle of Kosovo Polje
Mid-1400s	Bosnia comes under Ottoman rule
Late 1700s and early 1800s	National cultural and political awakenings
1844	Garasanin's Greater Serbia plan
1878	Congress of Berlin
	Serbia becomes independent
	Montenegro becomes independent
	Bosnia and Hercegovina come under Austro-Hungarian administration
1908	Bosnia and Hercegovina annexed by Austria-Hungary
1914	
June 28	Assassination of Archduke Francis Ferdinand in Sarajevo
July 28	Austria-Hungary declares war on Serbia
August 1	World War I begins

1914–1918	World War I
December 1, 1918	Kingdom of Serbs, Croats, and Slovenes established (Bosnia-Hercegovina and Kosovo included)
June 28, 1921	St. Vitus Day Constitution adopted
January 6, 1929	Royal dictatorship proclaimed; country renamed Yugoslavia
1931	Kingdom of Yugoslavia gets new constitution (Bosnia absorbed into *banovina* structure)
1934	King Alexander assassinated
1939	
August 26	Sporazum (agreement) with Croatia
September 1	World War II begins in Europe
1939–1945	World War II
1941	
April 6	World War II begins in Yugoslavia; Yugoslavia occupied and divided
April 10	Independent Croatia established (Bosnia-Hercegovina part of Croatia)
April–June	Resistance movements organize
November 29, 1943	Provisional government established by Tito's communists
November 29, 1945	FPRY proclaimed by communists (Bosnia-Hercegovina becomes one of six FPRY republics and Kosovo becomes an autonomous region within the Serbian republic)
1948	Yugoslavia and USSR Cominform split
1968–1971	Liberal reform movements
1971	Reform movements suppressed
1974	Decentralizing constitution adopted
1980	Tito dies
1980s	Economic crisis in Yugoslavia; disturbances in Kosovo
1986	Serbian Academy Memorandum

April 1987	Milosevic speaks in Kosovo
September 1987	Milosevic takes over Serbian League of Communists
1989	
March	Kosovo loses autonomy; Serbian control established
	Kosovo leaders proclaim sovereignty; Rugova chosen leader
June	Anniversary of Battle of Kosovo Polje
Autumn	Collapse of communism in eastern Europe
1990	
January	14th and last LCY congress meets
April–December	Multiparty elections in republics
November	Bosnian nationalists win election
December	Milosevic raids Bank of Yugoslavia
1991	
March	Milosevic and Tudjman meet at Karadjordjevo
May 15	Federal presidency rotation blocked by Serbia
June 21	U.S. Secretary of State Baker in Belgrade
June 25	Slovenia and Croatia announce independence
June 27	JNA forces move against Slovenia
July 7	Brioni Agreement
July–December	JNA forces fight in Croatia; major assaults in Vukovar, Dubrovnik
September 25	UN bans weapons shipments to all Yugoslavia
Autumn	EC meetings at The Hague begin
October 8	UN names Vance as mediator
October 24	Bosnian Serbs proclaim separate republic
November 9–10	Bosnian Serbs vote to stay in Yugoslavia
December 20	Yugoslav Prime Minister Markovic resigns
1992	
January 2	UN cease-fire in Croatia; UNPROFOR established

Early January	JNA's General Kadijevic resigns
January 15	EC recognizes Slovenia and Croatia
Late February	EC's Lisbon meeting on Bosnia
February 29–March 1	Bosnian referendum on independence
March 27	Bosnian Serbs declare independent Serbian Republic within Bosnia
April 5	War begins in Bosnia-Hercegovina
April 6	EC recognizes Bosnian independence
April 7	United States recognizes Bosnia, Croatia, and Slovenia
April 27	Serbia and Montenegro become FRY
May 22	Bosnia, Croatia, and Slovenia become UN members
May 30	UN sanctions against FRY
Summer	News of concentration camps, ethnic cleansing
June	NATO approves action in Yugoslavia
August	FRY expelled from UN
September	EC, UN-sponsored Geneva talks begin
October	"No-fly zone" established by UN/EC
November	6,000 UNPROFOR troops sent to Bosnia

1993

January	Vance-Owen Peace Plan announced
	War crimes tribunal established at The Hague
	Clinton administration begins in United States
April	FYROM (Macedonia) becomes UN member
May	Vance-Owen plan rejected
November	War crimes tribunal begins work
December	KLA established

1994

February	Marketplace bombing in Sarajevo
March 1	NATO bombs for first time ever

Early March	Owen-Stoltenberg plan announced
March 18	Washington, D.C., Accords
	Muslim-Croat federation set up in Bosnia-Hercegovina
	Federation signs confederal agreement with Croatia
June	Contact Group peace plan announced

1995

February	Milosevic nixes Contact Group plan
May	Croatian army action in Slavonia
June 2	Serbs shoot down American plane
July 11	"Safe area" Srebrenica taken by Serbs; 7,000 Muslim men killed
August 5	Croatia captures Krajina area; local Serbs flee
August 19	Three U.S. diplomats die in Bosnia
Late August–early September	NATO air attacks on Bosnian Serb objectives
September 8	Warring parties agree to talk peace
September	War crimes tribunal issues first indictments
September 26	Warring parties agree on framework for Bosnian constitution
November 1–21	Dayton (Ohio) peace talks
December 14	Peace agreement signed in Paris
Late December	IFOR (NATO) troops arrive in Bosnia

1996

January 19	IFOR completes separation of combatants and weapons
February 18	UN and FRY sanctions on Bosnian Serbs lifted
March 19	All of Sarajevo comes under Bosnian governmental control
April	KLA begins sporadic activity
June 19	UN ends four-and-one-half-year arms embargo on former Yugoslavia

August 15	Sarajevo airport reopens (closed since 1992)
September 14	Federal elections in all Bosnia (municipal elections postponed); nationalist parties win
October 1	UN ends sanctions on FRY
November 17	Municipal elections in FRY; opposition wins 14 cities; Milosevic refuses to accept outcome; street demonstrations begin
November 30	First war crimes conviction
Mid-December	NATO establishes SFOR (to replace IFOR) for 18 months

1997

January 3	Bosnian government holds first meeting
February 4	Milosevic accedes to opposition parties after 77 days of street protests
September–October	KLA funerals with mass participation

1998 Serb-Albanian tensions in Kosovo increase; UN and NATO try mediation

1999

January	Massacre of Kosovo Albanians in Racak
February 6–23	Rambouillet conference
March 15	Kosovo Albanians sign Rambouillet agreement
March 23	Serbs reject Rambouillet agreement
March 24	NATO war with Yugoslavia begins; lasts 78 days
June 3	Milosevic capitulates
June 10	UN Security Council Resolution 1244; postwar settlement for Kosovo
December	President Tudjman of Croatia dies

2000

January	Social Democrats come to power in Croatia
Summer	Yugoslav consititution altered to allow Milosevic third presidential term
September 24	Presidential election in Yugoslavia; Kostunica wins

September 24– October 5	Demonstrations in Yugoslavia
October 5	Milosevic ousted; Kostunica becomes president

2001

January	Djindjic becomes prime minister of Serbia
March	Milosevic arrested
June	Milosevic sent to The Hague as war criminal
Spring–November	Macedonian tensions; skirmishes with local Albanians
Autumn	SFOR (NATO troops) in Bosnia reduced from 34,000 to 18,000
November	Constitutional settlement for Macedonian Albanians

2002

February 14	War crimes trial of Milosevic begins
September	Macedonian Albanians included in government
Autumn	Croatia's President Mesic testifies against Milosevic at The Hague
September–December	Presidential elections in Serbia and Montenegro invalidated
November	Slovenia invited to join NATO and EU

2003

January	Speakers of parliament in Serbia and Montenegro become acting presidents
March	Serbian Prime Minister Djindjic assassinated
February	Yugoslavia ceases to exist; new state named Serbia and Montenegro replaces it
March	Announcement that EU will take over administration of Bosnia in 2004
April	EU troops replace NATO in Macedonia

THE BREAKUP
OF YUGOSLAVIA
AND ITS
AFTERMATH

1

The Breakup and the War: A Historical Overview

There was no Yugoslavia before the end of 1918. The territory of that future state was ruled or dominated for centuries either by the Habsburgs or by the Ottoman Turks. In the thirteenth century the Habsburg dynasty started assembling an empire in the northern and western regions of what would become Yugoslavia, while the Ottomans began conquering the southern and eastern portions in the fourteenth century. Expansionist ambitions moved them gradually toward each other. By the early 1500s the two empires became locked in military conflict over this Balkan land in wars that would continue off and on through the nineteenth century. The Ottomans dominated the area in the early centuries. In the 1500s and 1600s their empire extended to the very boundaries of the Habsburg-ruled Holy Roman Empire, and on several occasions Ottoman forces even reached the outskirts of the Habsburg capital, Vienna. The Habsburgs rebounded in the later centuries after having consolidated power at home by defeating rebellious feudal nobles and Protestant reformers; they then sent their armies southward to reconquer lost territories and to liberate others from Turkish rule.

In the 1700s and 1800s Habsburg power reasserted itself in the region, while the Ottoman armies and state suffered defeat and internal dissolution. The declining Ottoman state and the Habsburg Empire (known as

Austria-Hungary after 1867) would both collapse during World War I; that conflict began in 1914 in the area that would become Yugoslavia and was partially caused by a quarrel over who should control Bosnia.

In the late eighteenth century and the early nineteenth century, new ideas that had developed in the western European Enlightenment began penetrating the region of the future Yugoslavia. The new intellectual climate led to the development of national consciousness among the inhabitants. The peoples of the area, whether they lived in the Habsburg Empire or the Ottoman, began to have a sense of belonging to national cultural entities. Linguists, historians, and writers—many of them members of the clergy or of a newly developing intelligentsia—were in the forefront of defining each of the groups. Whereas before this time most Europeans identified themselves primarily in terms of religious affiliation—which made sense, since most lived in multinational empires—now people started thinking of themselves as belonging to national groups. They became Serbs or Croats or Slovenes; yet others identified themselves as Montenegrin, Bosnian, or Macedonian. Not all identities were completely formulated before World War I; some refining would continue well into the twentieth century. But in general the region was populated primarily by southern Slavs, or Yugoslavs (*yugo* = southern), of which there were several branches.

The Serbs of Vojvodina, the Croats, and the Slovenes developed national consciousnesses ahead of the others, partly because they lived in the more advanced Habsburg lands and also because the Enlightenment, and later Romanticism (which gave national idealism a tremendous boost), moved from west to east across Europe. The Serbs and the Croats acknowledged that each belonged to separate cultures, but by the mid-1830s they adopted a common literary language, Serbo-Croatian, based on a dialect of Hercegovina. It would be written in Cyrillic by the Serbs, who had gotten their religion and alphabet from the East, and in the Latin alphabet by the Croats, who had been Christianized from the West. In the 1830s and 1840s the Slovenes, too, established their own national identity with a separate language also written in the Latin script. The Montenegrins and Bosnians adopted Serbo-Croatian as their literary medium, but the Slavic Macedonians, whose language is closely related to Bulgarian, moved gradually toward establishing their own written language. The Slavic Macedonian nationality and language (with a Cyrillic orthography), however, were not officially recognized until after World War II, when the communists came to power in Yugoslavia.

As in western Europe, national cultural awareness soon generated national political programs. Like the Italians and the Germans, whose cultural awakenings in the first half of the nineteenth century were followed by military campaigns to unify Italy and Germany—accomplished in 1860 and 1871, respectively—the southern Slavs also forged ahead with political goals. Those who lived in the Ottoman state had an advantage. The empire was declining. Contemporaries even called it the sick man of Europe. Russia, France (in the mid-nineteenth century), and later Austria-Hungary did what they could to destroy it, which included assisting Balkan subjects of the Ottoman sultan in rebellions against him. Serbia, whose grand medieval state had long ceased to exist, achieved semiautonomy early in the nineteenth century (1815) after a Russo-Turkish war; after subsequent regional wars it either added to its territory or gained greater freedom. In the last third of the century, Serbia's cause was strongly promoted by imperial Russia and the Pan-Slavs, Russian backers of Slavic unity and Russian expansion into the Balkans who greatly influenced Russian foreign policy.

In 1878 both Serbia and Montenegro (the latter a semiautonomous theocratic state headed by a prince bishop from 1515 to 1851, when it was

Political Boundaries in the Balkans following the Congress of Berlin (1878). From *Bosnia and Hercegovina* by Robert J. Donia and John V. A. Fine, Jr., Copyright © 1994 by Columbia University Press. Reprinted by permission of the publisher.

secularized and became a hereditary principality ruled by the Petrovic dynasty) were granted official international recognition by the Treaty of Berlin. Once an independent Serbia (ruled alternately by two rival political dynasties, the Karadjordjevic and the Obrenovic) was established, the goal was to include all Serbs within that state, or, at least initially, all Serbs who were or had been Ottoman subjects. The plan for a Greater Serbia had its roots in one drawn up in 1844 by Ilija Garasanin, a liberal constitutionalist, government minister, and adviser to Serbian princes. His plan also had included Vojvodina, which was in southern Hungary and under Habsburg control. Serb statesmen in the later nineteenth century and the early twentieth, however, could not openly risk designs on Vojvodina given Serbia's then subordinate, soon-to-be hostile, relationship with the Austro-Hungarian great power. Yet in the decade before World War I Serbia took ever bolder stances with respect to Austria, and in this it was supported by the patron of Orthodox Slavs, Russia.

The Habsburg South Slavs also developed political agendas, first expressed in the 1840s, particularly during the revolutions of 1848. The Slovenes (who had never had a state) first proposed their United Slovenia program that year, calling unsuccessfully for the administrative unification of all ethnically Slovene lands and for the use of the Slovene language in schools and administration. The Croats, who had had a state in medieval times and had joined with Hungary (1102) and later Austria (1527) when dynasties died out, maintained that their state still existed legally (constitutionally). They worked for official acknowledgment of that status. To the Croats' dismay, their triune kingdom (Croatia, Slavonia, Dalmatia) remained under the tight control of Vienna between 1815 and 1867, after which, when a political compromise between Vienna and Budapest created the dual monarchy Austria-Hungary, most of the Croats came under even tighter rein from Budapest.

The most the Habsburg southern Slavs could dare under such circumstances was to press for cultural advances and limited political autonomy within Austria-Hungary. In some cases, in hopes of gaining greater leverage in the empire, they tried to cooperate with one another. This is how some Yugoslav political programs were born. The best known is the one called *trialism,* which was a plan to unite all southern Slavs of the empire (after 1908 it included Bosnia-Hercegovina) in a separate and third component of the Habsburg state. (Most southern Slavs in that state remained loyal to it and are sometimes known as Austroslavs.) Trialism was interpreted in various ways, but in general it was believed (falsely) that Archduke Francis Ferdinand, the heir to the Habsburg throne, was sympathetic to the basic idea. Some would even contend that it was because he was thought to favor autonomy for the Yugoslavs of Austria-Hungary that he was assassinated by a Bosnian Serb who passionately believed that all Serbs should live in Serbia. The killing took place in Sarajevo on June 28, 1914.

World War I determined what happened to the southern Slavs. It began in the summer of 1914, one month after the Habsburg archduke and archduchess were assassinated by a Bosnian Serb, Gavrilo Princip, who belonged to a secret society whose terrorism was supported and financed by the government of Serbia. Although this could not be proven at the time, Austria-Hungary, which had pursued an expansionist policy in the Balkans after 1878, when it was awarded the administration of Ottoman Bosnia-Hercegovina (annexed in 1908), blamed the Kingdom of Serbia for the archduke's death. Austria demanded immediate response to an ultimatum that the Serbs basically complied with, even though it infringed upon Serbian sovereignty. Without waiting for a reply, Austria initiated mobilization against the small Balkan state, which it expected to subdue with little difficulty. War was declared against Serbia on July 28.

The war that began in the Balkans very quickly became a general European war for reasons only peripherally related to Serbia. European great power rivalries had been building for decades. Among the most important was the Austrian-Russian one over control of the Balkans, where the Ottoman state was dying. By 1914 the powers had sorted themselves into two opposing camps. Open and secret alliances stood behind the groupings. Germany was allied with Austria-Hungary; Britain and France backed Russia. When Austria attacked little Serbia, alliance commitments brought Russia to Serbia's defense, Germany to Austria's defense, and Britain and France to Russia's defense. Most believed that war was inevitable and that it would be short and reinvigorating for Europe (Social Darwinist thinking had persuaded many that the fittest proved their abilities in business and on the battlefield; most who thought that way also believed that the theory would favor their side). What came to be known as World War I lasted four years and was the most devastating conflict Europe had ever experienced. In addition to the staggering economic and social upheaval of total war was the political consequence: the collapse of Europe's four empires. Austria-Hungary and the Ottoman Empire completely disappeared, while Germany and Russia (the latter a member of the winning alliance, but disabled by a communist revolution) lost territory and acquired new forms of government. In the center of Europe, from the Baltic Sea to the Black and Adriatic seas, emerged a string of small independent national states. Yugoslavia was among them.

The map of the new Europe was drawn up in Paris in 1919 at a peace conference dominated by the Big Four powers: Britain, France, Italy (which had joined the Entente alliance in 1915), and the United States (which had entered the war on the Entente side in 1917). Woodrow Wilson, the U.S. president whose Fourteen Points served as a guideline for the settlement, championed the principle of national self-determination and personally helped mark out the boundaries of Yugoslavia. Influenced by advisers and experts, some of them southern Slavs who believed in Yugoslav unity, the peacemakers packaged Serbs, Croats, and Slovenes into one national state. There were, however, some important territorial omissions. Where Italy's interests conflicted with the principle of southern Slav self-determination, Italian claims generally prevailed. (In the 1915 Treaty of London the British and French had promised Italy territorial compensation in return for joining the Entente.) Hence Trieste, the Istrian peninsula, and islands and coastal regions along the northeastern Adriatic were incorporated into Italy in spite of their predominantly Slovene and Croat populations.

The first Yugoslavia began life precariously. The Kingdom of Serbs, Croats, and Slovenes announced its existence on December 1, 1918. The Paris Peace Conference and subsequent internationally approved adjustments legalized the boundaries. Croats and Slovenes resisted the new arrangement, yet they had little choice but to go along. (The Entente powers had refused to recognize the Austrian South Slavs' State of Slovenes, Croats, and Serbs, which had been proclaimed in October 1918.) The Habsburg South Slavs were tainted by having fought for Austria, although there had been significant wartime defections to the Serbian side. Essentially, they came to the new state with little bargaining leverage. On the other hand, Serbia, with a state of its own before the war, had been cast as the southern Slav Piedmont (the Italian state that had enabled the unification of Italy in 1860). Also, Serbia was among the war's victors and to a certain extent regarded the new state as an enlargement of Serbia, a fortuitous fulfillment of the Greater Serbia idea. Serbs regarded the addition of the former Habsburg lands as a reward for Serbia's wartime sacrifices. Thereafter Serbia cherished its image as an Entente power and evoked it regularly in the 1990s, when war raged in the former Yugoslavia.

The key issue for the Yugoslavs between the two world wars was how the state should be run. The Croats, the Slovenes, and the Bosnian Muslims, or at least their leading political parties, favored a federal arrangement because it could guarantee them some autonomy. The Serbs, because they were the largest and most powerful group (there were 6 million Serbs, 3.5 million Croats, and 1.1 million Slovenes), naturally preferred a strong central power. Unitarism thus became the cornerstone of the 1921 constitution. The document, based on the Serbian constitution of 1903, established a parliamentary monarchy under the rule of the Karadjordjevic dynasty and centered in the Serbian capital, Belgrade. This assured Serb and Orthodox dominance in the new state, which now included the former Habsburg southern Slav lands. The constitution was called the St. Vitus Day Constitution because it was proclaimed on June 28, a day of particular significance to the Serbs (on that day in 1389 Serbs had been beaten by the Turks at Kosovo Polje [Blackbird Field], initiating 500 years of Ottoman domination; on St. Vitus Day in 1914 Gavrilo Princip shot Francis Ferdinand in order to prevent another foreign power, Austria, from ruling over the Serbs). Among those boycotting the vote on the constitution were the communists, the Slovene People's Party, and the Croat Peasant Party. The Slovenes eventually worked with the Serbs in return for some local autonomy and government appointments, as did the Bosnian Muslims, who voted in favor of the new constitution with the understanding that there would be minimal land reform in Bosnia. The Muslims also acquired monopoly control of the state's railroads. The Croat Peasant Party, however, was not compliant. It was the Croats' most powerful political organization and was headed by Stjepan Radic, who favored a republican form of government and publicly opposed the creation of a Kingdom of Serbs, Croats, and Slovenes when it was announced in 1918. Radic called instead for an independent Croatia. The country was thus off to an inauspicious beginning.

The problems facing the new state were enormous. Its task would be no less than to integrate into a viable state diverse social, religious, cultural, language, and ethnic groups who before 1914 had lived in eight different states. The new state's most serious problems, however, were economic. Its resources, including human ones, had been devastated by four years of war (six years, if one counts the two Balkan wars fought in the southern regions of the new kingdom in 1912 and 1913). The economy was in general very backward. Industry existed primarily in the former Habsburg lands, particularly in Slovenia, but it was now cut off from former markets and not yet integrated into the new political unit. Agriculture was primitive: peasant plots were too small and were regularly subdivided due to population pressures; the land was uneconomically managed (cooperatives were resisted except in the former Austrian lands); mechanization was generally unheard of, as was agricultural education; and transportation infrastructure, where not virtually nonexistent, was obsolete because it linked parts of the new kingdom with former political units now in other—usually unfriendly—states. The depression of the 1930s compounded the economic woes. Rural poverty was widespread, money went out of circulation, and peasants resorted to barter. Taxes could not be collected.

Between 1921 and 1929, when a royal dictatorship was proclaimed, the kingdom had 24 governments. Most failed to deal with the state's dire problems and ended in turbulence or political deadlock. Major obstruction came from non-Serb political opponents, particularly the Croats, the country's second-largest ethnic group. In 1928 the Croat leader Radic was shot in parliament by a Serb radical, and soon thereafter King Alexander took control. Parliament was disbanded. The country was renamed the Kingdom of Yugoslavia (intended to deemphasize the state's national components) and divided into nine administrative units (six with Serb majorities) named after rivers and the seacoast. In 1931 a new constitution permitted parliament to reconvene, but only "Yugoslav" parties were allowed to offer candidates. Political extremism of the left and the right flourished underground. The rightist Croat Ustasha movement was the most dangerous, demonstrated by its successful collaboration with Italian, Hungarian, and Bulgarian (Macedonian) rightists in assassinating King Alexander when he was on a state visit to France in 1934.

The Croat resistance to Belgrade's centralism continued and needed to be dealt with if Yugoslavia were to survive. Alexander was succeeded by his son Peter, who was a minor when he became king and thus ruled through an appointed regency. It, together with Serb government officials, managed the Croat issue clumsily. One idea that was discussed for several years was a Concordat, an agreement with Rome that would grant the church certain privileges in the kingdom, which it was hoped would please the Roman Catholic Croats. It only made the Croats suspicious and the Orthodox Serbs furious (the Orthodox patriarch died during the debates, causing Serbs to suspect foul play), so the matter was dropped in 1937. With Croat-Serb tensions mounting (while Hitler and Mussolini pursued their imperialistic acquisitions on Yugoslavia's periphery), the Serb prime minister, Dragisa Cvetkovic, concluded a pact known as the Sporazum (agreement) with Croat Peasant Party leader Ivan Macek on August 26, 1939. Croatia was given its own province (*banovina*) within Yugoslavia. It was large, encompassing 27 percent of the area of Yugoslavia and 29 percent of its population and included parts of Bosnia-Hercegovina. A Croat was made head of its autonomous parliament (*sabor*), and Macek was given the vice premiership of Yugoslavia. It was Belgrade's way of accommodating the moderate Croats. In the end it did not work. Other Yugoslavs demanded similar agreements, it did not weaken the separatist fascistic Croat Ustasha movement, and ultimately the Croats did not support the state when World War II began there in 1941.

Although World War II began in Europe with the invasion of Poland on September 1, 1939, the war came to Yugoslavia only in the spring of 1941. By then Yugoslavia was surrounded by Italian- or German-controlled territories (some, like Albania and Austria, had been annexed; others, like Bulgaria, Hungary, and Romania, had signed agreements with one or both of the Axis powers). On March 25, 1941, the Germans tried to impose a Tripartite Pact on Yugoslavia. The government that accepted the agreement was ousted by air force officers who preferred war to a pact with Germany. The coup leaders installed Peter Karadjordjevic, not yet 18, as king. War began within days, and the royal government fled into exile. Each of Yugoslavia's neighbors took a share of the country, generally claiming ethnic rights to the area they annexed. In addition, Montenegro became an Italian protectorate, the nucleus of Serbia became a German protectorate, and Croatia, enlarged from its Sporazum boundaries to include most of Bosnia-Hercegovina, became an independent state. In reality it was a puppet satellite of Italy and Germany, headed by the Croat Ustasha (fascist) leader Ante Pavelic. The first Yugoslavia, which had become an independent European state in 1918, had ceased to exist after only 23 years.

The story of the war years (1941–1945) is unbelievably complex. Each town and village, each family has a tale of heartrending tribulation to tell, for the Yugoslav lands experienced some of the worst of the conflict. Some would even contend that what happened in Yugoslavia determined the fate of Germany's drive to dominate Europe and conquer Russia (the Soviet Union), for Germans had no end of trouble in Yugoslavia, where they were compelled to maintain many divisions rather than use them in a war on the eastern front. Resistance to the occupiers of Yugoslavia developed everywhere, but the two major movements were led by Colonel Draza Mihailovic and by Tito (Josip Broz). Mihailovic was an officer in the royal military whose followers, called Chetniks, went to the hills to organize opposition after Yugoslavia fell; Mihailovic, a Serb, was supported by the royal government in exile in London and fought for the reestablishment of the prewar regime. Tito (half Croat, half Slovene), a communist who had been trained in the Soviet Union, coordinated a Partisan resistance whose plans for a postwar Yugoslavia included elimination of the Serb-dominated monarchy and the establishment of a federation (of nations) and of communism (this goal was not stressed in the early stages of the resistance). Mihailovic and Tito, a genuinely popular figure who was affectionately known as "the old man," cooperated initially but soon parted ways. They and their followers began fighting each other, and, in the case of Mihailovic, who was executed for collaboration after the war, there was cooperation with the occupiers.

By 1942 civil war complicated the Yugoslav story. Partisans, for example, fought Italians and Germans, but also Croat Ustasha and Serb fascists (pro-German supporters of Dimitrije Ljotic who supported the Germans as long as the Axis powers were winning) as well as Mihailovic's Chetniks. They also fought other local opponents of a postwar communist regime. Among these were Albanian and Bosnian Muslim units organized by the Germans. (Muslim collaborators were often middle class or from Hercegovina.) National groups fought one another, members of the same group fought among themselves, and even members of the same family often found themselves on opposing sides. War casualties were enormous; 6.4 percent of the prewar population perished. Some of the worst fratricidal fighting took place in puppet Croatia, which included much of Bosnia-Hercegovina. Here, in concentration camps like Jasenovac (a place evoked regularly by Serbs in the 1990s), the Croats implemented ethnic purification policies against Jews, Gypsies, and especially Serbs. The Serbs were either deported to the Serb protectorate, exterminated, or forcibly converted to Catholicism. About 500,000 Serbs were killed. If the 1992–1995 war in Bosnia has historic roots, it is in this World War II period of political, ethnic, and religious brutality.

In the end Tito's communist-led Partisan forces prevailed. They stressed brotherhood and unity and found broad support among those who opposed the return of the monarchy. They fought the occupiers even while the Western allies only planned retaliation—which did not come until June 6, 1944 (D-Day)—and when the war was over they could claim they had successfully liberated the country from foreign rule. That the Partisans, not Mihailovic, got Allied supplies, advisers, and support also helped the communists. By 1942 the Partisans established administrative units in "liberated" Yugoslav territories, which sent delegates to a national representative assembly after it was created near the end of 1943. With this development the "revolution" aspect of Tito's operation was well under way. Thereafter, Tito would rule with a strong hand, ever mindful of balancing the country's political and national elements. In November 1945, with the war over, the communists proclaimed the establishment of the Federal People's Republic, and with that a second Yugoslavia came into being.

The new Yugoslavia was a federation of six republics—Serbia, Croatia, Slovenia, Montenegro, Macedonia, and Bosnia-Hercegovina—and two autonomous units—Kosovo and Vojvodina (both within Serbia). Each of the republics was a constitutionally recognized national unit, with the exception of Bosnia-Hercegovina. The latter, a kind of Yugoslavia in miniature with a very mixed national and religious composition, was given republic status because it had been so important to the Partisan resistance against the foreign occupiers and also in the fight against Croat Ustasha and Ser-

The Republics and Autonomous Regions of Socialist Yugoslavia (1945–1991). From *Bosnia and Hercegovina* by Robert J. Donia and John V. A. Fine, Jr., Copyright © 1994 by Columbia University Press. Reprinted by permission of the publisher.

bian Chetniks. The most intense struggle of the war had taken place there, and many Bosnians had fought committedly for a new kind of Yugoslavia. Tito needed this kind of commitment, for both Croats and Serbs had failed the first Yugoslavia (Croats supported separatism, while the Serbs' regime fled and Mihailovic's forces collaborated with the occupiers). The new government thus bet a good deal on this Bosnian-Hercegovinian republic and even made it the basis of its defense system and established the bulk of Yugoslavia's munitions industry there.

Tito's Yugoslavia, like most of the other small states created in the middle of Europe after World War II, became a people's republic and a satellite of the USSR. Under the supervision of the Cominform, a communist international organization controlled by Joseph Stalin, the head of the USSR, a Soviet model of development was introduced. That meant collectivization of agriculture, nationalization of industry, and centralized management of all economic development. Rapid industrialization (primarily heavy industry) was stressed for this essentially backward agrarian country. Institutions and social groups considered to be opposed to such developments were eliminated or persecuted. Among these were monarchists, wartime collaborators, the middle class (Marx's bourgeoisie), the church, and farmer-peasants who resisted collectivization. To generate enthusiasm for the new communist society being built by the workers (proletariat)—the favored class—a Communist Party propaganda agency, Agitprop, was established. The goals of the new regime were promoted in the arts, in education, in the media, and in cultural and sports organizations. The Yugoslav communist regime embraced the Soviet model with exceptional zeal and tried to set an example for the other Soviet bloc countries.

Neither the bloc satellites, where communist regimes were imposed by the USSR, nor Stalin appreciated the Yugoslavs' attitude. Stalin was especially worried that he could not control Yugoslavia and its genuinely popular leader. By 1948 a confrontation between Stalin and Tito, which with hindsight the Yugoslavs traced back to wartime disagreements, resulted in Yugoslavia's expulsion from the Cominform. Once outside the Soviet bloc, Yugoslavia began developing its own brand of socialism, sometimes known as Titoism. Its two main features were workers' self-management (through workers' councils) and nonalignment in the international community. The latter, nonalignment, which grew out of Yugoslavia's sense of isolation, attracted many nondeveloped states worldwide that rejected the colonialism of both West and East. By the early 1960s Tito had become leader of the Third World countries. He also gained the attention of the West, which in 1950 began financially supporting Yugoslavia (as well as supplying it with arms), for this former ex-Soviet bloc state became useful to the West as a pawn in the Cold War. When the Cold War ended in 1989, Yugoslavia lost its relevance, and in a way that also explains why Yugoslavia's breakup in 1991 deteriorated into a bloodbath. It was no longer of vital interest to the West to maintain stability there.

Yugoslavia was not like other communist states. After the break with the Soviet Union in 1948, it pursued its own course of economic development. There was constant tinkering with the economic and the governmental apparatus, punctuated each decade with a new constitution to legalize the adjustments of the previous years. Administrative structures devised for the self-management system were intricate and often bizarre—difficult to explain even to the Yugoslavs. But on the surface Yugoslavia appeared to be a post–World War II success story. By the late fifties the country was visibly modernizing and its population was living relatively well (as compared with the Soviet bloc countries) and with considerable harmony among former warring groups. The borders were open, allowing Yugoslavs to travel, shop, work (usually as guest workers in northern Europe, of whom there were 1 million by the end of the sixties), and study abroad. Consumer goods became quite plentiful, and the measure of the arts was no longer socialist realism. Power in Yugoslavia, however, remained in the hands of the Communist Party, or the League of Communists, as it was renamed in 1952. The old guard in the party, together with Yugoslavia's managers and bureaucrats (a "new class" that emerged in communist society, something a leading Yugoslav critic, Milovan Djilas, faulted both the Russian and Yugoslav communists for), was able to maintain fairly tight control. In the mid-1960s, however, after yet another round of economic reforms and another constitution (1963), there was a good deal of anxiety in the country regarding the state's economic viability, and it led to considerable turmoil, including upheaval within the party.

The reformism of the 1960s was similar to what was then happening in Czechoslovakia, where the movement was known as socialism with a human face. Yugoslav reformists wanted to liberalize the economic system (beyond market socialism, which had been introduced in the early sixties) and to decentralize economic planning to give greater control to the six republics. The reformers also frequently argued for greater intellectual freedom. The national factor became very important in this decade, for the liberals were often "nationalists" (even within the party) who wanted greater economic and political autonomy for Slovenia, or Croatia, or Bosnia-Hercegovina. The Croats at this time also began to stress the uniqueness of Croatian culture and language (as distinguished from Serbo-Croatian, which they now considered an artificial creation). Between 1968 and 1971 Croatia became a hotbed of opposition in the country. Led by its reformist communists, it was in virtual revolt against Belgrade and the old guard of the party. For a time it was not clear how things would turn out, because Tito himself seemed to be wavering over which course to pursue. In the end he settled on the side of the old guard. Liberals and reformists were ousted, and "national" communism was suppressed. Hardliners returned to power. Together with the secret police and the army, Belgrade's dominance was reinforced.

Tito continued to dominate Yugoslavia until his death in 1980 (the 1974 constitution made him president for life). He had ruled for 35 years, always with an eye to balancing the many elements (political, ethnic, social) that comprised his diverse state. In the short run he succeeded. Yugoslavia did not disintegrate when he died, as many had predicted. But latent weaknesses—national and political issues left unresolved after the 1971 repression—coupled with major economic troubles and the collapse of communism in eastern Europe in the 1980s would cause Yugoslavia to implode. Tito's successors were less committed than he was to preserving Yugoslav unity; some even plotted the state's dismemberment. Tito in a way was the country's last unifying force; for many he was the glue that had held Yugoslavia together until 1980.

2

The Collapse of Tito's Yugoslavia

Tito's death in 1980 marked the end of an era. At the time no one could even have imagined the dramatic changes that would be in store for Yugoslavia in the next decade. Forces primarily external to the country would help undo Tito's state. Some, like the dangers of mounting foreign debt, could be foreseen. But others, such as the devastating effect of the worldwide rise in oil prices, could not. For a country like Yugoslavia, which was greatly dependent on imported fuel paid for in hard currency, the oil price crisis alone could have resulted in financial ruin. Attempts to deal with Yugoslavia's economic woes in the 1980s produced "stagflation" and a marked drop in the standard of living. Steadily rising inflation rates charted the country's economic ill health. By 1987 the rate had reached 200 percent per year; by August 1989 it was nearly 200 percent per month.

The 1980s also brought amazing changes to Europe's communist bloc. Innovations in the USSR began with Mikhail Gorbachev, who became party head in 1985 and soon embarked upon a policy of *glasnost* (openness) and reform intent on restructuring (*perestroika*) the Soviet economy. He was widely hailed, particularly by Western statesmen and women (e.g., Prime Minister Margaret Thatcher of Great Britain) and by Western investors. For *perestroika* to work Gorbachev needed to rid Russia of institutions and obligations that financially strained the country. Hence the east

European satellite states, long a burden on the Soviet economy, were urged to restructure as well. Throughout the decade Poland's reformers (Solidarity) had pressed for change with little success; by 1988 Gorbachev seemed to give them his blessing. In the last half of 1989, one by one, the other Soviet bloc countries—East Germany, Hungary, Bulgaria, Czechoslovakia, and Romania—went beyond restructuring, declaring themselves free of communism and of the USSR as well. It was surely not what Gorbachev had intended, yet it happened nevertheless. So it was that the Cold War ended without a bang, a surprise to virtually everyone.

If 1989 was the year of the anticommunist revolutions, 1992 was the year all of Europe eagerly anticipated. That year the European Community was to become the European Union (EU), fulfilling a dream first articulated after World War II by the Frenchman Jean Monnet. In 1992 twelve states would be joined in a customs union that would soon have a common currency; together they would represent a formidable world economic power. Some predicted that those living in the EU countries would reap untold economic benefits. By the late 1980s a 12-star circle, the symbol of European economic unity, already served as an inspiration for better things to come. For the east Europeans, the lure of that symbol helps account for some of the frenzy that accompanied the abandonment of communism and the series of "divorces" from the Soviet Union in 1989. The east Europeans wanted passionately to be a part of the future European Union. They longed for the prosperity it promised, and they wanted to be recognized as true Europeans, a dignity they felt they had been cheated of after World War II.

Yugoslavs also dreamed of prosperity and of being part of the new Europe, but Yugoslavia, which in 1948 had been the first to leave the Soviet bloc, faltered badly in the 1980s. While the bloc countries were breaking with the Soviet Union and renouncing communism, the Yugoslavs were quarreling bitterly over how the country should proceed. The issue of centralism versus federalism, so poisonous in the years between the world wars, was back with a vengeance. With Tito gone, there was no one strong enough to stand for the whole; meanwhile, the republican leaders—political talent had shifted to the republics during the 1970s—pushed harder than ever to assert themselves. This is how nationalism reemerged in Yugoslavia and ultimately helped tear the country apart. Two republics, Serbia and Slovenia, stood at the center of the confrontation over Yugoslavia's future. In the end, their respective positions turned out to be irreconcilable.

The Greater Serbia idea was revived in the 1980s. Its essence was incorporated into a 74-page Serbian Academy of Sciences Memorandum made public in 1986 that became a rallying point for Serb nationalists. The memorandum maintained that Serbia's economic woes were the result of a deliberate policy, pursued after 1945 by Tito (a Croat/Slovene) and his chief adviser, Edvard Kardelj (a Slovene), to keep the Serbs divided and underdeveloped economically. The academy's document gave the situation in Kosovo special attention. In 1974 Kosovo and Vojvodina, autonomous provinces within Serbia after World War II, had been granted a status equal with that of Yugoslavia's six republics by a new constitution. The new status had moved them a step away from Serbian control. But Kosovo was for the Serbs sacred territory, for it was here, at Kosovo Polje (Blackbird Field), that Serbs were defeated and subjugated by the Turks in 1389. It had been the heart of their medieval state, and Serbs believed that it must forever be part of Serbia, even though its population by the mid-1980s was 90 percent Albanian. In April 1981 there was a mass riot in Kosovo, and the province, where ethnic tensions between Serbs and Albanians had been brewing for a decade, became a major trouble spot.

Since the late 1960s Serbs had feared they were losing control of Kosovo. Some believed that Kosovo's Albanians would secede in order to join their conationals in the independent neighboring state of Albania. (About one-third of all Albanians lived in Kosovo.) Most Albanians of Kosovo were probably not eager to join the isolated, backward Albanian state, whose only ally was China. However, Kosovo Albanians, particularly the growing town and student population, were anxious for autonomy and generally favored a separate republic for themselves. By the 1980s their political demonstrations had begun turning into riots, and the police (mostly Serbs) and the military (generally from the northern republics) were installed permanently to keep Albanian political movements in check. In the late 1970s and the 1980s considerable numbers of Serbs and Montenegrins left Kosovo; their exodus was portrayed in the Serbian media as a flight for life from Albanian terror and oppression. The Kosovo Albanians, for their part, felt that they were living in a police state. By the late 1980s, outsiders were characterizing Serbian treatment of Kosovo Albanians as apartheid.

Slobodan Milosevic, a virtually unknown communist bureaucrat, used the Kosovo situation to capture control of the Serbian Communist Party in September 1987. Earlier that year he had gone to Kosovo Polje to discuss Serb complaints about Albanian oppression. Local Serb party agitators provoked demonstrations that resulted in the expected police response. Milosevic was rushed to the scene and made an impassioned speech about how Serbs must not submit to Albanian pressures, must not leave their historic homeland. "No one should dare to beat you," he shouted, evoking wild cheers from the crowd. Belgrade's Serbian media featured the event later that day. The result was an outpouring of Serb national pride, and later that year Milosevic and the "nationalists" took control of the Serbian republic's Communist Party. Taking advantage of the momentum, Milosevic soon limited the autonomy of Kosovo and Vojvodina in favor of Serbia by pushing constitutional amendments through the provincial assemblies, which had been packed with Milosevic cronies. Thereafter Milosevic would control the two assemblies and, more important, the votes of Kosovo and Vojvodina in federal government bodies. Serbian nationalism continued to swell, and Milosevic continued to gain power and popularity. On June 28, 1989, the 600th anniversary of the Battle of Kosovo Polje, 1 million Serbs gathered to hear the communist leader evoke romantic myths about Serbia's past. Non-Serbs in Yugoslavia began to worry about where all this would lead.

Slovenia, which worried that Great Serbism would capture the federal government apparatus, became the chief adversary of Serbian nationalism. Slovenes feared both cultural extinction and political domination. First, in 1987, Slovene intellectuals countered the Serbian Academy memorandum with *Nova Revija 57,* a volume subtitled *Contributions to a Slovene National Program.* In the summer of 1988, when four Slovenes charged with betraying state military secrets were tried in the Slovene capital, Ljubljana, in Serbo-Croatian rather than in Slovene, the Slovenes organized mass demonstrations. They were particularly riled when they learned that the secret military documents outlined a crackdown against Slovene "separatists." Slovenes began to draw parallels between themselves and the Kosovo Albanians. More and more it appeared to them that the two Belgrades (capital of Serbia and capital of Yugoslavia) were in cahoots. Slovenes began strongly promoting human rights and became a main defender of the Albanians. Milosevic, unable to dissuade the Slovenes from their stance on Kosovo, initiated an economic blockade against Slovene products in late 1989. Earlier that year, in May, Slovene intellectuals had charted their future course. They issued a declaration promoting sovereignty for Slovenia and establishment of democracy, to be grounded in political pluralism and based on human rights and freedoms.

Slovene political leaders, now reformers who were increasingly swept up by the national program, took matters to the Yugoslav communist congress in Belgrade in January 1990. The Serb-Slovene confrontation was played out there, with Milosevic's people leading a relentless opposition to Slovene proposals for party reform. The Slovenes, led by their president, Milan Kucan, in the end walked out of the meeting; the Croat delegation (which included Croatian Serbs), followed, to Milosevic's dismay; and thus the League of Communists of Yugoslavia collapsed forever. The party as well as the country was splintering along republic lines. Slovenia and Croatia, the wealthy northern republics, went ahead with planned multi-party elections announced for the spring. The other republics would also need to decide whether to opt for political pluralism or continue with communist rule. A larger issue was also looming: should republics or national groups be the base for sovereignty in Yugoslavia? In the case of the Slovenes, where the national and republican boundaries were essentially the same, the answer was simple: sovereignty for the republic. For the Serbs, who lived in Serbia, Montenegro, Croatia (12 percent Serb), and Bosnia-Hercegovina (31 percent Serb), the answer was not easy. Milosevic chose both: Serb control of Serbia, including Kosovo (90 percent Albanian) and Vojvodina (44 percent non-Serb, of which about 20 percent were Hungarian), and also Serbian national self-determination for Serbs outside Serbia. This meant a redrawing of republican boundaries so that all Serbs could live in Serbia. Given the mixed national composition of some areas of Yugoslavia—particularly Bosnia-Hercegovina—determining national boundaries was going to be a real problem.

Each of Yugoslavia's republics held an election in 1990. The results help explain why the country reached a political impasse in 1991. Slovenes voted in April. The former communists, now renamed the Party of Democratic Renewal, were defeated by DEMOS, a six-party coalition. A center right government made up of moderate nationalists and economic reformers was formed; however, the communists were not entirely thrown out. Many still held seats in parliament, and the former communist Milan Kucan was elected president by a wide margin. Croatia followed Slovenia to the polls in May. There the former communists were badly beaten while the overwhelming winner was the Croatian Democratic Union (CDU) with 60 percent of the vote, led by Franjo Tudjman, a former communist general turned ultranationalist. Tudjman had organized the CDU the previous year, and by the end of 1989, Croatia, like Slovenia, had spawned a dozen or so viable political parties. The CDU's campaign had been highly nationalistic and recalled for some the tone of the World War II Croat Ustasha excesses. When Tudjman and his party assumed power, they talked of Croatia's "historic and natural" boundaries (more than 1 million Croats lived outside Croatia, some in Serbia, but most in Bosnia-Hercegovina), and they also spoke, ominously, about new ties with Bosnia-Hercegovina. For Serbs, such talk raised the level of national fervor; they were especially concerned about the fate of some 580,000 Serbs who lived in Croatia. For Bosnia-Hercegovina, which was unprepared for such developments, it raised fears about the future of the Yugoslav federation.

Bosnia-Hercegovina's election was held in November. Its three major parties represented national groups—Muslim, Serb, and Croat—and each won seats in parliament in approximate proportion to the percentage of each national group living in the republic. Former communists got a mere 10 percent. Bosnia's parliament elected Alija Izetbegovic, a Muslim, its president. Macedonia's election that month also rid its republic of communist rule, although its new president, Kiro Gligorov, was a former communist. This republic's new government was nationalist and acutely conscious of Macedonia's Albanian population, which captured 21 percent of the vote in the election. Both Bosnia-Hercegovina and Macedonia, troubled by the growing nationalistic rhetoric of Serbia and Croatia, would attempt in the months ahead to chart a moderate course. Their only hope, as they saw it, was to preserve federalism, or, alternatively, to sponsor a confederation for Yugoslavia, which they did belatedly the following year.

Montenegro and Serbia voted in December 1990, and both returned communists to power. Momir Bulatovic, a young reformist Montenegrin party member, became Montenegro's president. He was also, however, committed to Milosevic and alone would stick by Serbia in April 1992 after the rest of the Yugoslav republics had broken away. Milosevic and the former communists, renamed the Serbian Social Democratic Party, won in Serbia. Milosevic, as expected, was elected president. Part of his success was due to the Serbian nationalist appeal, but communism's attraction should not be underestimated. In Serbia, where many feared losing jobs in unprofitable enterprises should a market economy be introduced, the answer was a vote for former communists who promised job security and a continued social security net. Milosevic, who understood his electorate well, secretly raided Yugoslavia's federal bank in December 1990 to the tune of $1.8 billion to provide subsidies for his constituents and Serbia's ailing economy, thereby assuring his party's electoral victory. It was a coup of sorts for Milosevic, but it earned him and Serbia the wrath of the other republics as well as the anger of Ante Markovic, who headed the fading Yugoslav federal government structure as its prime minister.

Many forces were at work in Yugoslavia by the beginning of 1991. Some were holding the country together; others were pulling it apart. One unifying factor was the federal government, but there had not been elections on that level in 1990, so those who sat in the federal assembly had been chosen in the days when the whole country was still communist. The prime minister was Ante Markovic, a former president of Croatia. His predecessor had resigned at the end of 1988 after an unprecedented vote of no confidence in the assembly. The issue was Yugoslavia's financial problems, which Markovic promised to remedy. At the end of 1989 he implemented a comprehensive reform plan that tied the Yugoslav currency, the dinar, to the German mark, made it convertible, and dramatically, but alas temporarily, lowered the inflation rate. Those who still believed in Yugoslavism continued to support Markovic. Unfortunately, their numbers at home were diminishing rapidly. Among them were the Yugoslav National Army (JNA), which, of course, had a commitment to preserve the state, and those who feared the direction nationalism might take if the country began to break apart. This included many of mixed nationality as well as committed communists. The strongest support for Markovic and a united Yugoslavia came from abroad, from the European governments, the U.S. government, and the International Monetary Fund (IMF); all had political and economic interests at stake there.

The forces working against a united Yugoslavia ate away at the federal institutions. Markovic and his reforms, for example, were undermined by the republics. The most audacious case was Milosevic's "Great Serbian bank robbery" of December 1990, noted above. Milosevic publicly continued to support central institutions, for he hoped to infiltrate and capture control of them as a power base for an enlarged Serbia. He, however, disliked the federal prime minister, Markovic, who wanted to move the country toward market reforms; for the Serbs, Markovic was simply a tool of foreign agents. The northern republics, Slovenia and Croatia, who by October 1990 were proposing a loose confederation of republics, also opposed Markovic, but because he was a centrist. Slovenia held a successful plebiscite on independence in December 1990, and in late February 1991 nullified crucial federal laws in preparation for "disassociation" from Yugoslavia in June. Croat leaders began saying that Croatia, too, would break away if Slovenia did. Both republics were working on new constitutions; Serbia had already adopted a new one in March 1989. Nothing was happening on the federal level in response to these developments, for Markovic had wanted to wait until the republics held elections in 1990. By the time they had, it was too late for federal elections or federal constitutional reform. And by the end of March 1991 it was too late for Markovic as well, at least as far as Milosevic and Tudjman, the presidents of Serbia and Croatia, were concerned. The two plotted secretly on March 25 to get rid of him.

The unity of the federal military was also weakening. The JNA was the supreme defense institution, but after the late 1960s there were also territorial or local defense units. These were a kind of national guard controlled by the republics. Slovenia took this national guard very seriously, declared it independent from the JNA in autumn 1990, and began adding to its arms supply. Croatia was also buying weapons for its "Specials" paramilitary forces. The JNA, meanwhile, was being manipulated by Serbia. In March 1991 the Serbs who lived in the Krajina area of western Croatia seceded from that republic. Fearing that their rights would not be protected under the new Croatian constitution, they declared their land a Serbian autonomous region. They hoped for protection and eventual union with Serbia even though their territory was several hundred miles from Milosevic's republic. The Krajina Serbs had been encouraged by Milosevic into declaring independence from Croatia. When the Croat police tried to stop them, violence broke out, and some were killed. The JNA, given the job of quelling ethnic fighting, intervened on behalf of the Serbs. The collective federal presidency, not the federal assembly headed by Markovic, directed the JNA to do so. That federal executive body had been taken virtually hostage by Milosevic and Serbia.

The federal presidency became the focus of events in the spring of 1991. Its powers (including command of the army) and its composition had been spelled out in the 1974 constitution. It had eight members of equal status, one from each of the six republics and the two autonomous provinces. The members took turns heading the presidency; each served one year according to a preestablished order of rotation. This system decentralized power, gave the provinces equal weight with the republics (to the Serbs' dismay), and provided for a peaceful succession when Tito, who had been elected president for life in 1974, died. In the 10 years after Tito's death in 1980 the system worked well enough. But in 1991 the rotation of presidents, which was due on May 15, was blocked by the Serbs. The president at the time was Borisav Jovic, a Serb and close collaborator of Milosevic; the next in line for the office was Stipe Mesic, a Croat. Jovic refused to be replaced by Mesic. This was in effect a Serbian coup d'etat. Jovic was backed by Serbia's allies on the presidency: Montenegro, and Kosovo and Vojvodina (controlled after 1989 by Milosevic people). Since the beginning of the year the presidency had in fact been deadlocked—four to four—on most issues. Political paralysis had set in; Jovic's May 15 challenge forced Croatia's hand. On May 19 Croats voted for sovereignty, and on May 29 a vote for independence was coupled with the establishment of a Croatian national guard. Croatia's Krajina Serbs boycotted both votes.

Last-minute attempts were made to head off the breakup of the country. Macedonia and Bosnia-Hercegovina, which had remained fearful and in the shadows, offered a compromise between the Slovene-Croat position and that of Serbia: a confederation (known as the "asymmetrical federation") to be named Union of Yugoslav States. James Baker, the U.S. secretary of state, met with Markovic and with each of the republic presidents on June 21, urging them to keep Yugoslavia together. Markovic also spoke to the Croat and Slovene assemblies, urging them not to secede. The two northern republics refused to turn back. On June 25, 1991, Slovenia and Croatia announced their independence.

The immediate result was war in Slovenia. On June 26 Prime Minister Markovic, with the presidency no longer functioning, ordered the JNA to take control in Slovenia. But the JNA was no match for the Slovenes, whose national guard and police had prepared for the confrontation. In 10 days the war was over. Deaths and casualties were minimal. A truce was brokered by the EC, and the Brioni Agreement of July 7, signed by EC representatives and the heads of Yugoslavia's republics, settled matters for Slovenia. (The EC also persuaded the republics to accept Mesic as head of Yugoslavia's presidency, an office he assumed on July 1 but never really controlled.) The truce in Slovenia held for the stipulated three months, the republic was allowed to be independent (October 8), and JNA forces were evacuated by late October.

In Croatia there was no truce. Hostilities there were only just beginning in July 1991, and matters would go very badly for Croatia, for the Yugoslav government authorities (Markovic, Mesic) had lost control over the JNA, whose officer corps was 70 percent Serb. The JNA soon began supporting the Serbs in the Croatian war, where fighting raged in several areas until the end of the year. In the north and west (Krajina and the Dalmatian coast) the fighting split Croatia in two, cutting off the main part of the republic from its lucrative coastal resort areas. The southern Adriatic Sea's tourist mecca, Dubrovnik, attacked in October, was bombed from the air and the sea, its resort hotels destroyed. In the east (Baranja, along the Hungarian border, and Slavonia, which had borders with Serbia and Bosnia-Hercegovina) the war between Serbs and Croats, which had begun in late summer, was reminiscent of World War II's bestial fratricidal killing. Civilians bore the horrors of the conflict. Eastern Croatia, which had a mixed population and a border contiguous with Serbia, experienced some of the most vicious fighting. Croatia's fourth-largest city, Osijek (population 158,000), and Vukovar (population 40,000) suffered terribly. In Vukovar, under siege for 87 days, only a fourth of its traumatized inhabitants who had not fled or been driven out survived, mostly by living in cellars. There were 2,300 dead; the town itself was totally leveled.

The EC tried to stop the war, holding weekly meetings, usually in The Hague, and brokering more than a dozen failed truces. Only after mid-October, when special envoy Cyrus Vance, representing the United Nations, got involved, was headway made toward peace. In late November there was at last a UN cease-fire that stopped most of the fighting. By then the Serbs controlled one-third of the Croatian republic. Ten thousand had been killed; 30,000 soldiers and civilians had been wounded; and 730,000 (500,000 Croats, 230,000 Serbs) had become refugees and now lived in other Yugoslav republics or elsewhere in Europe.

Terms of the settlement were prepared by the United Nations, whose troops, UNPROFOR (UN Protection Force), would monitor the truce. Its envoy, Cyrus Vance, gained the commitment of the Serb Milosevic, which was critical. Most agree, however, that the Serbs, who were winning at the time, complied precisely because they had taken what they wanted and now hoped to secure their gains. The idea of a United Nations peace-keeping force was appealing because it would constitute a thin blue line— UNPROFOR forces were called blue helmets or blue berets—separating Serb-held areas from the rest of Croatia. In a way, the UN safeguarded Serb military gains, allowing Milosevic to attend to other matters. The Croats, of course, hoped to get back the occupied areas. (This did not occur until August 1995, when Croats launched a rapid military assault against the Serbs, who then fled Croatia.) The cease-fire agreement was signed in early January 1992. UN Resolution 743 established a peace-keeping force to supervise the cease-fire and the withdrawal of JNA troops. By mid-February the number of UNPROFOR troops was set at 14,000, and in early March 30 nations began deploying forces to serve under General Satish Nambiar of India in four different areas of Croatia. Because it was important to keep the management of UN operations away from possible hostilities, UNPROFOR headquarters was set up in Sarajevo. The UN was clearly ill-informed and ill-prepared for the imminent war in Bosnia, which began the next month.

By late 1991 Tito's Yugoslavia was coming to an end. In December Mesic resigned as president of the presidency and Markovic resigned as prime minister. In early January 1992 Veljko Kadijevic, the JNA head, who was still a Yugoslav at heart, resigned as well. The central authorities had caved in to Milosevic and the nationalistic forces. The international community, after much wrangling (which will be discussed in a later chapter), began acknowledging Yugoslavia's demise. Some began accepting the independence of the northern republics. On January 15, 1992, the EC states jointly recognized Slovenia and Croatia. Bosnia-Hercegovina held a referendum on independence at the end of February 1992. It declared independence and was recognized by the EC on April 6, and, together with Slovenia and Croatia, by the United States on April 7, one day after war broke out in Bosnia. The three former republics of Yugoslavia became members of the United Nations on May 22, 1992. Macedonian UN membership came only in April 1993, while the EU (formerly EC) recognized its independence in November 1993. The remainder of Tito's Yugoslavia,

Serbia and Montenegro, chose to remain together and officially adopted the name Federal Republic of Yugoslavia (FRY) on April 27, 1992. This third Yugoslavia, for which international recognition was not forthcoming, continued Milosevic's Great Serbist policies. With Serb areas of Croatia under Serbian control and protected by the UN, the FRY turned its attention to the Serbian-populated lands of Bosnia and Hercegovina.

3

The War in Bosnia-Hercegovina

Of Yugoslavia's six republics, Bosnia-Hercegovina was the most diverse. It was Yugoslavia in miniature. Unlike the other republics, it had neither a majority national group nor a majority religious community. The 1991 census recorded a population of 4,364,574, of which 43.7 percent were Muslim, 31.4 percent Serb, and 17.3 percent Croat; 5.5 percent identified themselves as Yugoslav. (Most Bosnians were descended from southern Slavs who had migrated to the area in the sixth and seventh centuries A.D.) Because it is a key to understanding the area, it should be underlined that Muslim was a *national* identification in Bosnia. Yugoslavia's 1974 constitution listed Muslim among the country's nations, and to say one was Muslim in Bosnia was similar to someone, say in Chicago or New York City, saying he was ethnically Jewish. In neither case is religious affiliation or practice assumed. Like its national composition, Bosnia's religious picture was also complex. Religious identification generally, but not always, corresponded to national affiliation. Serbs were usually Orthodox, Croats were usually Catholic, and the Muslims were generally Sunni Muslim. Bosnia also had a small Jewish community, descended mostly from Sephardic Jews, exiles from Spain who settled in the area in the sixteenth century. After fifty years of socialist rule, however, many Bosnians no longer practiced religion—or at least not regularly. This was most often the case in urban centers.

Bosnia and Hercegovina's political experience was also diverse, more so than that of Yugoslavia's other republics. They were the only lands that were first under Ottoman and then under Habsburg administration before becoming part of Yugoslavia in the twentieth century. They had been independent or autonomous medieval states that came under Ottoman Turkish rule by the mid-1400s. Ottoman administration, which lasted there until 1878, allowed the Bosnians relative autonomy within their respective religious communities. Those Bosnian Slavs who accepted Islam, however, were somewhat better off than the others, since they shared the ruler's faith and often themselves became members of the ruling elite. Habsburg rule in Bosnia-Hercegovina, or "Bosnia," came next, and although it lasted only until the end of World War I, it brought many Western influences. Catholicism was promoted by the regime, as were business and modernization, and Bosnia was drawn economically northward.

After World War I, Bosnians became part of a southern Slavic state where for the first time they experienced the expansionist ambitions of the Serbs, who regarded the Kingdom of Yugoslavia as though it were an enlarged Serbia, and of the Croats, who were hoping to resurrect a state of their own. Both Serbs and Croats regarded Bosnia as potentially theirs. During World War II, Bosnia was part of the Croat Ustasha state, and it was in Bosnia that Tito's Partisans clinched their victory for a new (socialist) Yugoslavia by defeating the occupiers. Most important, Tito also beat the Croat Ustasha (fascists) and the Serbian Chetniks (royalists); both groups were ultranationalist. The bloody civil war that raged in Bosnia during this time was one of Europe's horrors. Anyone reminded of these events fifty years later should have been very worried about what would happen in Bosnia if Tito's Yugoslavia began to disintegrate, for Tito had insisted upon a separate republic for Bosnia-Hercegovina. One way of looking at Yugoslavia's history since World War II involves seeing its survival as depending upon a strong Bosnia acting as a political buffer between Serb and Croat ambitions. Unfortunately, in 1990 Bosnia was neither strong nor politically stable.

In November 1990 the Bosnians held a multiparty election, a half year after Slovenia and Croatia and a month before Serbia. The communists were ousted, and members of three national parties replaced them in Bosnia's assembly. The three winning parties were all nationalist and won seats in approximate proportion to the size of their respective national groups. They were the Party of Democratic Action (PDA) (Muslim), the Serbian Democratic Party (SDP), and the Croatian Democratic Party

(CDU-BH), a branch of the CDU of Croatia. The three also won all the seats on the presidency, and Alija Izetbegovic (PDA) was chosen to head it. For Bosnia to hold together, all the parties would have to remain committed to Bosnian unity. But events had overtaken Bosnia, and maintaining unity was to prove difficult. Slovenia had held its referendum for independence (December 1990); Bosnian Croats were being drawn toward Croatia, which was also considering separation; and the Bosnian Serbs were being swayed by the Greater Serbia rhetoric of Radovan Karadzic of the SDP, who would ultimately lead them into war. When Slovenia and Croatia declared independence (June 1991) and war with the JNA ensued, President Izetbegovic rejected suggestions that Bosnia cantonize so that its national communities might have autonomy. Thus in September 1991, the Bosnian Serbs acted, as had the Croatian Serbs the previous year, by declaring enclaves of Bosnia to be Serbian autonomous regions (SARs). On October 24, 1991 the assembly's Serbian deputies proclaimed a separate assembly of the Serbian nation.

For the next six months Bosnia was pulled in two directions: it could remain part of a rump Yugoslavia, which Bosnian Serbs favored in a referendum of November 1991, or it could declare independence, which Bosnian Croats and Muslims voted for on February 29/March 1, 1992. The independence vote, which tallied 99.4 percent positive responses from 63 percent of the electorate, had been prompted by an international community proposal that offered all Yugoslav republics the option of being independent. But by spring 1992 Bosnia was damned if it remained in Yugoslavia, and damned if it declared independence. Left in Yugoslavia, it would become another Kosovo or Vojvodina, a part of Greater Serbia and subject to Milosevic's political will. Committed to independence, it was certain to face military force, particularly since the JNA was available for war, having stopped fighting in Croatia in January. Izetbegovic tried to keep his republic free of Serbia and free of war, but in the end it was clear he could not do both. Tragically, the mild-mannered and somewhat naive Izetbegovic would not believe war could come and was unprepared to deal with it when it did. At a mid-March meeting in Lisbon the EC attempted to head off a confrontation by proposing to create a Bosnia with three constituent parts. All parties, even Izetbegovic, agreed, although he reversed his position a week later. The Bosnian Serbs countered by declaring a Serbian Republic of Bosnia-Hercegovina on March 27. War began 10 days later, a day before the EC recognized Bosnia-Hercegovina as an independent state.

Something not known at the time was that both Serbia and Croatia had express designs on Bosnia. Presidents Milosevic and Tudjman had met in

September 1991 and secretly agreed to divide their neighboring republic. Memoirs and interviews with key players in the Yugoslav breakup have confirmed this collusion. Croatia's Tudjman, moreover, conceded as much when he drew the former Yugoslavia's new boundaries on a napkin for a British statesman at a dinner party in London in May 1995. Wartime developments (both Serbs and later Croats, too, fought against the Bosnian army) and the various proposed peace agreements would all stipulate a division of Bosnia in some manner or other. In general, the agreements, including the peace treaty produced in Dayton in November 1995, had the support of Milosevic and Tudjman (some were even proposed by them), and all diminished the multinational unity and strength of Bosnia while providing Serbia and Croatia with opportunities for expansion. It will be easier to understand some of the complexities of the Bosnian war if one keeps in mind the political ambitions of the republic presidents of the former Yugoslavia.

The war in Bosnia began in April 1992 and ended in October 1995. During the first year of fighting, until about May 1993, the leading combatants were the Bosnian Serbs and the Bosnian government. The government, although multinational (Croat, Muslim, and Serb), was usually misleadingly identified as Muslim, partly because its president, Izetbegovic, was Muslim. It had a small (50,000), poorly armed and poorly organized fighting force. (By summer 1994 it had 110,000 troops and was much better organized; the Bosnian Croats, at times allies of the Bosnian army, had 12,000 national defense troops in 1992 and 50,000 by mid-1994.) The Bosnian Serbs were led by Radovan Karadzic, head of the Serbian Democratic Party, and had an army of 80,000, a number that remained constant. These were troops that technically had been released from the JNA but continued to be supported and supplied by Belgrade (rump Yugoslavia or FRY). They concentrated their attacks in eastern and northern Bosnia with the goal of creating a continuous arc of Serb-held territory that would link Serbia with Serbs in western Bosnia and western Croatia (the Krajina area). Karadzic's forces also repeatedly targeted Sarajevo, Bosnia's capital, with an eye to establishing postwar headquarters there. The Bosnian government, unprepared for war, appealed to the United Nations for assistance. The UN responded by recognizing Bosnia-Hercegovina as an independent state on May 22; on May 30 it imposed sanctions against the aggressor, the FRY (Serbia and Montenegro), for its involvement in the conflict.

In spite of the UN actions, the war continued, and in the late summer and autumn of 1992 reports of concentration camps and crimes against civilians began to fill the media. That summer Bosnians fleeing "ethnic cleansing" and genocide caused refugee numbers to swell, so that by November the figure for all national groups reached 1.5 million (a third of Bosnia's population). When the International Red Cross obtained access to the camps, its investigators concluded that the Serbs were most to blame for the human rights violations, including at least 20,000 rapes. In September the EU and the UN established a permanent Geneva conference to deal with the Bosnia problem. By November 6,000 UNPROFOR forces were dispatched to the area to process war prisoners and refugees and to dispense humanitarian aid. The previous month the UN Security Council had attempted, rather lamely, to deal with Serb aerial attacks by declaring Bosnia a "no-fly zone." Early the following year the UN had also established an international court to try war criminals. It passed a resolution to allow NATO to fire on violators of the no-fly zone, and it declared six cities, Sarajevo, Bihac, Gorazde, Srebrenica, Tuzla, and Zepa, "safe areas" under UN protection. For the most part the UN pronouncements were empty gestures that were not enforced and were regularly defied and brazenly violated by Karadzic's Serbs.

Ethnic cleansing, as a Serbian war policy, had first been implemented in late summer 1991 in eastern Croatia. It aimed at Serbianizing certain Croatian territories by ridding them of non-Serb inhabitants, primarily Croats. The policy of ethnic cleansing, however, was most rigorously applied in Bosnia, beginning shortly after that state's independence was proclaimed in April 1992. Muslims became the primary target of the policy, which active perpetrators have maintained was prepared well in advance and carried out calmly and systematically. Ethnic cleansing became a defining factor in Radovan Karadzic's newly proclaimed Serbian Republic of Bosnia, and Bosnian Serbs became its agents. However, the first "cleansers" were Serbs from Serbia, many of whom belonged to special paramilitary forces (Arkan and Vojislav Seselj led such units), who had refined their cleansing techniques in Croatia the previous year. The policy in Bosnia, implemented first in Muslim villages, began with harassing and terrorizing local inhabitants (civilians), many of whom, fearing for their lives, left voluntarily. The less fortunate were tortured, raped, mutilated, and murdered; their homes and other property were confiscated. By the fall of 1992, the policy was extended to towns and cities, where systematic destruction of Muslim culture and history was undertaken. Mosques, libraries, schools, and public places important to Muslims were all targeted for destruction. Anti-Muslim propaganda played an important role in implementing the policy.

Western governments and the UN were already aware of what was happening in Bosnia in April 1992, but they chose not to reveal it or to intervene on behalf of the victims. The Western media discovered the detention and death camps of Omarska, Trnopolje, and Manjaca in July of that year and widely publicized the horrors, which they compared to the Holocaust against the Jews during World War II. Genocide was occurring again in Europe, and no one was doing anything about it. Yet in spite of a massive media exposé, little would be done to stop the anti-Muslim genocide. As late as summer 1995, when Srebrenica was "cleansed" of its Muslims (roughly 7,000 men were executed, while the rest of the town's inhabitants were forced to flee), the powers still failed to act. They continued to treat the Bosnian situation as a humanitarian crisis, sending food to feed the hungry, while looking the other way when it came to identifying and punishing those responsible for the crimes. Granted, it might have been difficult to determine exactly who was behind ethnic cleansing. But even Vojislav Seselj, one of ethnic cleansing's boastful agents in Croatia and Bosnia, admitted that the policy was planned in Belgrade and suggested a connection with the Serbian Ministry of Interior. The finger of responsibility pointed ominously to President Slobodan Milosevic of Serbia. But even in late 1995, at the Dayton peace conference (discussed below), the great powers would conveniently relegate the issue of genocide to a virtually powerless war crimes tribunal. The great powers at the end of the twentieth century would prove unwilling to act on behalf of universally held moral principles when it was clearly not in their basic self-interest.

By January 1993 the international community produced a first comprehensive peace proposal, the Vance-Owen plan. It proposed dividing Bosnia into 10 provinces—3 for each national community and a separate UN-supervised province for Sarajevo. It was difficult to sell the plan to the combatants and their supporters. The negotiators, Cyrus Vance, who represented the UN, and Lord David Owen, who acted on behalf of the EU, traversed the former Yugoslavia seeking compliance while peace talks and truces came and went. In May 1993 the assembly of the Bosnian Serbs, who were the key combatants and in control of about two-thirds of Bosnia, decisively rejected the Vance-Owen proposal.

The next phase of the Bosnian war lasted nearly a year, until March 1994. It began with a new peace proposal—the Owen-Stoltenberg plan—on the table. (Owen had continued as EU envoy, while Thorvald Stoltenberg, a former Norwegian foreign minister, took over Vance's UN job.) The new plan proposed that Bosnia be reconfigured into a confederation of three ethnic units. Serbia's Milosevic and Croatia's Tudjman encouraged adoption of the plan; they had in fact been its coauthors. Bosnia's Izetbegovic, still hoping to maintain a united multinational state (one that the

UN, after all, had recognized), boycotted the peace talks; he was firmly opposed to dividing Bosnia along ethnic lines. Until the spring of 1993 the Bosnian government chiefly had the Serbs to worry about, but for the rest of that year Izetbegovic also had to deal with hostile Bosnian Croats, renegade Muslims in the Bihac area, and civil disorder among Muslim crime lords in Sarajevo. The criminals of the capital were dealt with in the autumn in an effective crackdown executed by Bosnia's new prime minister, Haris Silajdzic. The Muslims in northwestern Bosnia (adjacent to Croatia), led by Fikret Abdic, a popular local figure and rival of Izetbegovic, who proposed an autonomous province for the Bihac area, were a more complicated issue. Abdic, who also favored an agreement with Karadzic's Serbs and the Bosnian Croats, continued to be a problem for Bosnian unity until the end of the war.

Izetbegovic's greatest problem in 1993 was the Bosnian Croats, led by Mate Boban. By July 1992 they had established an autonomous Croat state—Herceg-Bosna—centered in southwestern Bosnia. (Tudjman's Croatia later admitted to supporting this move.) In spring 1993, with the Owen-Stoltenberg peace plan on the table, the Bosnian Croats decided to enlarge the territory of their proposed ethnic unit through military action and at the Muslims' expense. This meant ending a formal alliance with the Muslims and fighting against the Bosnian government. Many Croats left Izetbegovic's government at this time, and fierce combat raged between former allies who had until then fought together against the Serbs. The Croat-Muslim war was most vicious in the area of Mostar, a city whose elegant sixteenth-century bridge—a symbol of ethnic and religious harmony—was destroyed by Croat fire in November 1993. Mostar was almost totally destroyed and became a divided city. Civilians on both sides, Croat and Muslim, were killed, "ethnically cleansed," terrorized, or forced to flee. The refugee flow surged again, and the Owen-Stoltenberg plan collapsed.

At the beginning of 1994 prospects for peace were slimmer than ever. Fighting continued and took on the character of a civil war. All parties engaged in ethnic cleansing and atrocities against civilians. The early victims adopted the aggressors' tactics in dealing with the enemy. Representatives of the international community, working through EU bodies and the UN, scurried about, hoping that diplomatic means would bring about an end to the fighting. In February 1994 there was yet another Serbian bombing of the marketplace in Sarajevo, a bloody massacre filmed by ABC television crews who were in the city at the time.

That bombing marked a turning point in the handling of the Bosnian situation. NATO was brought in to frighten the Serbs, who were given an ultimatum to vacate a 20-kilometer exclusion zone around Sarajevo. In late February, NATO shot down four Serbian planes near Banja Luka. It should be noted, however, that NATO's move was made in defense of UN personnel only. Bosnian victims of aggression were still without a defender, a situation all the more exasperating because the Serbs, who had inherited the arsenal of the JNA, had the military advantage. The September 1991 UN ban on sale of weapons to the republics of the former Yugoslavia still held. It had been imposed by the UN at the request of the Yugoslav federal government—still headed at the time by Prime Minister Ante Markovic—in hopes of saving a united Yugoslavia. Only in 1994 were the Muslims and Croats able to smuggle in adequate weapons to challenge the Serbs.

March 1994 saw the beginnings of a new phase in the Bosnian conflict, the product of intense U.S. diplomatic efforts. The overall plan, which gained the cooperation of the Contact Group (France, Germany, Great Britain, Russia, and the United States), which was organized the following month, was to bring the Croats and Muslims together, and then drive a wedge between the Bosnian Serbs and Serbia. Muslim and Croat hardliners (e.g., the Croat Mate Boban) were ousted, and the two groups officially ended hostilities against one another and were reassociated in a Bosnian federation. The outlines of a confederation with Croatia were also drawn up, and both federation and confederation were formalized in a signing ceremony in Washington on March 18, 1994. Peter Galbraith and Victor Jackovich, the U.S. ambassadors to Croatia and Bosnia, respectively, acted as facilitators. In May the leadership of the Bosnian federation met for the first time; its president, Kresimir Zubak, was a Croat, and its vice president and prime minister, Ejup Ganic and Haris Silajdzic, were both Muslims.

Bosnian Serbs denounced the new federation and continued their defiance of the EU, the UN, and NATO. They violated Bosnia's safe areas (especially Gorazde), expelled Western journalists, abducted UN troops, fire-bombed UN humanitarian relief offices (UNHCR) in Belgrade, and in April shot down a British plane that was evacuating Muslim war victims for the Red Cross. The Contact Group consequently began applying to Serbia, protector of the Bosnian Serbs, a "carrot and stick" tactic. Milosevic and Serbia were offered an easing of the UN sanctions against Yugoslavia in return for a Yugoslav embargo against Pale, the Bosnian Serb capital on the outskirts of Sarajevo. Milosevic, the JNA, and Yugoslavia's police instigated a campaign against Karadzic and his supporters. The latter were railed against in Serbian newspapers as "killers of civilians," and the FRY put an embargo on trade with the Bosnian Serbs (August

1994). Milosevic was rewarded with a partial easing of sanctions. The Bosnian Serbs, who still controlled two-thirds of Bosnia, remained cocky and defiant. Intense fighting took place around Bihac in northwestern Bosnia in October, and in November Sarajevo was again hit hard; the Serbs, commanded by General Ratko Mladic, a Bosnian Serb, began to appear invincible. In November, too, they again took UN hostages, some of whom (55 Canadians) were released in December. Secretary of Defense William Perry of the United States began saying that he felt Serbian war gains to be irreversible, and the UN began talking about abandoning its Bosnian humanitarian mission, which it was beginning to regard as hopeless, as well as life-threatening to its personnel.

By December 30, 1994, Bosnia had been at war for 1,000 days. The estimated number of deaths was 200,000; there were 2 million refugees, 1.1 million of whom now lived abroad. The Bosnian Serbs appeared to be the victors. The year 1995, however, brought a reversal of fortunes for the Bosnian Serbs, and it also produced a peace agreement. Three interlocking developments determined the course of events: military action in Croatia, NATO bombing in Bosnia, and diplomatic efforts of the Contact Group as orchestrated by the United States.

In Croatia, which became the center of renewed activity in 1995, the war had ended in January 1992. For three years one-third of the country had continued to be occupied by Serbs, while the truce lines between Serbs and Croats were monitored by UNPROFOR troops. In January 1995 Croatia's president, Franjo Tudjman, announced that he planned to end UNPROFOR's presence in his country when its mandate came up for renewal at the end of March. It was a clever move that resulted in a redefinition of the UN mission in Croatia. Richard Holbrooke, the U.S. diplomat who later in the year micromanaged the Dayton peace process, rushed to Croatia and persuaded Tudjman to renew UNPROFOR's mandate until the end of the year (the United States, which had promised to supply 25,000 troops should the UN need to evacuate the former Yugoslavia, was reluctant to fulfill that commitment and therefore wanted UNPROFOR to stay). In return for his compliance, Tudjman got the force reduced from 12,500 to 5,000 and had UNPROFOR's task of monitoring truce lines changed to monitoring the republic's borders. The UN forces were relabeled UN-CROC (UN Confidence Restoration Operation in Croatia), thus acknowledging that the territory belonged to Croatia. Tudjman, now with international approval, could reassert claims to Croatia's occupied territories.

In May Croatian troops went on the offensive in Croatia's western Slavonia area, attacking Serbs. Most Serbs there put up little resistance and either fled or surrendered. The area, which was quickly reincorporated into Croatia, was soon flooded with Croat engineers, bankers, and businessmen arriving to reestablish the region's infrastructure. In early August Croatia's army turned to the Krajina, the major stronghold of Croatian Serb separatism. The Croatian army, 100,000 troops recently trained by retired U.S. army officers, dispatched the Serbs in a matter of days. On August 5, Knin, capital of the Serb Krajina, fell, and as many 170,000 Serbs fled the area, mostly to Serbia. The FRY might, in fact, have directed the Croatian Serbs not to resist Tudjman's forces, which could partly account for Croatia's rapid successes. In any case, the FRY did not come to the rescue of the Croatian Serbs, and to many it looked as if Milosevic had betrayed them for his own political gain. The international response to the Croat blitz offensive through the Krajina was generally benign; there even appeared to be tacit endorsement of it. The Croatian army then crossed its borders into western Bosnia (the Bihac area), where it joined efforts with the Bosnian army against the Serbs. The combined armies then quickly reduced Serb-held territory in Bosnia from 70 percent to about 50 percent by mid-September.

During the spring and summer of 1995, while Croat and Muslim forces were rallying in the north and west, the Bosnian Serbs kept fighting, primarily against Bosnian Muslim enclaves in eastern Bosnia and, of course, against Sarajevo. Treated mercilessly, civilians continued to be victims of an ethnic cleansing policy for which Radovan Karadzic and Ratko Mladic, among others, were named war criminals by a war crimes tribunal being organized in The Hague. In mid-July the Bosnian Serbs took Srebrenica, humiliating Dutch UN forces who were guarding it, and perpetrated mass atrocities against Bosnian Muslims living there at the time. (Many were refugees who had sought protection in that city, which had been declared a safe area by the UN.) An estimated 7,000 Srebrenicans, mostly men, were unaccounted for and presumed killed by Bosnian Serbs. After Srebrenica, Mladic's forces moved on to Zepa, another "safe area."

The Bosnian Serbs also escalated their defiance of both the UN and NATO. In late May and early June, they took 370 UN hostages, many of whom were then chained to NATO target objectives and tauntingly displayed on Serbian television. This was the Serb response to NATO's rather belated and mild use of force against them when UN regulations, for example, no-fly zones, were violated. About this time also, a U.S. pilot, Scott O'Grady, was shot down and spent a week successfully proving his survival skills somewhere in the Bihac area. The UN hostages were eventually released to Milosevic in Belgrade, from which they were then transported to Zagreb, Croatia's capital. The Serbs also tried to assassinate EU representative Carl Bildt, the Swede who later became responsible for implementing the civilian objectives of the Dayton peace agreement. Thus NATO gradually stepped up its bombing of Bosnian Serb targets during the course of the summer. By late summer it focused especially on the Sarajevo area, attacking ammunition and fuel dumps as well as radar and communications objectives. In mid-September the Serbs finally pulled back their weapons from Bosnia's capital.

Diplomatic efforts to end the war in Bosnia also heated up in spring and summer 1995. All members of the Contact Group were engaged, although the Americans led the mission. In mid-August three U.S. diplomats who had been involved in shuttling between Serb, Muslim, and Croat factions were killed in an accident on Mt. Igman (between Sarajevo and Pale) while hurrying to meet with a Bosnian government delegation. After their deaths, the peace mission went into even higher gear and became the preserve of Richard Holbrooke, who managed through determination and a forceful personality to accomplish what had been undoable for four years. On September 8 the warring parties agreed to participate in peace talks, based on an accord issued in Geneva. Its broadly drawn basic provisions were (1) that Bosnia-Hercegovina would continue to exist as a legal entity within its existing borders, and (2) that it would consist of two parts—the Muslim-Croat federation that had been established in March 1994, and the Serbian Republic (Republika Srpska) of Bosnia-Hercegovina—each having its own constitution and the right to establish separate relationships with neighboring states.

It is important to stress that in the accord the Serbian Republic, Karadzic's renegade self-proclaimed state within Bosnia, was granted recognition for the first time. The fact that each of the two entities would have separate institutions and the right to separate foreign policies, implying that they would be closely linked to different neighboring states, is also notable. In the future the federation and the Serbian Republic might well become satellites of Croatia and the FRY, respectively, opening the door for a possible division of Bosnia—a fulfillment of the Milosevic-Tudjman agreement of September 1991 to divide it. The warring parties also accepted the accord's general provisions about establishing commissions to deal with elections, human rights, refugees, joint public corporations (e.g., for transportation systems), preservation of national monuments, and an arbitration system for the resolution of current and future disputes.

In October, while preparation for peace talks proceeded in earnest, isolated fighting continued. In mid-October Wright-Patterson Air Force Base, near Dayton, Ohio, became the venue for the deliberations. The talks, which began on November 1, lasted three weeks and were subject to a news blackout. Anxious journalists busied themselves with human interest stories about the local community or hung around outside the air force base "waiting for the white smoke"—an allusion to the smoke that appears from a Vatican chimney when a new pope has been elected. The representatives of the warring factions were housed separately (and virtually held captive during what were referred to as "proximity talks") while the international community's spokespeople went from delegation to delegation seeking agreement on specific points. It was an arduous three weeks for the negotiators, but Holbrooke and Secretary of State Warren Christopher of the United States, who shuttled back to Dayton from remote parts of the world whenever reluctant Serbs, Croats, or Muslims required additional arm-twisting, were unrelenting. Agreement was finally reached and initialed in Dayton on November 21. Official signing took place on December 14 before an imposing array of world leaders at the Elysée Palace in Paris.

Before the Dayton agreement was initialed, several odds and ends were taken care of. Two matters dealing with Croatia pretty much resolved all outstanding issues regarding the war in that state. On November 10 the confederation between Croatia and the Muslim-Croat federation of Bosnia-Hercegovina (of March 1994) was reconfirmed; and on November 12 a settlement was reached on eastern Slavonia. The status of that area within Croatia (location of the fierce fighting in Vukovar and Osijek in late 1992) was still as a Serb-occupied territory. The agreement provided for a 12- to 24-month transition to Croat control and a return of refugees to their homes. Also, on November 17, Richard Goldstone, head of the war crimes tribunal in The Hague, reconfirmed indictments of war criminals, including those against Radovan Karadzic and Ratko Mladic, the civilian and military leaders of the Bosnian Serbs.

The Dayton agreement confirmed the sovereignty and independence of Bosnia-Hercegovina, now a dual or two-part state. The Muslim-Croat federation would control 51 percent, and the Serbian Republic 49 percent of Bosnian land. There would be a central government and a collective presidency, while each of the two component states would have its own legislative and executive bodies, all to be chosen through internationally supervised free and democratic elections, to be held within six to nine months. The Dayton document also spelled out a military settlement to be supervised by IFOR (Implementation Force), headed by NATO and commanded by a U.S. general. Troops were to withdraw behind cease-fire lines within 30 days, and both heavy weapons and troops were to be removed to their barracks within 120 days, both of which were accomplished within the allotted time. The agreement also guaranteed refugees

Bosnia and Hercegovina after the Dayton Agreement (1995).

the right to return to their homes or to be compensated for losses of property. IFOR's mission was to last one year, until December 1996. The implementation of the civilian aspects of Bosnian reconstruction was assigned to a joint civilian commission headed by Carl Bildt, a former conservative prime minister of Sweden. The task of this body was rather vaguely defined, yet its duties (economic reconstruction, restoring law and order, promoting human rights, and holding free elections) were crucial to the success of the Dayton peace. Implementation of auxiliary provisions of the treaty, such as facilitating the work of The Hague war crimes tribunal, was also going to be extremely difficult.

None of the warring parties was wholly satisfied with the agreement. The Muslims were unhappy that Bosnia was divided; the Serbs were extremely upset with the loss of certain territories, particularly Sarajevo. Yet Izetbegovic of Bosnia, Tudjman of Croatia, and Milosevic, who negotiated for the FRY (Serbia-Montenegro) and also for the Bosnian Serbs, signed the agreement that the Contact Group pressed upon them. Each could return home a hero, having at least attained peace, although not a perfect one. The Bosnian Serbs held out for several days before signing, but afterward Karadzic continued to threaten trouble for Sarajevo, predicting that it would become another Beirut; meanwhile, Ratko Mladic, the Bosnian Serb military commander, vowed to fight on.

Whether the peace would hold and order would be restored was dependent upon many things, not the least of which was the will of the political leaders of the area. Whether peace would hold after IFOR left in December 1996 and whether Bosnia survived as an independent state was up to them. The September 1991 agreement between Milosevic and Tudjman to divide Bosnia between them remained ominously on the minds of many. Time would tell whether these leaders could be trusted and whether the Dayton agreement would be the basis for a final settlement for the area or only a prelude to the ultimate division of what had been Yugoslavia's multiethnic, multicultural, multireligious republic. The larger issue of whether the people of Bosnia and of Croatia could overcome the horrors they had experienced depended on whether the causes of the war were made clear and whether those responsible would be held accountable.

4

A War of Myths, Propaganda, and Balkan Politics

The breakup of Yugoslavia and the war that followed were the direct result of a series of power struggles. Federal and republican political figures grappling for economic and political domain are responsible for what happened to the country. Yet both the breakup and the war have often been portrayed in terms quite removed from the very real factor of politics. This is partly because the leaders themselves wished to mask their motives, and partly because they needed popular support that could be mobilized only by evoking nationalist and religious causes. Outside observers, including journalists and representatives of foreign governments, frequently accepted such explanations for Yugoslavia's tragedy without much questioning. Some did so out of naivete, others because the area was exotic to them and because such cultures, in their view, seemed to be governed by inexplicable, nonrational forces. The representatives of foreign governments, of course, sometimes had their own political motives for preferring to interpret the Yugoslav crisis as one driven by nationalism and religious hatred. Such forces, they cautioned, were uncontrollable, and the meddling of foreign powers (whose voters would probably oppose their country's involvement in Yugoslavia) would certainly be counterproductive. So it was that myth and propaganda were often used to explain and perpetuate the ongoing Yugoslav crisis.

It was said and written right from the beginning that "age-old ethnic hatreds" caused Yugoslavia's breakup and its bloody war. The phrase has been repeated so often, as if by rote, that hardly anyone bothers to think about its meaning or its validity. The fact is that historically there has been little fighting among these peoples. Wars before the nineteenth century were generally fought by noble warriors or mercenaries. Byzantine Greeks and Hungarians were the foes of the medieval states in the area. These were followed by the Ottoman Turks, who, after their conquests in the Balkans between the mid-1300s and the mid-1400s, established relative peace in the area (Pax Ottomanica). The wars of the 1600s and 1700s were between the Habsburgs and the Ottomans, also fought by noble armies and hired soldiers. Among the latter were the local inhabitants of the Habsburg military frontier (Vojna Krajina), who were generally Serb fighters. They had been commissioned by the Habsburg ruler in the mid-1500s to defend the southern border of the empire (and Christendom) from Turkish invasions. In return, the frontiersmen, whose villages were strung from the northern Adriatic coast to Hungary, were granted local political autonomy and the right to collect booty from the enemy. The former areas of the military frontier figured prominently in the recent war in what was Yugoslavia, but it should be remembered that the frontiersmen historically fought the Turks.

Moreover, in getting back to the "age-old ethnic hatreds" charge, it should be noted that ethnic divisions among the southern Slavs were not established until modern times. The South Slavs, including the Slavic Muslims of Bosnia, all belonged to the same ethnic group; their ancestors had all settled in the area in the sixth and seventh centuries. They did not even begin consciously to sort themselves into branches of that southern Slavic family until the late 1700s and early 1800s, and then it was largely the intellectuals—those who wrote about linguistic, cultural, and historical differences—that understood how Serbs, Croats, Slovenes, and perhaps others might be distinct from one another. The people began to learn about and nurture their ethnic or national identities much later. Granted, the Serbs had a national (Serbian Orthodox) church that was separate from the Byzantine church at Constantinople (from 1566 to 1766 as permitted by the Ottomans), and the Serbs also had a rich tradition of oral folk literature that evoked a Serbian loyalty. That identity, however, was not truly focused until Serb intellectuals of the turn of the nineteenth century, such as Vuk Karadzic, accentuated the Serbianness of the poetry, of the language, and of the Serb people. Literacy, education, and the media in the late nineteenth and early twentieth centuries later helped sharpen the ethnic or national awarenesses of the subgroups of the Balkan Slavs. This was as true for the Yugoslav peoples as for other Europeans (e.g., Italians and Germans) who were experiencing national awakenings slightly ahead of the Yugoslavs.

As for the "age-old religious hatreds" allegation, which is also commonly cited as a cause of Yugoslavia's woes, there is little to substantiate this assertion either. Most of the South Slavs lived in the Ottoman state, where the *millet* system prevailed. After their conquest of the Balkans, the Ottomans divided peoples into religious communities (*millets*), allowing each to be governed by their own religious laws. There was an Islamic *millet,* to which, of course, the rulers belonged. In the Balkans it also included those, like the Bosnian Moslems, who had converted to Islam. (Some historians of Bosnia-Hercegovina prefer to depict the Bosnian Moslems as "accepting" rather than "converting to" Islam, thus implying that becoming Moslem was less of an ideological or religious choice than it was a conforming to social and political realities.) The Orthodox *millet,* which was initially under the jurisdiction of the Greek patriarch of Constantinople/Istanbul, included all of the state's Orthodox Christians. However, as noted above, a separate Serbian patriarchate also existed for two centuries; it had been established by an Ottoman grand vizier, a Serb convert to Islam who had appointed his brother to head the Serbian church. A Roman Catholic *millet* also existed for those of the Catholic persuasion. In Bosnia the Catholics were represented by the Franciscan order, which had received an empowering charter from the Ottoman sultan in 1463. All in all, there was a great deal of religious toleration in the Ottoman Empire at the height of its power, and there was little cause for religious hatred or religious wars. Sephardic Jews, many of them fleeing persecution in Spain, settled at this time in the Ottoman lands—a good number in Sarajevo, Bosnia's main city. Indeed while the wars of the Reformation raged in western and central Europe, even Protestants sought refuge in the Ottoman Empire.

Since much of the war that began in Yugoslavia in 1991 was fought for control of Bosnia-Hercegovina, many myths have been propagated specifically about that former Yugoslav republic. One myth aims at undermining the legitimacy of Bosnia as a political unit and asserts that Bosnia has never been a state or had an independent political tradition. Those who take this position (mostly Serbs) maintain that Bosnia was Tito's creation, an administrative convenience of socialist Yugoslavia designed to thwart the rights of the larger national groups, especially the Serbs. Another broadly drawn allegation rejects the depiction of Bosnia as a multiethnic, multicultural society. It maintains furthermore that Bosnian Muslims were converts from Orthodoxy (the Serbian view) or from Catholicism (the Croat view) and that therefore they were really Serbs/Croats. The allegation rejects outright the notion of a separate ethnic or "national" identity for the Slavic Muslims of Bosnia.

In fact, however, Bosnia does have a political history. It begins in the thirteenth century with the establishment of a monarchy, which survived

The Medieval Bosnian Kingdom at Its Greatest Extent in 1391. From *Bosnia and Hercegovina* by Robert J. Donia and John V. A. Fine, Jr., Copyright © 1994 by Columbia University Press. Reprinted by permission of the publisher.

until the Ottoman conquest in the mid-fifteenth century. The boundaries of that state, moreover, remained more consistently fixed than those of the medieval Serbian or Croatian states. Under the Ottomans, Bosnia, Hercegovina, and a third unit, Zvornik, constituted administrative divisions (*sandzaks*) of the empire. Thus the political continuity and the names of Bosnia and Hercegovina were preserved, as they also were under Austria-Hungary between 1878 and 1918. Bosnia's status was even partially retained during the first decade of the Yugoslav kingdom—the Serbian dynasty concluded an agreement with the Muslims in exchange for supporting the new state—but was lost after King Alexander established a dictatorship in 1929. The Bosnian territories were subsequently divided among four of the kingdom's new administrative units, known as *banovinas*. During World War II the Bosnian lands were part of independent Croatia but lacked a separate political identity. Bosnia-Hercegovina was reconstituted (not artificially created) as a political entity after World War II, becoming one of socialist Yugoslavia's six republics. It was, however, the one republic that had no national/ethnic or religious majority.

History also affirms the fact that Bosnia has had a long multicultural tradition where religious and ethnic differences were not generally reasons for hostility. Most historians maintain that before 1918, when the first Yugoslavia came into existence, there was little or no religious or ethnic conflict here. To the contrary, the inhabitants of Bosnia generally joined together against the common enemy, usually Istanbul or Vienna. The seeds of conflict, however, were sown when the Ottoman state began to deteriorate and the equitable treatment of the religious communities under the *millet* system was compromised. The independent status of the Serbian church ended in 1766 when the Serb patriarch was replaced by Greek church administrators; increasingly thereafter the Orthodox Serbs stressed their Serbianness. Thus, during the nineteenth century the Bosnian Orthodox identity was slowly superseded by a Serbian national one. The Catholics of Bosnia experienced a similar transition from religious to national identity, as more and more Catholic clerics in Bosnia (especially after 1878, when Austria-Hungary took over the area) were trained in Croatia, where Croat national consciousness was blossoming. By the turn of the twentieth century in Bosnia, the Orthodox had become Serbs, the Catholics had become Croats, but the Slavic Muslims remained Muslim. They did not adopt a national identity. After all, as Muslims they already (or still) belonged to the dominant social and political class.

The first real evidence of ethnic tensions among the peoples of Bosnia came during the 1920s and 1930s, after the first Yugoslav state came into being. It was nurtured by political extremists, particularly in the 1930s.

World War II, which also spawned genocidal policies elsewhere in Europe (e.g., Nazi German treatment of Jews, Slavs, and Gypsies), brought fierce ethnic and religious conflict to Yugoslavia. Most analysts of current events in the former Yugoslavia maintain that if there is a precedent for the horrors of the fighting of the 1990s, it can be found in the early 1940s—in other words, the ethnic conflict is not age-old but a half-century old, and within the memory and experience of many who raged in Bosnia-Hercegovina after Tito's death.

Throughout occupied Yugoslavia during World War II, there was incredible fratricidal fighting and killing. Much of the worst of it occurred in Bosnia, which was then part of "independent" Croatia (a fascist satellite of Italy and Germany). The confrontation in Croat-ruled Bosnia featured a struggle between Croats and Serbs. The Serbs, who were singled out by the Croats as the enemy, suffered terribly. They were executed, deported, or converted to Catholicism. For the Serbs, Jasenovac, where tens of thousands of Serbs were brutally killed, stands as a symbol of Croat extermination policies. In the recent war in Yugoslavia Serbs frequently evoked the memory of Jasenovac as a reason for the 1990s conflict. However, they inflated the number of Serbian casualties, just as some Croats greatly minimized them. Serbs claim that 1.1 million of their nation died there, while Franjo Tudjman, president of Croatia after 1990, has written that only 70,000 Serbs perished in the camp. (In fact, a little over 1 million Yugoslavs altogether—6.4 percent of the population—died in all of World War II. Serb deaths account for nearly one-half of the total [487,000]. Of these, 125,000 were Croat Serbs and 209,000 were Bosnian Serbs, or 17.4 percent and 16.9 percent of the Serb populations of Croatia and Bosnia, respectively.) There is no doubt, however, that both ethnic and religious cleansing policies were implemented in Yugoslavia during World War II and the accompanying civil war.

Nationalists tend to simplify the history of the war in Yugoslavia, yet it is anything but a simple story. True, there was a Croat fascist state, led by the Ustasha Ante Pavelic, but not all Croats were Ustasha. Many joined Tito's Partisans because they wanted to fight against the foreign occupiers and/or because they welcomed Tito's promise of a federal postwar Yugoslavia. The chief Serbian leader during the war was the royalist Draza Mihailovic, head of the Chetniks; however, once he stopped fighting against the occupiers (in order to fight the communists), many Serbs also joined Tito's forces. Some Bosnian Muslims worked with the Ustasha, and a small group became part of a Nazi SS unit, but many Bosnian Muslims fought with the Partisans, who promised Bosnia its own republic and the Muslims a special status within it. "Brotherhood and Unity," a myth with a dubious history of its own, was the slogan of Tito's forces. Several things are certain about this war/civil war: the ultranationalists (Ustasha and Chetniks) fought the internationalists (Partisans); the Partisans fought the foreign occupiers with Allied help; and all sides—Ustasha, Chetniks, and Partisans—wanted control of Bosnia.

If national stereotypes and symbols emerged during World War II, they were greatly embellished and widely used during the recent war in Yugoslavia. The Serb nationalists promoted a heroic image of their nation. They glorified the medieval Serbian state, which had been defeated by the Ottoman Turks in 1389 at Kosovo Polje, and romanticized the Serb heroes who died valiantly in that battle. (There is a rich tradition of epic poetry about these warriors, known to all Serbs because the poems have been passed on orally from generation to generation.) Serbs saw themselves as defenders of Christendom against the "infidel Turks," and later as fighters against Austro-Hungarian (World War I) and German (World War II) imperialism. In the recent war Serbs claimed to be fighting the same array of enemies: the Bosnian Muslims, whom they called "Turks"; Austria, Germany, and the Vatican, who, they believed, were backing Slovenia and Croatia with the aim of establishing a Fourth Reich or empire in the Balkans; and, of course, the Ustasha (Croats), who, in the Serb view, were again allied with Germany and on the verge of exterminating Serbs just as they had at Jasenovac. The Albanians of Kosovo (90 percent of its population) also were a constant irritant, for they inhabited the heart of medieval Serbia—where the heroes had fallen in 1389—whose soil was so soaked with the blood of valiant Serbs that it could not possibly belong to any other nation. The Albanians, Serbs claimed (wrongly), were latecomers to the area and were engaged in an Albanian conspiracy to wipe out the Serbs (Albanian women, whose job it was to produce an Albanian population explosion, were said to be part of the anti-Serbian plot). The Serbs also claimed that they were being victimized by the United States, which backed the Bosnian Muslims because it did not wish to offend Muslim oil-producing powers.

Serb paranoia dwelt on the image of Serbia as a permanent victim. Old symbols were resurrected to rally the nation: a cross with four Cyrillic S's—one S in each crux of the cross—which was an acronym for the slogan "Only Unity Saves the Serbs"; Chetnik attire; the royal double eagle; and also the Yugoslav flag without a star, a detail that had been added during the socialist period. The image and the symbols were used as propaganda for "Greater Serbia," an idea that had historic roots and whose program had been resurrected in the mid-1980s by the Serbian Academy of Science and Arts. Greater Serbia was to include all of the

Serbian republic (including Vojvodina and Kosovo, where there were large non-Serb populations) and all of the areas of the former Yugoslavia where Serbs lived. This included Montenegro, a good portion of Bosnia (including its Muslim areas), and probably Macedonia, which was traditionally looked upon as southern Serbia. The academy's statement, which was made public in 1986, is imbued with a strong sense of Serbia as the age-old victim, but one that was now about to take destiny into its own hands.

The Croat self-image was also rooted in its medieval state, founded by King Tomislav in the tenth century and sanctified by the head of the Church at Rome. The state known as the "triune kingdom" consisted of three parts—Croatia, Slavonia, and Dalmatia. Although its components were separated (e.g., Dalmatia soon came under the rule of the Venetian state, where it remained until the end of the 1700s), and although its dynasty died out in the year A.D. 1102, Croatia continued to exist as a political entity. It accepted the rulers of Hungary when its own royal family line ended, and when the Hungarian dynasty expired in 1526 (when its last king was killed by the Turks at Mohacs), the Croats (their nobility) accepted Habsburg rulers. They maintained that Croatia's integrity continued because of contractual arrangements with the Hungarians and later with the Habsburgs, although the Croats were not always treated as genuine political partners. The Croat identity continued to be bound up with a sense of being Catholic and therefore a part of Western civilization.

Like the Serbs, the nationalist Croats developed stereotypes of their Yugoslav neighbors. The Slovenes were regarded as "mountain Croats" rather than as a nation in their own right. Bosnian Muslims were Croats who had converted to Islam, while Serbs were reprehensible—backward, Eastern (therefore uncivilized and uncultured), and untrustworthy. As the nationalist rhetoric escalated in the 1980s, and particularly after 1990, when Franjo Tudjman and his party, the Croatian Democratic Union (CDU), came to power, the outlines of a Greater Croatia program surfaced. There was talk about restoring Croatia's "historic boundaries," which for Bosnia at least boded no good, since that republic's lands had in recent history (the 1940s) been a part of Croatia. Croatia's new constitution, its adoption of the red and white checkerboard emblem for its flag, and the introduction of the *kuna* as a monetary unit frightened non-Croats. The flag and the *kuna* were reminiscent of Ustasha Croatia; the constitution, which declared Croatia to be the state of the Croat people, concerned the Croatian Serbs, who worried that they had become a minority in their own country.

The traditional image of Bosnia, generally shared by its constituent ethnic and religious communities, was one of a multiethnic, multicultural, and multireligious state. It was where diversity was tolerated, and members of different groups intermarried and even celebrated each other's religious holidays. This character was particularly evident in urban centers, where there was a long tradition of civilized society. Greater Serb and Greater Croat nationalists, who coveted Bosnian lands, were viewed with suspicion and as interlopers and destroyers of civilization. Sarajevo, Bosnia's capital, had acquired a special image all its own. It had hosted the 1984 Olympics, an international event that complemented Sarajevo's "international" character. During the war that began in 1992, the city came to symbolize civilization under attack, becoming the Spanish Civil War of the 1990s for liberal intellectuals abroad. Writers went to Sarajevo to produce plays (e.g., *Hair* and *Waiting for Godot*) under siege conditions; journalists romanticized the violinist who played classical music daily at the site where Sarajevans in a bread line had been killed; and a Sarajevo schoolgirl named Zlata Filipovic became famous for her *Diary* (comparisons with Anne Frank came to mind), which was quickly translated and published abroad, although Bosnians were left to fend for themselves in the three-and-one-half-year Serbian siege.

In the 1990s propagandists and nationalist politicians exploited the myths and stereotypes for their own ends. The media in Serbia and Croatia became tools of the ruling parties and their leaders—Milosevic in Serbia, Tudjman in Croatia. The leading newspapers (e.g., *Politika* in Serbia) bowed to nationalist politics, or were censored or shut down (e.g., Serbia's *Nin* and Croatia's *Danas* and *Slobodna Dalmacija,* respected liberal forums that had been open to diverse views and opinions). In Bosnia *Oslobodjenje* continued in its liberal tradition, but its headquarters in Sarajevo was bombed. The nationalists also controlled television, which became the most important medium in the countryside, where in some areas literacy was minimal. The medium was used to spread lies and fear about the enemy (false war information was regularly broadcast) and about political opponents in elections. Both Milosevic's and Tudjman's reelection campaigns used the media effectively to their advantage.

Film was also a factor in stirring up ethnic passions. However, it was not local films but rather American imports that stimulated unsavory segments of the population. The criminal, antisocial element, which in normal, peaceful times is monitored by law and the police, flourished during the war. The thugs became killers and plunderers who served the leaders' political ends by terrorizing the ordinary citizen. The Tigers and White Eagles, paramilitary units among the Serbs, for example, drew their membership from among this criminal element. Many became rich from thieving from ethnic enemies or smuggling embargoed goods from abroad.

They adopted a glitzy lifestyle characterized by powerful foreign cars (Mercedeses and BMWs), sexy women, big guns, and bravado, styling themselves after the shoot-em-up heroes of American westerns and after Rambo. The embargo against selling weapons to former Yugoslav republics and the more comprehensive embargo against exchanges with Serbia made these criminals valuable to their respective states, but in many cases a real danger to the populace in general.

The Bosnian Serbs, whose leader was Radovan Karadzic, were masters at using myth and propaganda. For them, the Croats were Ustasha or fascists, while the Bosnian Muslims were Turks and Islamic fundamentalists. These Serbs propagated the assertion about age-old ethnic and religious hatreds until nearly everyone believed it. Karadzic regularly declared that Yugoslav peoples were like cats and dogs who could not live together. A psychologist by profession, Karadzic was the ultimate propagandist, using myth and stereotypes to rally local supporters but also to frighten foreign powers. His aim seemed to be to scare the pants off the U.S. Defense Department (other powers were not potential intruders in the Bosnian Serb grab for territory). He used all of the right buzz words: Vietnam, quagmires, Beirut, Mogadishu, body bags, Islamic fundamentalism, and religious jihad. He reminded the outside world that world wars began in the Balkans, alluding to the fact that Francis Ferdinand, the Austrian archduke, was assassinated in Sarajevo by a Bosnian Serb in 1914 and that the act had precipitated World War I. He boasted that Serbs had defeated the Germans in World War II by keeping 20 German divisions occupied in Yugoslavia at the time. (In fact, some Serbs collaborated with the Germans, while others, like Mihailovic's Chetniks, stopped fighting against them and also collaborated; the Germans in Yugoslavia were defeated by Tito's Partisans, a multinational force, with the help of money, supplies, and support from the western Allies. The West, however, had a poor historical memory about these wartime events.) When in spring 1993 the Bosnian Serbs seemed cornered, with even Milosevic appearing to abandon them, Karadzic played the humble card: Yes, Serbs, were now alone, but God was on their side. He slightly modified his position with regard to the Croats, saying that perhaps Serbs could live with them, but not with the Muslims. He longed, he said, for the day when war would end and he could return to work in his old hospital job, treating mental patients—even Muslim ones.

In the Federal Republic of Yugoslavia (FRY), or rump Yugoslavia, which since April 1992 has been comprised of only Serbia and Montenegro, Slobodan Milosevic was the ultimate politician. Although he was portrayed in the West as the evil force ("the Butcher of Belgrade") that had destroyed Yugoslavia and caused its bloody war, Milosevic survived. In Serbia the opposition was unable to unite or make headway in deposing him. Milosevic used opponents to his advantage. Vojislav Seselj, a hardened Chetnik who was known for his grisly rhetoric about killing Croats, was let out of prison and allowed to run for parliament. Seselj's paramilitary thugs did Milosevic's dirty work for him in eastern Croatia and eastern Bosnia. Vuk Draskovic, the opposition political leader with the largest following, who had helped organize massive demonstrations against Milosevic, was beaten up and thrown into prison along with his wife, Danica. (Danica Draskovic and Slobodan Milosevic's wife, Mirjana Markovic, a sociology professor at the University of Belgrade, were bitter enemies—with Danica's family representing the Chetnik tradition and Mirjana's defending the communist/Partisan heritage. Mirjana was a strong supporter of her husband, although only a behind-the-scenes force in the early 1990s.) Milosevic tolerated the dramatic return of Prince Alexander, who arrived in October 1991 to rally support for peace and a restoration of the monarchy, knowing no doubt that Alexander, who had been born in London and spoke Serbian poorly, would find few backers. Milosevic even appointed Milan Panic, a Serb-born Californian pharmaceuticals executive, as prime minister of Serbia in mid-1992. The Panic interlude in Serbian history was a bizarre one, for Panic, whose personal adviser was John Scanlon, a former U.S. ambassador to Yugoslavia and then a board member of Panic's drug company, was clearly unsuited for the job. He often spoke gibberish and displayed an ignorance of Yugoslav politics. Milosevic could confidently sit back until Panic was defeated in elections later that year.

The FRY and Milosevic courted Western, particularly U.S., support. (The Panic experiment was a bow toward U.S. approval.) In the early years of the war the media were filled with reminders of past good relations between Serbs and the West. After all, Serbia and the West had been allies in both world wars. The argument worked fairly well with the French and the British, but was less effective in the United States. Lacking American support, the Serbs played on U.S. fears by raising the specter of Russian solidarity with Serbia, a prospect that threw Washington policy makers into chaos. The Serbian press regularly attacked American enemies of the FRY. Senator Robert Dole, for example, was singled out as an Albanian lackey for being critical of Serb treatment of Kosovo Albanians. In general the United States was blamed for the embargo against the FRY, which had brought economic hardship to Serbia and Montenegro. The trade embargo, which also prohibited cultural exchanges and the like, even banned Disney comics; parents could hardly believe the cruelty of it, and many preferred to tell their children that Donald Duck had died rather than reveal American heartlessness. The Serbs blamed the West for its woes rather than Milosevic, who even allowed renegade banks (e.g., Dafiment Bank) to promote get-rich-quick schemes that bilked patrons in order to help finance the Serbian war effort. The syndrome of Serbs victimized by foreigners prevailed; it was easier to accept that than to acknowledge that Milosevic had misled them or that they had been fools.

By the summer of 1993, Milosevic, under pressure from the West and with a promise to ease the embargo, changed his hype. It was evident in party-controlled papers and television. The Bosnian Serbs, particularly Karadzic, were attacked as killers and ethnic cleansers. Karadzic was portrayed as an adventurer and a gambler, said to have run up huge debts in Belgrade casinos. Milosevic began supporting a deal with the Croats to bring about peace. All this led eventually to Dayton, Ohio, in November 1995, where Milosevic worked on his image as peacemaker. He was certainly portrayed more favorably in the U.S. media than any of the others attending the peace talks, and at home he was credited with bringing about an end to the war. The embargo against the FRY ended, boutiques reopened, the Serbs were again friends with the West, and the FRY was again a part of Europe. The story in the official media had a happy ending.

But the impact of the war on the FRY, even though no fighting had actually taken place in Serbia or Montenegro, was significant and far-reaching. Serbia, in particular, underwent radical social transformation. It experienced a serious brain drain as many young people and intellectuals left the country to avoid serving in the military or to escape economic depression and political intolerance. At the same time, the FRY has become home to hundreds of thousands of refugees, mostly villagers from backward areas of Croatia (Krajina) and Bosnia, who would infuse the country with a new cultural image and no doubt nurture resentment of Belgrade (and Milosevic) for having abandoned them in the fight against the Croats and the Muslims.

The West's image of the Yugoslavs, the breakup of their country, and the war that followed was also often based on stereotypes and acquired myths. The book most widely read by those hoping to understand the Yugoslav crisis was Robert Kaplan's *Balkan Ghosts,* published in 1993. Yugoslavia is covered in about 75 pages, and the portrayal of its peoples relies very heavily on Rebecca West, the English writer who in the 1930s published a two-volume opus on Yugoslavia. The Yugoslavs are depicted in both works as exotic, passionate, noble, but mysterious beings—ones to whom one might easily affix the "age-old ethnic and religious hatreds" label. For a time in the early 1990s, Kaplan's book was all the rage. It was widely acclaimed by popular reviewers, although academic critics panned it, and it became a favorite selection of ladies' reading societies; even President Bill Clinton and his wife, Hillary, were said to have read it. The conclusion most often drawn from the reading of this book was that these exotic peoples were no match for rational, civilized Westerners; the ethnic passions and the resulting barbarism, combined with a foreboding, rugged mountainous terrain, were something the West ought to avoid. On television talk shows and in the press Kaplan has regretted the inferences drawn from his book. He did not intend for policy makers in the West to be frightened away from intervention in Yugoslavia; instead, he had hoped to convince them that involvement was necessary.

A more general fear that gripped the West was that intervention in the Yugoslav crisis would lead to an expansion of the war. The rationale was that it is natural for wars to grow and get out of control, so it is best not to get involved. There was fear that the war would move to other parts of southeastern Europe: to Kosovo, Macedonia, Albania, and NATO allied countries Greece and Turkey. Here was a Balkan version of the "domino theory" that had influenced policy makers during the Vietnam War. There were even some who predicted that World War III could start here—after all, had not both previous world wars begun in this part of Europe? The phrase "Balkan tinderbox" was often used by the doom-sayers, who failed to remember that in both previous world wars the major European powers were itching to fight each other and used the crises of their smaller neighbors to precipitate the fight. In the 1990s this was decidedly not the case; if anything, the great powers shrank from military involvements, having found them expensive and sometimes embarrassing ventures.

Others images of the war, particularly in Bosnia, evoked historical analogies. Those who favored intervention on behalf of the Bosnian state depicted the big power position as a sellout, another "Munich," a comparison to the British and French allowing Hitler to have his way with Czechoslovakia in 1938. Ethnic cleansing, after it was revealed in the summer of 1992, was compared to the Holocaust, the genocidal policy of the Nazis against Jews in World War II. The Holocaust analogies continued. World leaders present at the opening of the Holocaust Museum in Washington in April 1994 were reminded that after World War II they had pledged "never again" to allow national or racial genocide. The case of Bosnia was brought up, but the will of the international community was lacking, perhaps because other possible historical analogies—Algeria, Vietnam, Beirut, Afghanistan, Somalia, Northern Ireland—were more vivid.

One thing is certain: the breakup of Yugoslavia and the war in Bosnia put a heavy damper on the euphoria that swept across Europe and the

United States when the Cold War ended in 1989. By 1992 there was already lamentation about a "New World Disorder," a reference to American President George Bush's "New World Order." By it, Bush had meant that nations would live in harmony now that communism was dead; tyrants in the post–Cold War world would be dealt with by multinational alliances acting together against blatant evil. The Desert Storm coalition that defeated Iraq in 1991 was regarded as an example of this. When it came to Bosnia a year later, the cooperative spirit of the new order had fizzled. In the United States this brought out the isolationists, who insisted that America was not the world's policeman. Also questioned was the view of an article widely read in academic circles entitled "The End of History" by Francis Fukayama, where it was maintained that conflict in society would fade with the end of communism and the triumph of liberal democracy. The idealistic image of the world and its peoples living in accord with one another proved short-lived. It was replaced by the image of innate and passionate nationalisms, long repressed by communism, pursuing their respective destinies. In 1996 one widely read pundit, Samuel Huntington, took a different, but no less gloomy tack. For the future of the world he predicted growing religious or culturally based divisions and an inevitable clash of civilizations.

5

The Response of the International Community

When Yugoslavia was created after World War I, the United States and the victorious European powers played a major role in defining its boundaries and its character. The south Slavic lands of the former Habsburg and Ottoman empires were joined with the small independent kingdoms of Serbia and Montenegro into one state. The justification was national self-determination for the local inhabitants, a principle that President Woodrow Wilson of the United States had championed when outlining a plan for the postwar period in his Fourteen Points. Wilsonian idealism, however, was modified with pragmatism by the statesmen who dominated the Paris Peace Conference in 1919. Pragmatism could be described as exercising realism or self-interest in international politics, in this case the self-interest of France, Great Britain, Italy, and the United States. The powers at the time were particularly intent on creating a buffer between themselves and their former ally, Russia, which was in the throes of a communist revolution. Hence Yugoslavia came into existence as one of a string of small "national" states that were to act as a barrier (*cordon sanitaire*) against the ominous East. Besides Wilsonianism and pragmatism, a good dose of cynicism and a sense of Western superiority also governed the day-to-day negotiating at Paris.

A similar combination of motives influenced the Allies' attitude toward Yugoslavia during and after World War II. The Allied powers backed the local forces who fought against the Axis villains Italy and Germany. By 1943 this meant throwing exclusive support to Tito's communist-led Partisans. The West accepted communism in Yugoslavia as the lesser of two evils (fascism/Nazism being the other). Prime Minister Winston Churchill of Great Britain, on a trip to Moscow in late 1944, even accepted Joseph Stalin's imperialistic ambitions in the area, putting his check mark next to Stalin's note about a fifty-fifty division of influence in Yugoslavia between West and East. When Roosevelt later questioned the wisdom of this action, Churchill cynically suggested that, unless one was planning to live in Yugoslavia after the war, what happened to that country internally should be of little concern. His argument was that the immediate war effort and postwar geopolitical concerns should take policy-making precedence. In 1948, when Yugoslavia was expelled from the Moscow-led Cominform, the international communist organization, Tito's regime was welcomed by the West as an enemy of the enemy. A Yugoslavia outside the communist bloc could serve as a valuable tool in the West's Cold War against the USSR. It became a propaganda example to the European communist satellite countries. It was a thorn in the side of Stalin, and it thus became a recipient of massive Western military assistance beginning as early as 1950. As the West overlooked the communist nature of Tito's regime (by the 1960s that regime was even praised in the West for its novel institutions), Yugoslavia rapidly became a significant military power. Its army, with financial aid from the West, became the fourth largest in Europe.

Toward the end of the 1980s, two developments changed the framework of international relations as it related to Europe. One was the collapse in 1989 of communism in the USSR's European satellites: Poland (August), Hungary (October), East Germany, Bulgaria, Czechoslovakia (all in November), and Romania (December). The other was a growing anticipation of European unification, projected for 1992. The latter was eagerly embraced by the former satellite states once they were disentangled from the Soviet community but left floundering in search of economic security. At the same time—the late 1980s and early 1990s—there emerged a new international outlook that was promoted by the great powers, particularly the United States. The unification of the two Germanies, the victorious Gulf War against Iraq, and the restructuring (*perestroika*) taking place in the USSR under Mikhail Gorbachev had produced an infectious euphoria about the future. It was said that a "New World Order" was emerging. Problem states (like Iraq) would be dealt with through "collective engagement," and in the end all states would reap a "peace dividend" (monies no longer needed for defense would be used for domestic programs).

Yugoslavia, too, wanted to become part of the new European Union, and the northern republics at least were also anxious to be rid of communism and federal government controls. The Yugoslavs, however, could not agree upon how to proceed. Yet the fact that in terms of the international community Yugoslavia belonged neither to the East nor to the West put it in a unique and what would prove to be a very precarious position. With the Cold War virtually over, Yugoslavia ceased to be of strategic interest. Troubles in Yugoslavia, even a bloody war, would no longer be of major interest to either East or West. The United States, for example, might abhor the evils that would be perpetrated in Bosnia, but its military could no longer justify intervention in Yugoslavia as being in America's own national interest.

In this regard, it is instructive to compare developments in the USSR and Yugoslavia, both federations being pulled apart by centrifugal forces. In 1991 the West's policy in both cases was to oppose separation. It backed Gorbachev in Moscow and Ante Markovic in Belgrade, standing behind the central governments of the two states even if it meant opposing democratic movements in the fractious republics. So it was that Secretary of State James Baker of the United States traveled to Belgrade on June 21, 1991 (only days before war broke out in Yugoslavia), to lecture Yugoslavia's republic presidents against secession. President George Bush made a similar plea to Ukraine less than two months later on a visit to Kiev. Yet both countries disintegrated, Yugoslavia violently and the USSR almost uneventfully at the end of 1991. Since the West's response to the new situation in the former Soviet Union was fairly positive, it is interesting to speculate on what it might have been if the Yugoslav split had occurred after the Soviet one. If the sequence of events had been reversed, would Baker have arrived to chide the Slovene and Croat separatists (by implication encouraging the federal forces to do anything necessary—even using military force—to keep the country united), or might Yugoslavia have been allowed to split peacefully, as would the USSR and Czechoslovakia?

When the war began (in Slovenia) in late June 1991, the European Community (EC) scurried to the rescue. The foreign ministers of Italy, Germany, the Netherlands, and Luxemburg (Great Britain, France, and also the United States stood in the wings) met with Yugoslavia's leaders. A flurry of diplomatic activity brought about the Brioni Agreement on July 7, which ended the fighting in Slovenia but failed to achieve the same for Croatia. With Slovenia effectively out of the war, the JNA moved more forcefully against Croatia, and the war produced a flood a refugees. In August the Conference on Security and Cooperation in Europe (CSCE) met in Prague to discuss the war and the refugee problem, while the IMF and the World Bank froze funds destined for Yugoslavia. The European Community continued its initiative with regard to the Croatian war, holding a series of almost weekly meetings beginning in early September. Britain's Lord Peter Carrington was named the EC's official mediator. Early in its deliberations the EC discussed deploying the military forces of the Western European Union (WEU) in Yugoslavia, but this proposal was defeated. (The United States was vehemently opposed to European forces acting on their own and conveyed its concerns to its European allies: the future of NATO and the U.S. role in it was at stake.)

The United Nations involved itself in Yugoslav affairs more gradually. The prodding of France seems to have been important here. On September 25, 1991, the United Nations Security Council banned arms sales to all parts of Yugoslavia, an action that in the long run gave a military advantage to the Serbs, who inherited the JNA and its weapons. (In the three-and-one-half-year war in Bosnia, those who felt that Bosnia was at peril because of the UN ban argued forcefully but in vain to lift the arms embargo against it. It was not lifted until June 18, 1996.) In early October the UN asked an American, Cyrus Vance, to act as its mediator in Yugoslavia. By late November Vance had achieved a cease-fire, and discussions began on using UN troops to monitor the peace. The proposal was backed by Britain and France. The EC, the United States, and the UN then cooperated in imposing economic sanctions on Belgrade, first introduced in November 1991, but expanded and tightened several times after that. In September 1992 Yugoslavia, made up by then of Serbia and Montenegro only, was also expelled from the UN.

In the final month of 1991, four months before the war would begin in Bosnia, the debate over whether to recognize Slovene and Croat independence divided the Western powers. The French and the British opposed recognition, with Lord Carrington leading the debate against it, while Germany, whose spokesman was its foreign minister, Hans Dieterich Genscher, strongly favored it. (Vance, the UN mediator, was also against it, believing that it would "damage the peace process.") The battle lines over the issue were reminiscent of World War II's European alliances: it was Britain and France against Germany all over again. But behind the question of Yugoslavia's future was also the future of European leadership, for Slovene and Croat independence was being discussed at the same time as the Maastricht Treaty, the document that would finalize the European Union. Germany, whose economic might frightened the French and the

British, won on the recognition issue; the EC voted to accept independence for the two former northern republics of Yugoslavia and would announce it on January 15, 1992. But in the end Great Britain and France would have their revenge. The management of the cease-fire in Croatia was turned over to the United Nations' UNPROFOR forces in early January. Thereafter the UN, where Germany had less clout (it was not a member of the UN Security Council), would have a greater say than the EC in the affairs of former Yugoslavia.

The United States refused to recognize Slovenia and Croatia in January, maintaining that all of Yugoslavia's republics should have been offered the option of independence. The Americans seemed to be miffed at Germany's carrying the issue in December, but in part the U.S. leadership must have also resented having to deal with so controversial an issue in a presidential election year. In February both Bosnia and Macedonia held referendums to determine popular support for independence, and although the vote was positive in both republics, only Bosnia was recognized that spring. (Macedonian independence was vehemently opposed by Greece, a NATO power; bringing the Greeks on board on this issue would require skillful diplomacy.) The United States strongly supported Bosnian independence, and may even have urged the Bosnian government to seek it. Very likely the Bosnians got the impression that independent status would protect them from war and JNA aggression. Bosnian independence was recognized by the EC on April 6, while the United States recognized all three former Yugoslav republics—Slovenia, Croatia, and Bosnia-Hercegovina—the following day. The UN would accept the three as members on May 22. Neither recognition nor UN membership, however, saved Bosnia from the JNA; the war began there on April 6.

The war in Bosnia started nearly one year after Yugoslavia's disintegration began, by which time the major powers' positions, motives, and policies toward the area were pretty much set. For the British and French, the recently reunited Germany was the central concern. It loomed as a potential economic and political colossus, threatening to dominate the emerging European Union. Therefore Germany's sponsorship of independence for Slovenia and Croatia was seen as a traditional thrust southeastward by German expansionism. The British and French also worried about how the success of separatist movements in Yugoslavia might influence disaffected groups in their own states—in Northern Ireland, for example. In supporting Yugoslavia's unity, Great Britain and France stressed their historical ties with Serbia (e.g., in World War I), and though they may have been pressured by world opinion to send peacekeepers and humanitarian aid to Bosnia in the months to come, both were opposed to substantive commitment there. Only in spring 1995, after Jacques Chirac assumed the presidency of France, did the French focus any serious attention on resolving the Yugoslav crisis.

In the United States, the Bush administration formulated policy toward Yugoslavia until January 1993, and it favored Yugoslav unity and opposed involvement in that country after it began to disintegrate. Bush's prestige and popular support had peaked in spring 1991 with the successful war against Iraq, but both Bush and Baker, his secretary of state, who was soon to become head of Bush's reelection campaign, seemed reluctant to risk a Balkan version of Desert Storm against the JNA in spring 1992. In August of that year, when Lawrence Eagleburger replaced Baker, U.S. policy took on a cynical tone. Eagleburger, who had once been U.S. ambassador to Yugoslavia, took the tack that the Yugoslavs were barbarians governed by passions no civilized state (like the United States) could hope to deal with; his argument was that America must stay out of the conflict and let the natives kill each other until they were tired of the slaughter. At the least it was inappropriate language for a former diplomat in describing the peoples of another nation, but it served well enough as a justification against U.S. involvement while the Bush-Baker team focused on the election. Many believe, however, that Eagleburger and Brent Scowcroft, a member of Bush's National Security Council and a former diplomat who was once also assigned to Yugoslavia, held on to the Yugoslav unity position too long.

The Clinton administration, which came into office in early 1993, was also reluctant to tackle the inherited Yugoslav tough nut, even though during the election campaign Clinton had been very critical of Bush's inaction there. Clinton's foreign policy team was new, learning on the job, and dealing with what Warren Christopher, the new secretary of state, called a "problem from hell." They rejected the Vance-Owen plan (see below) for Bosnia because they opposed rewarding the Serbian aggressor, yet they offered no alternative. Thus for nearly a year the Europeans were left to handle the problem virtually alone. In both the Bush and Clinton administrations important voices in the State and Defense Departments were at odds over how to deal with Yugoslavia. At State the tendency was to support the separatists and to punish the Serbs, with military action if necessary. A number of policy analysts resigned from that department because their counsel was not heeded. The Defense Department, however, was very cautious toward Yugoslavia. Bush's chief of staff, Colin Powell, who opposed involvement in unwinnable conflicts, set the policy tone that was essentially followed by his successor, John Shalikashvili.

The USSR, as well as its successor, the Commonwealth of Independent States (CIS), was at first only a peripheral player in the Yugoslav arena. In 1991, while Gorbachev was still in power, he met with the presidents of Serbia and Croatia, Milosevic and Tudjman, hoping to mediate between them. Later, with Boris Yeltsin in power, the Russians resurrected their traditional role as protector of the Serbs. This seems to have been prompted largely by Yeltsin's need to quell domestic pressures from Russian rightists like Vladimir Zhirinovsky. The West appeared to accept this Russian position—after all, with the Cold War ended, how much of a threat could Russia be?—and it hardly blinked in February 1994 when Russian peacekeeping soldiers were moved into Sarajevo unilaterally. (The Russian move, incidentally, boosted Russian self-esteem, which had been flagging since the disintegration of the USSR in 1991.) Germany, meanwhile, continued to urge greater international involvement on behalf of the separatists and against Belgrade. Germany, newly united and coping with the economic consequences thereof, was also bearing the major load of the Yugoslav refugee problem, having admitted as many as a half million of those (mostly Croats and Muslims) fleeing the war. Germany, however, was in a weak position vis-à-vis the other powers, all of whom (except the United States) had troops in the former Yugoslavia, for Germany was prohibited by its constitution from engaging in military operations abroad.

When the war began in Bosnia, the international community was in agreement on one thing: it opposed military involvement in the area. Instead, it supported the diplomatic missions that had been initiated by the UN and the EC (now the EU). Cyrus Vance and Lord David Owen, who had replaced Carrington, represented the UN and EU, respectively. Their work, crisscrossing the former Yugoslavia, threatening and cajoling devious politicians into accepting the regularly violated cease-fires, was tedious and frustrating. It was a thankless job whose efforts produced a settlement of sorts in January 1993. The Vance-Owen plan proposed the reorganization of Bosnia-Hercegovina into 10 cantons—3 for each of the national groups and a separate one for Sarajevo—while still preserving Bosnia's unity and multiethnic character. The plan was turned down by the Americans because it granted too much to the Serb aggressor, and by the Bosnian Serbs because they wanted more. The Croats, expecting the war to end soon, immediately launched a military operation against the Muslims, their former allies, hoping to be awarded a larger portion of the republic when the conflict ended.

The next diplomatic initiative, headed by Owen and Thorvald Stoltenberg of Norway (Vance's replacement), produced results a year later, in

March 1994. Their plan for a Bosnian peace settlement featured a Bosnia with three ethnic components and was based on an outline proposed by Milosevic and Tudjman. In the United States it was portrayed as a sellout to the aggressors (both Serb and Croat) and a sanctioning of ethnic cleansing policies. The Muslims held out on accepting it, and the Bosnian Serbs, after holding a referendum, turned it down. The United States then belatedly cranked up its own diplomatic efforts after having stood on the sidelines for more than a year. It threw its support behind the Muslims and the Croats, pressuring the two to stop fighting each other in order to create a Muslim-Croat federation within Bosnia. This was hastily put together, as was a confederal association of the new federation with independent Croatia. The federation and confederation agreements were sealed with a signing ceremony in Washington in March 1994. The following month a new association, the Contact Group, was established to deal with the on-going Yugoslav problem. Its members were Britain, France, Germany, Russia, and the United States. Together they pursued a French-German plan, proposed in June 1994, to apply a policy of inducements and punishments toward Serbia, hoping that Serbia would then put pressure on the Bosnian Serbs and thereby bring an end to the conflict. In June 1994 the Contact Group produced yet another proposal for redrawing the map of Bosnia-Hercegovina. It allowed the Serbs only 49 percent of the territory, although they held about 72 percent at the time. The plan, rejected by the Serbs that summer, was expanded the following year and adapted for the U.S. mission, headed by Richard Holbrooke. The Contact Group, with the United States in the lead, thereafter handled the international community's dealings with former Yugoslavia.

Within Bosnia itself the international community had an established presence in the UNPROFOR body. That UN agency had set up its headquarters in Sarajevo in March 1992 in order to monitor the Croatian peace from a safe place. But even before the UN commander, General Lewis MacKenzie of Canada, arrived in Bosnia's capital, war had already begun there, and UNPROFOR troop numbers had to be increased. (UNPROFOR began with 14,000 troops in Croatia, but by spring 1994 had 30,000 in the areas of the former Yugoslavia. In Bosnia-Hercegovina there were 16,300, of whom 5,000 were assigned to Sarajevo.) UNPROFOR was a ragtag group, often ill trained and poorly supplied by the various countries who had sent them. The Bangladeshis arrived without winter clothing, others came without weapons, and many became involved in black marketeering, an activity that thrived because of the UN arms embargo (against all of the former Yugoslavia) and the trade embargo (against the FRY). UNPROFOR was billed as a peacekeeping force, but it had no authority to use weapons even to defend its own troops, much less to defend the local inhabitants. Its troops were shot at, killed by snipers, and taken hostage (mostly in late 1994 and 1995); and UNPROFOR watched, or stood by, as others were raped and killed, even those in its care, like the Bosnian deputy prime minister, Hakija Turajlic, who was murdered by Bosnian Serbs in January 1993, and the roughly 7,000-plus Srebrenicans who were executed in July 1995. Its UN-authorized charge was to remain neutral, to treat all sides equally. Those who took sides, like the French UNPROFOR commander General Philippe Morillon, who espoused the cause of the people of Srebrenica, under Bosnian Serb attack in spring 1993, were recalled.

UNPROFOR occupied itself primarily with dispensing humanitarian aid. But humanitarian convoys were regularly sabotaged, aid was confiscated, and supplies often failed to reach the needy, prompting the United States unilaterally to initiate air drops of food in spring 1993. More than a few Bosnians as well as foreign journalists began to look upon this humanitarian aid quite cynically: it was a device designed to keep the victim fed until the aggressor could kill him. It also helped feed and supply the fighters, whose front men regularly raided the convoys and exacted tolls from their drivers. At least one American reporter concluded that UNPROFOR's presence in Bosnia was actually prolonging the war: Bosnia's saviors had become its jailers.

If UNPROFOR had little control over the brigands who looted humanitarian convoys, it had no authority over the perpetrators of crimes against civilians. Such crimes violated the Geneva Conventions that had been spelled out after World War I. Most of the transgressions against civilians were characterized as "ethnic cleansing," a policy first used by the Serbian aggressor, but also later by others, especially by the Croats, on a lesser scale, during their military blitz against Slavonia and the Krajina in 1995. In spring 1993 the UN tried to deal with the crimes against the larger civilian communities by establishing "safe havens" to protect at least the towns of Bihac, Gorazde, Sarajevo, Srebrenica, Tuzla, and Zepa, whose prewar numbers had been swollen by refugees. The Bosnian Serbs virtually ignored the UN pronouncement about the safe havens, defiantly violating them in 1994 (Gorazde) and 1995 (Srebrenica, Gorazde, and Zepa). Tadeusz Mazowiecki, a former president of Poland acting on behalf of the UN, who had proposed and defended the safe haven idea, resigned in protest when the UN failed to defend the safe areas when they came under attack in 1995. In the end, ethnic cleansing and crimes against civilians (including at least 20,000 rapes) became a matter of business that was delegated by the UN to a war crimes tribunal. Established in October

1992, the war crimes body assembled in The Hague began its work in November 1993, but it acquired a head magistrate (a South African, Richard Goldstone) only in summer 1994, while it issued its first indictments only in September 1995 on the eve of the Dayton peace talks.

Throughout the war, civilians, in fear of being violated or killed, continued to flee the area. About 60 percent of Bosnia's prewar population, 2.7 million people, left their homes. Many went abroad, while others sought refuge in other former Yugoslav republics or sometimes in other areas of Bosnia. In the latter cases, many engaged in voluntary ethnic restructuring, resettling in communities where their own group predominated. In some cases, exchanges of property—a house in a Serb village traded for a house in a Croat one—were prearranged. Wherever the refugees went they put an economic strain on the host country. The UNHCR (UN High Commission for Refugees), headed by Sadako Ogata of Japan, struggled to deal with the massive humanitarian problem.

In the former republics of Yugoslavia and in states that accepted large numbers of those fleeing the war, the problem also became political and even affected European stability. Many in the international community argued that ethnic cleansing and the war could end if the Bosnians were only allowed to defend themselves. To this end many called for lifting the arms embargo against Bosnia—creating a "level playing field," it was called—while others went further, demanding that the international community assist an armed Bosnia against the aggressor. For them, "lift and strike"—removing the arms embargo and using NATO air power to hit strategic targets—was the answer. That policy was not popular among the European powers who had troops in Bosnia against whom Bosnian Serbs might retaliate, but "lift and strike" was strongly advocated in the United States, particularly by liberal journalists and conservative politicians, and it gained wide popular support as reports of war atrocities dominated media coverage. In summer 1995 both houses of the U.S. Congress voted to lift the arms embargo against Bosnia, but most congressmen continued to oppose sending U.S. troops to Bosnia.

Throughout the ongoing war in the former Yugoslavia, there had been a fear that the conflict would spread. One area generally mentioned in this regard was Macedonia, the former Yugoslavia's southernmost republic. War in Macedonia might then spill over into Albania or Greece, and could involve NATO allies Greece and Turkey on opposing sides. Macedonia, which had voted for independence in February 1992 and which met the EU's qualifications for independence, was not immediately recognized internationally. Greece objected to recognition, partly because it felt that it alone had a historical right to use the name "Macedonia." The powers allowed Greece to exercise a virtual veto here. The UN, meanwhile, sent 1,000 troops, about half from the United States, into the area to keep a vigil for peace. (This was the only UN contingent with American troops in it.) Gradually Greece's position was moderated through international pressures, and Macedonia was recognized by the UN in April 1993 and by the EU in late 1993. It was required, however, to use as its name the cumbersome designation "Former Yugoslav Republic of Macedonia" (FY-ROM). Diplomatic pressures (Cyrus Vance was the active mediator here) brought about further accommodation, so that by the fall of 1995 Greece and Macedonia had reestablished trade relations, while the latter state had agreed to change its flag to suit Greece. In October 1995, shortly after this development, assassins who no doubt opposed improved Greek-Macedonian relations tried to kill the Macedonian president, Kiro Gligorov, following his visit to Serbia. Tensions remained, but Macedonia escaped war.

Military involvement in the former Yugoslavia was an issue the international community debated throughout the course of the war. The UN, of course, occupied itself exclusively with humanitarian peacekeeping activities. The EC/EU had discussed using the Western European Union (WEU) forces, but NATO—and the United States in particular—was much opposed to it, so the idea was dropped. NATO's position on the eve of the war, presented by John Galvin, an American general who then headed NATO, was that Yugoslavia was outside NATO's jurisdiction and that therefore NATO did not intend to get involved here. By the spring of 1993, Manfred Woerner, then head of NATO, urged military action, but the powers were reluctant. The states with UN troops on the ground feared Serbian retaliation, and the United States worried about embarrassment or worse if military intervention failed. Margaret Thatcher, former prime minister of Great Britain, together with many world leaders not then in power and with no constituents' support to lose, spoke in favor of an aggressive policy and the use of military means to deal with the Serb aggressors. By default, and rather reluctantly, NATO began to get involved. NATO action was approved in June 1992, and its ships began cruising the Adriatic Sea the following month. In October 1992 the UN established a no-fly zone, but NATO air patrols began only in April 1993. After much discussion, bombing missions were approved in January 1994, but NATO bombs were used (for the first time in the history of the organization) only on March 1 of that year, and then only sparingly.

International involvement in the Yugoslav war was closely followed by the media, which exposed the bureaucratic bumblings of the world powers. The paralysis that seemed to tie the hands of both the UN and NATO was widely broadcast. A "dual key" arrangement with respect to command and control issues, which required NATO to get UN approval for any action, was the journalists' focus. UN Secretary-General Boutros Boutros-Ghali, a Coptic Egyptian, shied away from assertive UN involvement in Bosnia, calling it a "rich man's war." The Japanese special UN envoy Yasushi Akashi, who met regularly with representatives of the combatants, was portrayed as wimpy and somewhat dazed by the whole experience. Akashi tended to let the Bosnian Serbs manipulate him. Decisions to bomb (to protect UNPROFOR forces only), when the bureaucrats finally could agree, usually required warnings to the Serbs that often dragged out for days. The public image of both the UN and NATO began to suffer greatly. As the war in Bosnia entered its third year, and as NATO continued to puzzle over its role in a post–Cold War Europe, a rationale was gradually built for NATO military action. NATO at last understood that, as Richard Lugar, a prominent member of the U.S. Senate Foreign Relations Committee, put it, NATO would have to "go out of area" or "go out of business."

The all-out push for peace, which came in the second half of 1995, included NATO bombings that were at last more determined and freer of UN control, particularly in September 1995. The Europeans had been threatening since October 1994 to pull out their troops, who were regularly under threat; and the United States, to Clinton's regret, had pledged to help evacuate them. The Americans, who worried about casualties, opted to push for peace; then occupying troops, at least, would have a better chance of surviving. The Croat offensive against the Serbs in Croatia's Krajina region in early August and the joint Croat-Muslim offensive in Bosnia—both successful operations—paved the way for the Americans and NATO to make a positive strike. The Contact Group pulled itself together. The United States worked out arrangements with the Russians (Serb protectors); and in September, France, for 20 years a reluctant partner in NATO, formally rejoined NATO's military operations. Bosnia became the test of NATO's relevance, leading some to wonder whether NATO moved in order to save Bosnia or in order to save itself. Cynics said it was definitely the latter.

The Dayton agreement (discussed earlier) was concluded on November 22 and came to be known as the "American Peace," for special envoy Richard Holbrooke and Secretary of State Warren Christopher, both of the United States, played the major roles in obtaining a treaty. All Contact Group members, however, were actively engaged in the deliberations, and all were given a special role in the postwar peacekeeping or rehabilitation (economic, political, and military) of Bosnia. Primary effort was put on achieving peace, while the goal of a multiethnic, multireligious, multicultural Bosnia faded into the details. Few noticed, perhaps because there was a news blackout for three weeks during the conference, that Bosnia was in fact being dismembered and that the aspirations of Milosevic and Tudjman of dividing Bosnia between them were still a real possibility in the future. But then the Contact Group in summer 1994 had already prepared the world for compromises; the group had already "jumped over the moral bridge in the interests of wider peace," as one U.S. envoy had described the new diplomatic approach toward the Bosnian war.

The peace agreement was signed in Paris on December 14, 1995. In addition to the presidents of Bosnia, Croatia, and the FRY, all of the presidents and foreign ministers of the Contact Group powers were in attendance. (Only the ailing Russian Boris Yeltsin was absent; he was represented by his prime minister, Viktor Chernomyrdin.) Also present were Javier Solana, the new head of NATO; Filipe Gonzales, the head of the EU; Abdellatif Filali, a Moroccan who spoke for the Islamic states; and Carl Bildt, the former Swedish prime minister, who was about to become the EU envoy to oversee Bosnia's civilian rehabilitation. It was an imposing assemblage that was gathered in the resplendent Elysée Palace. Its members pledged $6 billion in international aid, warning the recent combatants that they would not tolerate renewed hostilities. They hoped to scare the Yugoslavs into behaving. The powers also congratulated one another on their respective contributions to peace. Each president took his turn at the podium; Bill Clinton spoke last. The symbolism of this is remarkable, for it not only acknowledged a new relevance for NATO but affirmed U.S. leadership of NATO and of the post–Cold War world. The Bosnian peace, if nothing else, had produced the framework for a new international order.

6

Back to Kosovo, Where It All Began

In March 1981, less than a year after Tito's death, students began demonstrating in Kosovo's capital, Pristina. Their demands were relatively modest: edible cafeteria food and better, less crowded dormitories. It began as a small disturbance at Pristina University, which had been established in 1969 to accommodate Albanian as well as Serbian students there. The liberal communists then in power in Yugoslavia, who approved the new institution, could hardly have predicted its rapid growth and disruptive potential. By 1981, the university had 36,000 students, not counting 18,000 enrolled in extension programs. Most students signed up for humanities courses and were generally unemployable when they finished their studies. At the time, in 1981, Yugoslavia was experiencing severe economic problems, including a groaning foreign debt and massive unemployment (25.7 percent in Kosovo, a figure that reached 57 percent by 1989).

The federal government in Belgrade sent in troops and declared a national emergency. By the end of March, violence had erupted, hundreds were arrested, and some students accused of counterrevolutionary motives began voicing the larger economic, social, and political goals that they were being accused of having. The government overreacted, thereby encouraging Serbian hard-liners in the administration to exact revenge against Albanians. The university was closed down, as were elementary and secondary schools (ostensibly for an early summer break). Education for Kosovar Albanians came to a stop. The university students returned home, and the countryside and nearby towns were politicized by them. Kosovar intellectuals soon began drafting reform programs. During the 1980s, Kosovo, a province of two million, came under police rule. By the end of the decade, 584,373 Kosovo Albanians, one-half the adult population, would be arrested, interrogated, or interned. In the West, human rights monitors were writing that Kosovo had come under apartheid rule. A vicious circular process had been unleashed.

Throughout the 1980s, the Serbian response to developments in Kosovo was highly charged, as though emotions long pent up had begun spilling out uncontrollably. The student demonstrations had irritated a festering wound, and now that Tito was gone, Serbs were determined to get their due. Serbs experienced a nationalist resurgence that was expressed in the media and in public life. When Alexandar Rankovic, the Serb vice president and interior minister of Yugoslavia from 1945 to 1966, who had been removed by Tito in 1966 for secret police activities against the government, died in 1983, 100,000 Serbs turned out for "their" man's funeral in Belgrade. As things heated up in Kosovo, Serbs got on the "Let's Go to Kosovo" bandwagon. It meant supporting Serbian resettlement of the province in order to help assert Serbian claims to it. It also meant giving notice that Serbs intended not to be victims any longer, that Tito's policies were going to be reversed, and that "past mistakes," such as constitutional accommodations to the Albanians of Kosovo, would be erased. The nationalist newspapers and television fed the mob's frenzy. When, in 1985, a Serbian farmer in Kosovo, named Martinovic, charged (probably falsely) that he had been sexually assaulted by two Albanians, it was played up by the nationalists to stimulate anti-Albanian feelings. Similarly, when, in 1987, an Albanian recruit named Aziz Kelmendi went berserk in his barracks in Paracin, killing four (only one was a Serb), the media used the "massacre" to heighten anti-Albanian sentiments. It was in this context that the Serbian Academy of Science and Arts composed its memorandum (made public in 1986) and that Slobodan Milosevic took over leadership of the Serbian communists (1987).

The nationalism daring to express itself again, in this last decade of communist rule, necessarily refocused on national history. Hence both Serbs and Albanians sought to tie Kosovo to their respective pasts. This province of less than 11,000 square kilometers (12 percent of the Republic of Serbia), had a population of two million, about 90 percent of whom were Albanian, and both national communities claimed it for their own. For the Serbs it was the heart of the first Serbian state, founded in the late 1100s, and it became central to their spiritual past, when the Serbian Orthodox Church's Patriarchate was relocated there (to Pec) in 1346. In the 1980s, there were still dozens of Serbian monasteries in western Kosovo, which is why Serbs began insisting that Kosovo once again be called Kosovo-Metohija (*Metohija* meaning "monastic lands"). Kosovo was also the location of the battlefield where, in 1389, an encounter between Serbs and Turks brought an end to the medieval Serbian state, or so legend had it. In fact, other battles were more important to Serbia's decline—the final conquest of Serbian lands did not come until 1455—but the 1389 Battle of Kosovo Polje had acquired symbolic significance. Oral legends about it had enshrined Serbs as a chosen people of the New Testament.

Albanians, too, claimed Kosovo, since their ancestors, they maintained, had inhabited the area long before the Serb tribes arrived in the sixth century A.D. They believed their forebears to be Illyrians, and although some historians suggest a Thracian ancestry, most recent scholarship sides with the Illyrian position. Whatever the case, they were certainly there before the Serbs, although perhaps in smaller numbers; they probably even fought on the side of the Serbs in the legendary 1389 battle. In the 1980s they outnumbered the Serbs there by nine to one. Unlike the Serbs, the Albanians did not have a common religion or church that united them— a few were Catholic, some were Orthodox, while most (80 percent) over the years had become Muslim. They did, however, have a common legal/ moral code, the Kanun of Dukagjin, which had been codified in the 1400s. Highlighting the principle of personal honor, it was not published in its entirety until 1933.

In a perfect (nationalist) world, each nation would have a state of its own in which all its members would live, nurturing a common language, culture, and general well-being. In the nineteenth century, many believed that this ideal was visibly unfolding, as one national community after another established its own country. If Italy and Germany could come into being, why not Serbia and Albania? Indeed, as the Ottoman Empire's control of its Balkan lands ebbed, national states began emerging there. A small Serbia had appeared on the map already in 1817, although its independent status was not approved by the European powers until 1878. That very year, however, conservative Albanian leaders, many of them Muslim landowners, organized the League of Prizren. Recognizing the dangers, to them, of the nationalist ambitions of their neighbors, they formed the league as a bulwark against the expansionism of emerging national states in the Balkans. As elsewhere, nation building was clearly moving beyond the ideal, for as politicians and state builders sought wealth and power, they manipulated nationalism to serve their own selfish ends. By then, Serb statesmen had already forged their plan for a Greater Serbia, which demanded that Serbia include not only the lands where Serbs then lived but also those lands where Serbs may have lived or ruled in the past. Pursuing the Serbian nationalist goal put Serbs into conflict with the Ottoman Empire, the Austro-Hungarian Empire, and to a certain degree the state of Montenegro as well. Similarly, to achieve independence, Albanians would have to hold off the advances of Serbs, Montenegrins, Macedonians, and Greeks. Fortunately for them, Austria-Hungary came to their aid in late 1912. With Austrian sponsorship, Albania became a European state, although its borders were still being discussed when World War I interrupted the march of the Balkan peoples toward their own national states.

World War I was a great boon to Serbian nation building. After initial defeats, and several years of occupation and exile for the Serbian royal government, Serbia's enemies were routed and their respective states dismembered. Some Austrian and Ottoman territories were joined with Serbia to form the Kingdom of Serbs, Croats, and Slovenes (renamed Yugoslavia in 1929). Not only were all Serbs now together in one state, but other Southern Slavs were to be governed by Belgrade as well. The Serbs could hardly have wished for more. Kosovo was now included in this state, although its Albanians—400,000 of them—were not specifically mentioned in the state's name. In 1921 the Kosovars, unhappy with their lot, petitioned the League of Nations for Kosovo to be included in Albania, but the request was denied. A large Albanian state was not meant to be at that time. Kosovo Albanians lost their privileges, were allowed only religious instruction (Serbs identified them as Turks and encouraged them to emigrate from Kosovo to the new state of Turkey), and often had their lands expropriated in order to accommodate Serb colonists.

During World War II, Italy annexed Albania proper, and Yugoslavia, too, was invaded and partitioned by various enemy powers. Tiny Kosovo was divided among the Italians, Bulgarians, and Germans. During the war, Albanian nationalists formed the Balli Kombetar, a resistance movement favoring unification of Kosovo with Albania; it opposed the return of the Albanian king, but it also rejected working with the communists, who were, in their minds, too "Slavic." After the collapse of Italy in September 1943, Tito's communist agents were finally able to recruit some Albanians for their National Liberation Movement. They lukewarmly promised to support the unification of all Albanians. Final plans were not specified, but it was generally expected that after the war a unified Albania-Kosovo would become a part of a Yugoslav, or even a general larger Balkan, federation.

As it turned out, both Serbs and Albanians would be disappointed by the post-1945 Yugoslav state. Serbia became one of its six federal republics, but, to their dismay, numerous Serbs were absorbed into neighboring Yugoslav republics. Kovoso (also Vojvodina) became a part of Serbia, but because of a sizable Albanian population, it was given the status of "autonomous region." The new state structure was meant to promote equality among the federal units, but Serbs suspected that a balancing device had deliberately been put into play. Its purpose, they believed, was to keep Serbia weak. The Kosovars, at first, were not sure how to assess these developments. As matters were still in flux before 1948, some believed Kosovo could still be united with Albania; but should that not happen, Kosovars would be confined to an inferior status in the new Yugoslavia. Significantly, the 1946 Yugoslav constitution had categorized Albanians as a "nationality" rather than a "nation." Given that fact, they could never have a republic of their own; only "nations" were constitutionally entitled to have republics.

With the Russia-Yugoslavia split in 1948, Yugoslavia's borders were closed to both East and West. Yugoslavia was isolated. Kosovars were thus cut off from Albania, which thereafter experienced bizarre ideological associations, first with Russia and then with China. Prospects for Albanian unification—even if the Kosovars might have favored it—were slim. As the world settled into four decades of Cold War, the Kosovar Albanians were stuck in Serbia/Yugoslavia. They were illiterate and poor, and they had little hope for advancement or even autonomy. Only in the 1960s did things begin to look up for them. In 1963 the Yugoslav government upgraded Kosovo to the status of "province"; in 1965, with the establishment of a special federal fund for underdeveloped regions, Kosovo was allotted financial assistance (40 percent of the fund) for economic improvement; in 1967 Tito made a notable visit to the province; and in 1968 "Metohija" was dropped from the province's name. In 1969 Kosovo gained a new constitution, and also a new supreme court and authorization for a university in Pristina. Five years later, the Constitution of 1974 made Kosovo one of eight official units of the Yugoslav federation, giving Kosovo an equal vote in the national governmental bodies. All of these developments were greeted favorably by the Albanians, since their numbers had grown to an overwhelming majority in Kosovo and they would therefore be the prime beneficiaries of the changes. The Serbs, on the other hand, fumed, for their control over Kosovo seemed to be getting increasingly remote. Moreover, their power in Yugoslavia had been greatly diminished.

The Serbian national cause was resurrected in the 1980s. Tito's death in 1980 and student demonstrations in Pristina in 1981 were an impetus and early markers for its rise. At first, Serbianism was voiced very tentatively and usually by noncommunists. But the Serbian Academy Memorandum, and particularly the media's coverage of it, signaled a breakthrough to a broader base. Yet, as late as June 1987, Slobodan Milosevic, a "Yugoslav-minded" communist, denounced the memorandum as "darkest nationalism." This, in spite of his April 24 visit to Kosovo, where he was moved by the crowds to champion the province's Serbs—a fact that the media exploited shamelessly. The latter quickly advanced Milosevic's political fortunes, catapulting him to popularity and to the head of the Serbian party by the end of the year. As Milosevic abandoned party ideology for the "nationalist" cause, the nationalist press and state television became his ally, as did the Orthodox Church. Both urged Serbian (re)unification, and Kosovo was the obvious place to start, for it was Serbia's historical and spiritual heartland.

Throughout 1988 Serbian nationalism continued to escalate. The media beat the drums, while Serbs across the republic joined regular street demonstrations, some even wearing old Chetnik garb—including hats with the skull and crossbones—that had not been seen since World War II. Milosevic understood the message and proceeded with asserting Serbian power. In October and November 1988, he succeeded in purging the League of Communists (LCY) parties in Kosovo, Vojvodina, and even the republic of Montenegro, of their Yugoslav-minded leadership, in favor of persons loyal to him. In the cases of Vojvodina and Kosovo, the next step was to amend their constitutions, negating the 1974 constitutional provision that had given the provinces autonomy, though it left them within Serbia. Restoring them to undisputed Serbian control was paramount. In the case of Kosovo, autonomy was relinquished in March 1989 by a "packed" parliament. Milosevic's gains were swift and would have weighty consequences for all of Yugoslavia. With control over four of the eight federal units by 1989, Serbia now owned one-half the votes in the collective federal presidency, the eight-person body that rotated presidents annually and came to dominate Yugoslav politics in 1991. Serbia was clearly poised to pounce for control of all of Yugoslavia.

The Kosovars protested the November 1988 purge and arrest of their party leaders. One notable Albanian communist who was arrested at the time was Azem Vllasi; he was later tried unfairly, in a highly charged atmosphere, in a court surrounded by army tanks. His arrest and trial heightened Albanian-Serb tensions and aroused concerns in other Yugoslav republics, particularly in Slovenia. In November, Albanian miners from

Trepca (the Mitrovica area) demonstrated for five days, carrying both Yugoslav and Albanian flags and pictures of Tito. (The mines, which produced 50 percent of Yugoslavia's nickel, 48 percent of its lead and zinc, and 47 percent of its magnesium, in addition to other metals and coal, were of great actual and potential value to Serbia.) In early 1989, when a curfew was imposed on Kosovo, the Trepca miners went on an eight-day hunger strike, an action joined by shopkeepers, educators, and others who turned it into a national strike. The protests, however, were in vain; Belgrade met each resistance with severe police and military restrictions.

In the face of Serb pressures, the Albanians of Kosovo felt they had little recourse. Instead, they began leading a virtual life in a virtual state. They organized schools and hospital care when Belgrade cut off these services for Albanians; moreover, they collected the taxes needed to pay for them. They formed their own trade unions and also established a new leadership, which directed the political affairs of the province. A strong family structure kept the parallel institutions functioning well. Shortly after Kosovo lost its autonomy in March 1989, Albanian political leaders stood on the steps of a parliament whose doors were closed to them and issued a proclamation of sovereignty for Kosovo. Two years later, on September 22, 1991, when war was already in progress in Croatia, the Kosovars held a referendum on establishing a republic, an effort that met with overwhelming voter support. Thereafter school and university documents were stamped "Republic of Kosovo." Of course, none of these developments were acknowledged by Serbia.

The new Albanian leadership was comprised largely of intellectuals—mostly writers and professors—many of them former members of the LCY. The party they organized, in December 1989, was called the Democratic League of Kosovo (LDK). By 1991 it had 700,000 members, an astonishing number. Ibrahim Rugova, a professor of Albanian literature who was educated at the Sorbonne in Paris, was chosen to lead the LDK. A compromise candidate, his calm manner and ability to get along with others qualified him for the position. Some would characterize him as dull and affected, partly because of the silk neck scarf he wore at all times, except, apparently, in the month of August. For nearly a decade, Rugova set the political program for the Kosovars. Its cardinal principle was pacifism vis-à-vis the Serbs. His justifications were that Kosovo was poor (in late 1989 the Serbs had summarily appropriated $98 million from the Bank of Kosovo for Yugo Banka in Belgrade); that its people had no weapons, since Serbs had confiscated arms from Kosovo's territorial defense units; and that, because the Serbs were eagerly waiting for a pretext to move into Kosovo to put the Albanians down, it was best not to irritate them.

For Rugova, the optimum policy was to be calm and wait. Meanwhile, the LDK drafted its long-range program. For as long as Yugoslavia continued to exist, the goal would be a "republic" for Kosovo. If Yugoslavia were to collapse, the LDK would work for independence. A third possibility, union with Albania, was an eventuality put on hold. The chief reason was that Albania at the time was a huge question mark. It had virtually collapsed in February 1991, and its new leader, Sali Berisha, was facing economic catastrophe. For the interim, LDK established a party office in the new Albania.

Meanwhile, Milosevic and Serbia continued the triumphal march toward victory. On March 28, 1989, five days after Kosovo lost its autonomous status, the Serbs proclaimed Serbia to be whole again. On June 28, the 600th anniversary of the legendary Kosovo Polje battle, 1,000,000 Serbs gathered at the site, near Pristina, to greet Milosevic, who descended from above by helicopter—an image reminiscent of Hitler's plane emerging from the clouds, greeted by Germans assembled for the Nuremberg rally in 1934. Serbs in Croatia soon were drawn into the euphoria. With support from Serbia, they organized politically, and when Croatia adopted a new constitution (June 1990), the Croatian Serbs followed with a declaration of independence (August 1990). Soon the Serbs in Bosnia would jump on the bandwagon. The LCY of Yugoslavia had fallen apart in January 1990, and both Slovenia and Croatia had held republic elections that brought noncommunist governments to power. (Both, also, were greatly alarmed by Milosevic and the new Serbian nationalism, and had been severe critics of Serbian treatment of the Kosovo Albanians.) The course of events in 1990 and early 1991 are covered in chapters 2 and 3, and need not be repeated here. Clearly, what had begun in 1981 in Kosovo with the student demonstrations over cafeteria food had led in June 1991 to the onset of war among the peoples of the former Yugoslavia.

The war would last until November 1995, yet, surprisingly, Kosovo was hardly involved in the story. Little happened there in the war years. The Albanians lived their lives, ran their schools and hospitals, and paid their taxes. They boycotted elections in Serbia in 1990, 1992, and 1994, preferring to reject the legitimacy of Belgrade's rule. They continued to get financial assistance from the sizable Albanian community living abroad, often referred to as *Gastarbeiter,* or guest workers, because they had migrated mostly to western European states—especially to Germany and Switzerland—in search of jobs. (As many as 350,000 were working in Germany alone.) The Serbs, whose police still patrolled Kosovo, had little time for the sometimes unruly province; they were busy with a three-and-one-half-year siege against Sarajevo. Even the West ignored the Kosovars, although in the prewar years, many had staunchly defended the Kosovars' human rights. The Kosovar leadership, headed by Rugova, was meek and deferential. Its "virtual" government was headquartered in Ljubljana, Slovenia, until May 1992, after which it moved to Germany. In April 1992, at a meeting in London called to discuss impending war in Bosnia, the Rugova delegation came but its members were treated as observers. The group was not allowed to participate in deliberations and had to be satisfied with watching the discussion on a television monitor in a separate room. Kosovo, according to one observer, settled into a dull and "sullen stability" during the war years. The only development of note came from Washington in late 1992, a "Christmas Warning," drafted by President George Bush's Secretary of State Lawrence Eagleburger, who admonished the Serbs to leave the Albanians in Kosovo alone or be faced with the use of force against them.

The Dayton peace agreement of November 1995 was hastily concluded just weeks after the fighting ended. Kosovo's Albanian leadership was surprised that the status of their province was not even on the agenda. Except for a warning to Belgrade that the United Nations would continue sanctions against Belgrade until Serbia started to deal positively and directly with the Kosovars, Kosovo was deliberately side-stepped. Richard Holbrooke had wagered the Dayton settlement on Milosevic's cooperation. Negotiators understood that Kosovo would be treated as an internal concern of Serbia, which it put off the bargaining table. The West had even persuaded Berisha in Albania to support their position. The disillusionment felt by the Kosovars after Dayton was heightened the following April when the European Union officially recognized the Yugoslav state (Serbia and Montenegro) and especially when, in June 1996, the head of the newly established U.S. Information Office in Pristina lectured Ibrahim Rugova to the effect that Kosovo was regarded as a part of Yugoslavia and that it should continue so.

The lesson the Kosovars gained from the Dayton treaty was that pacifism led nowhere. The way was thus open to those elements who favored a more militant approach. In fact, already in mid-1993, such a group had founded the National Movement for the Liberation of Kosovo. By December it also established a military wing, the Kosovo Liberation Army (KLA), which was charged with preparing guerrilla operations against Serbia. The movement was especially strong among Albanians abroad and heavily financed by them. Few, however, knew about the existence of these organizations before 1995. Only in April 1996 did the KLA actually begin sporadic guerrilla activity, and it took credit for its killing of Serbs on a BBC Albanian-language broadcast in London. The organization stepped up its assassinations of Serb officials throughout 1997 and 1998, gaining in popularity among the Kosovar people as it did so. In October 1997, 13,000 mourners attended a funeral for a KLA man who was killed by Serbs, and 20,000 mourners attended one in November. At the November funeral, one of three masked KLA men in attendance removed his disguise and condemned the Serb killing of Albanians. The killings continued, the retaliations by KLA increased, and support for the KLA grew. More and more Kosovars were rejecting Rugova's pacifist policies.

The escalation of violence in Kosovo alarmed the West. Diplomats, like Robert Gelbart, the U.S. representative in Pristina, lectured the Albanians about engaging in violence. The Serbs interpreted this as a go-ahead to clamp down on "terrorists" in "their" province. Meanwhile, the British foreign minister Robin Cook traveled to Belgrade to persuade Milosevic to negotiate a deal with the moderate Albanians. Milosevic brushed him off and refused to see other envoys. Richard Holbrooke, Milosevic's drinking buddy from Dayton, however, was able to get the Serb leader to receive him. Holbrooke convinced Milosevic to talk with Rugova in mid-May; later that month, Rugova went to Washington to see President Clinton. In July, Holbrooke got Milosevic to agree to a monitoring force for Kosovo, the Kosovo Diplomatic Observer Mission (KDOM). This was one month after NATO, which continued to monitor events in the former Yugoslavia area after the Dayton peace, attempted to rattle Milosevic with aerial exercises, called "Determined Falcon."

In late September 1998, the United Nations Security Council issued its Resolution 1199, calling upon both the Serbs and Albanians to cease their violence. Anticipating that both sides, but especially Serbia, would ignore the UN resolution, NATO began discussing the legality of using force. Traditionally, NATO considered force only when one or more of its own members was under attack, but Serbia, the country in question, had not attacked a NATO member. Rather, the issue was whether NATO could justify intervening in what was to them clearly a matter internal to Serbia, a sovereign state. The United States, especially Secretary of State Madeleine Albright, favored intervention, and by the end of the month NATO also accepted that position, relying on the reasoning of the French president, Jacques Chirac, who argued that a humanitarian emergency allowed it. The matter was clinched on October 8, when Contact Group leaders meeting at London's Heathrow airport got a back-handed go-ahead from Igor Ivanov, Russia's foreign minister. He told the group that should intervention in Serbia be proposed to the United Nations, Russia (China, too) would veto it; however, if NATO intervened, Russia would protest but, naturally, would have no recourse. The Russians had pressing domestic problems to deal with and had grown exasperated with the Serbs; according to one observer, they were particularly weary of Milosevic's tedious brother, who was Serbia's ambassador to Moscow.

In 1999 violence escalated on both sides. KDOM and KVM (Kosovo Verifying Mission), an OSCE/NATO group that Holbrooke and Milosevic had agreed upon in October, cooperated in monitoring the violence. On January 8, 1999, 45 inhabitants of the Albanian village of Racak were massacred, and KVM quickly confirmed that Serbs were to blame. Racak was the turning point in the course of events. It convinced the Contact Group and NATO that intervention against Serbia was imperative. Great Britain, Germany, and the United States began preparing for an occupying force, later named KFOR.

Serbia and the Kosovars, however, were to be allowed one last chance to show they could behave. The Contact Group organized a peace conference at Rambouillet, not far from Paris. The Serbs and Kosovars were summoned to France and told they would have to agree to the conference agreement or face dire consequences. Besides the Bishop Artemije, the Serbs sent no one of importance; they could, of course, rely on Serbian embassy support from Paris. Initially, the Kosovars were afraid to come because the Serbs warned that they would be arrested if they did. The French saved the conference by providing them with travel documents and transportation. The Kosovar delegation of 16 was made up of a disparate group, individuals belonging to rival factions, who in some cases had never met one another. They would have to learn to get along. The leading Albanians at the meeting were the pacifist Rugova, the 29-year-old militant KLA head Hashim Thaci, and Veton Surroi, editor of *Koha Ditore*, who moderated between rival factions and helped build the consensus decisions that the delegation had agreed to support. An advising team, made up of influential Americans and Germans, assisted the Kosovars. The two delegations, incidentally, would never meet one another, and they even lived on separate floors at Rambouillet.

The meeting began on February 6 and lasted, after an extension, until the 23rd. One document on the agenda contained nonnegotiable principles. It guaranteed the territorial integrity of Yugoslavia, meaning that Kosovo would not be allowed independence at that time; it included human rights guarantees for both Serbs and Albanians; and finally, it stated that what was discussed and agreed to at Rambouillet could be revised after three years. A second document, which was intended as an interim agreement, dealt with matters such as a cease-fire, and a representative assembly for Kosovo and elections to it.

The Serbs treated the conference as a lark. They drank heavily, caroused, and sang late into the night. In order to get some attention to the matter at hand, the French took to cutting back on cheese courses at dinner, and even announced that they had run out of cognac. The Albanians took the conference more seriously, debating specific issues at length and expressing particular concern about provisions for a future referendum on independence. The United States, suspecting that the Serbs would not sign the agreement, worked hardest to get the Albanians to accept it. Jamie Rubin from the state department befriended Thaci, the KLA leader, and assured him that the Kosovars would benefit from signing. Secretary of State Albright arrived for the last days of the meeting and promised the Kosovars an independence referendum in three years. The pressure on the Kosovars finally bore results; they signed on March 18, after consulting with Albanians at home.

On March 23, the Serbs, as expected, rejected Rambouillet. The Americans could thus say that the Albanians were the "good guys." Some historians have suggested that Albright and the U.S. delegation wanted the Rambouillet meeting precisely for this purpose: to prove to Europe definitively that the Serbs were intransigent. Holbrooke was again in Belgrade with Milosevic on the 23rd; when they parted, it was clear to both that war was imminent.

The war in Kosovo, which had no UN Security Council resolution to back it, began on March 24. It lasted 78 days and ended on June 10. Like most wars, it was not the war either side had expected. NATO envisioned an action lasting a few days, basically confined to light bombing in the Belgrade suburbs. But the Serbs were not easily intimidated. Several days before the war's onset, Milosevic had purged his leadership, assuring that hard-liners would be in power in the government and in the army in the likelihood of a conflict. Forty thousand military and police were in or near Kosovo, where pressure against the local Albanian population quickly increased. As soon as the bombing began, Kosovars, who generally welcomed the NATO engagement, began leaving the province. In the first week alone, 300,000 fled; in all, during the conflict more than 848,000 crossed Kosovo's borders into Albania, Montenegro, and Macedonia. The latter, because it feared civil unrest and economic crisis due to the rapid influx of refugees, soon closed its borders. As the Albanians left, Serb authorities confiscated their personal and property ownership documents. This would make it difficult, if not impossible, for them to return. Inadvertently, NATO, whose bombing Serbia blamed for the refugee exodus, had given the Serbs a way to realize their hope of cleansing Kosovo of Albanians. NATO also had to scramble to help feed and house (in tents) the refugees.

Things went badly for NATO. The military action, for one, required the approval of 19 countries, which NATO's head, the Spaniard Javier Solana, secured on March 23. Once the fighting began, the military commander, U.S. General Wesley Clark, took over and directed the war from NATO headquarters in Brussels, based on e-mailed video reports of the previous day's missions. Twice daily he held teleconferences to coordinate what was essentially war waged by a committee. Various NATO powers had serious disagreements over how to execute the conflict. France, for example, was against bombing bridges; Greece, although reluctantly going along with the war, had to deal with overwhelming public opinion against it; and the United States opposed use of ground forces. The war was carried out exclusively by air, from heights of 15,000 feet or above, in order to avoid NATO casualties. A long spell of bad weather and the Serbs' knack for manipulating their radar so that allied planes could not "lock on" to Serb targets resulted in a sorry performance. The Serb public, rather than rise up to overthrow Milosevic, as some NATO statesmen expected or at least hoped, rallied behind Serbia's leadership. Meanwhile, NATO, holding on to the fiction that they were not taking sides in the Balkan conflict, refused to coordinate action with the KLA, which could have been of great help on the ground, especially where reconnaissance was vital. So NATO, which had "stumbled into war" without a real plan, and certainly no Plan B, escalated war efforts gradually. Eventually, the bridges were bombed, and electric facilities and civic structures became targets. Often NATO bombs went astray or targeted the wrong building. The biggest blunder was certainly NATO's bombing on May 7 of the Chinese embassy in Belgrade, an action that could have been avoided if the CIA, which chose the target, had updated its map of the city. The embassy bombing caused a major diplomatic crisis between the United States and China.

Milosevic had also expected a shorter war. He doubted NATO's cohesion and ability to persevere. He also counted on Russian help, which in the end he did not get. Boris Yeltsin, Russia's president, who was experiencing a variety of problems at home, politically could not survive a long NATO action. He feared Russian public opinion would push him toward helping Serbia. In mid-April, while NATO was holding its 50th-anniversary celebration in Washington, Yeltsin telephoned Clinton and told him he wanted the war to end. At the same time, NATO leaders, embarrassed by their feeble performance to date in Serbia, redoubled their resolve to win.

A month of allied and diplomatic efforts brought two important actions. NATO finally got its act together, agreeing that ground forces would have to be used if the aerial campaign continued to falter. The United States was key to this development. On May 18, President Clinton, who at the war's outset was still reeling from an impeachment proceeding against him, wrote a letter to the *New York Times,* publicly putting "all options on the table," meaning that the use of ground forces would be considered. The British immediately began planning a September invasion, while Clinton's National Security Council finally formulated a clear war policy: "Serbs Out, NATO and Albanians Back." At the same time, Russian diplomats were actively working to pressure Milosevic to give up. The Russian special envoy Viktor Chernomyrdin, together with his close friend Vice President Al Gore and the Deputy Secretary of State Strobe Talbot, who was fluent in Russian, prepared the way. Meanwhile, a neutral mediator, the Finn Martti Ahtisarri, was chosen to help deal with the Serbs. In early June, the Russians agreed to the critical NATO demand that all Serb forces *must* leave Kosovo. Chernomyrdin and Ahtisarri took the message to Milosevic, who a few days earlier, along with four key Serb government officials, had been indicted by the International War Crimes Tribunal. On June 3, Milosevic at last capitulated.

On June 9, military heads from NATO and Yugoslavia signed a Military-Technical Agreement ending the fighting. The document stipulated the withdrawal of all Serbian forces (military, paramilitary, and police) from Kosovo, a task that was expeditiously completed by June 20. It also provided for the presence of an international security contingent to monitor the agreement and facilitate the return of refugees. Incidentally, on June 12, hours before the Western forces were to arrive in Kosovo, Russians, who were among the occupying force in Bosnia, crossed into Kosovo with 50 vehicles and took over Pristina airport. They, perhaps correctly, expected NATO to exclude them from the postwar settlement in the area.

On June 10, NATO officially stopped the bombing, and the UN Security Council passed its Resolution 1244 outlining the postwar settlement for the area. The United Nations then set up a Mission in Kosovo (UNMIK) as prescribed by 1244. It was headed by the Frenchman Bernard Kouchner, a founder of the Medecins sans Frontiers (Doctors without Borders). His first task was to ease the Kosovars back into the idea of autonomy within Serbia/Yugoslavia. Ten thousand KFOR forces would be on hand in Kosovo and Macedonia to back him up. He also sought the cooperation of local leaders, both Albanian and Serb. In accord with Resolution 1244, the KLA demilitarized. Some weapons were actually turned in, and the Kosovo Protection Corps of 3,000, with 2,000 reservists, replaced the KLA. Human rights, although guaranteed by the resolution, were still abused—often this time by Albanian acts against the Serbs. Veton Surroi wrote eloquently about the need for all in Kosovo to honor human rights and chastised Kosovar Albanians for their transgressions against the Serbs.

By late autumn 1999, things had generally stabilized. Virtually all of the 848,000 Albanians who had fled in spring had returned, marking the most rapid resolution of a refugee crisis in modern memory. The Kosovars seemed to be adapting to what they expected to be a temporary condition of autonomy; assembly elections and a referendum on independence were hoped for in the near future. Unification with Albania proper appeared to be an abandoned goal. Since the fall of the Berisha regime in 1997, the Kosovars had no friendly leader to look to in Albania. Besides, economic conditions in Albania were dismal, worse than in Kosovo. Some Kosovar writers even began using the Kosovar Albanian dialect (Gheg, as opposed to the Tosk dialect used in Albania) in their publications. It seemed to signal a settling in for a separate Kosovo existence. Also settling in were the KFOR forces, who erected Camp Bondsteel, the largest U.S. military base since the Vietnam War. It had durable housing for five thousand.

As for the 78-day war, much has been written about its impact on warfare and on international law. One prominent British military historian has insisted that June 3, 1999, the day Milosevic capitulated, will mark a turning point in the history of warfare, for it ended the very first war in which air power alone was responsible for victory. Ground troops, although discussed, were never used. Others would disagree that air power was pivotal; diplomacy, particularly Russia's pressure on Serbia, was a very important, if not decisive, factor. All would agree, however, that the war was of a new sort. One side, NATO, fought with ultramodern technology using only limited manpower (15,000 NATO crew, assisted by 30,000 technicians), operating from great distances, in order to minimize pilot risk. (The Stealth B2 bomber, for example, flew its 14-hour missions from a base in Missouri.) There were only two NATO casualties, and these were the result of an Apache helicopter malfunctioning during a trial flight. The war for NATO personnel was what one observer calls a guilt-free turkey shoot. For those on the ground—Serbs and Albanians alike—the bombing was very real. Ten thousand died. Such a war raises various ethical issues. It presumes, for one, that the lives of one side are more valuable, more important than even the lives of those being saved.

Other legal and moral issues have also been raised by this war. It was fought in support of one group (Kosovo Albanians) in a civil war within a sovereign state (Serbia/Yugoslavia), a legally inviolable entity according to international law. It was undertaken without United Nations consent and, for that matter, without the consent of the peoples in those NATO states that participated in it. War was never officially declared, legislative bodies in the NATO countries were not consulted about military options, and since war was undeclared, its goals and strategies often changed from week to week—sometimes at the whim of the strategists it seemed. It was a "virtual" war, undertaken with "virtual" consent, and treated by the media as a spectator sport. Even victory was "virtual." The Serbs did not surrender; fighting concluded with a Military-Technical Agreement. Speculating on what future wars might bring, if Kosovo is any indication of things to come, one analyst worries that if Western nations could engage in violence with such impunity in Kosovo, they might be tempted to use it more often.

7

The Aftermath of a Decade of Conflict and War

In November 1996, on the first anniversary of the Dayton Peace Accords, the University of Dayton, in Ohio, hosted a commemorative conference. It began with a celebratory banquet, where Richard Holbrooke, the chief peace negotiator, spoke and also received the Desmond Tutu Award for Peace. One year after the initialing of the treaty, there was reason to celebrate. A truce among the warring parties had been achieved, and the fighting had not resumed. NATO's IFOR had successfully kept the hostile parties in Bosnia-Hercegovina separated for one year and had not itself experienced casualties. Peace continued to hold, and on the third anniversary of the treaty, Holbrooke was back at the University of Dayton to accept an honorary degree. In November 2001, Bill Clinton, who had only earlier that year stepped down from the U.S. presidency, traveled to Ohio to receive the first Dayton Peace Prize, an award of $25,000. By then, Bosnia had been relatively peaceful for five years, and the NATO team had once again proven itself by bringing Serbia to defeat in Kosovo in spring 1999. During the spring and summer of 2001, there had also been fighting in Macedonia between rebel Albanians and government troops, but that, too, had ended. NATO had kept vigilant, and Western diplomats meeting with Macedonian antagonists had fairly quickly helped defuse the conflict. It appeared that the West, through trial and error, had become skillful at handling trouble in the former Yugoslavia. Self-congratulations still seemed to be in order.

The work of dealing with the human devastation of war fell to the war crimes tribunal in The Hague. The tribunal had been established by the UN Security Council in 1993 and opened in that Netherlands city in 1994. It was slow to begin its work, often for lack of compliance from the signatories of the Dayton treaty. Slobodan Milosevic and Franjo Tudjman, sometimes themselves considered candidates for the tribunal's prosecution, were uncooperative, as were the various Bosnian authorities who were reluctant to give up those who they considered national heroes, no matter how bloody their deeds had been. NATO and UN authorities in Bosnia, too, seemed unable or unwilling to round up persons accused of war crimes. Radovan Karadzic and Ratko Mladic, considered by most to be the leading outlaws of the Bosnian war, were yet to be apprehended in late 2003. World public opinion was critical of NATO for this failure (some NATO sources blamed the French for protecting the guilty, especially Karadzic).

In spite of this lack of cooperation, the war crimes tribunal forged ahead, partly due to the persistence of two determined women, Louise Arbour and Carla del Ponte, judges from Canada and Switzerland, respectively, both of whom served terms as head of the tribunal. Painstakingly, evidence of crimes was and continues to be collected. The dead were found (sometimes exhumed), counted, and identified. The living victims were urged to recount the crimes perpetrated against them. Volumes of testimony were accumulated, and indictments were handed down against accused criminals, sometimes in secret so that the indictee could not have time to flee a surprise apprehension. The 16 permanent tribunal judges, backed up by teams of lawyers, crime experts, police officers, and analysts, began hearing cases. By the end of 2002, close to one hundred alleged war criminals were in custody and several dozen convictions had been issued. Since the tribunal does not recognize the death penalty, those found guilty are to serve prison terms in a host European country.

Initially, those indicted by the court at The Hague were generally from Bosnia, mostly Serbs, but they also included Croats and Muslims who were accused of grave breaches of the 1949 Geneva convention, violations of the laws or customs of war, genocide, or crimes against humanity. War crimes charges have also been extended to Croatian Croats and Serbian Serbs, but until Croatian President Tudjman's death in late 1999 and until Milosevic was himself sent to The Hague in June 2001, it was virtually impossible for the tribunal to apprehend indicted criminals in those two states. Sending the indicted to The Hague continued to pose problems for the new leadership in Croatia and Serbia. In February 2002, 100,000 Croats from across the country rallied on behalf of indictee General Mirko Norac and called for Ivica Racan, the new prime minister, to resign. Similar demonstrations in Serbia opposed transporting Milosevic to the Netherlands; the leaders of Serbia and Yugoslavia were significantly divided over the matter, with Zoran Djindjic, prime minister of Yugoslavia, favoring and Vojislav Kostunica, Yugoslavia's newly elected president, opposed to turning Milosevic over to the UN court.

At first, the court at The Hague tried only minor figures, those often directly responsible for crimes, such as detention camp personnel. Later, heads of state and those in high offices were also indicted. In spring 1999, for example, the tribunal, quickly extending its investigations to crimes in Kosovo, handed down indictments of not only Milosevic but also five of his key advisors. One of them, Milan Milutinovic, still president of Serbia in late 2002, surrendered to the court in early 2003 when his term in office was up. Only one woman has been indicted: Biljana Plavsic, the first president of the Bosnian Serb Republic after 1996. Once indicted, Plavsic turned herself in, and eventually pled guilty, but during her trial prominent Western political leaders offered favorable character testimony on her behalf because she had expressed remorse for her actions. The charges against her were reduced. In February 2003, Plavsic was sentenced to 11 years in prison.

The war crimes tribunal was the first such international body to meet since military courts in Nuremberg prosecuted the Nazis after their defeat in World War II. In judgments the court at The Hague has handed down, international law regarding war crimes has been expanded to include rape as a crime against humanity. Two legal precedents were advanced to enable this development. One was to accept a woman's testimony although she might be experiencing posttraumatic stress; and, two, sexual assault was categorized as torture and therefore punishable as a war crime. In early 2001, three Bosnian Serbs were the first to be convicted of this charge. The tribunal also took up the issue of journalists being subpoenaed to testify against the accused. A prominent U.S. lawyer who specialized in cases involving First Amendment rights, presenting a case on behalf of a *Washington Post* reporter and backed by dozens of prominent Western newspapers, argued that journalists should be exempt from testifying, lest their lives be endangered. At the end of 2002, an appeals court agreed to dismiss the subpoena.

Apart from proceedings at The Hague, there was an interesting development regarding Bosnian war crimes that involved the government of the

Netherlands. The Dutch had commissioned an investigation of the Srebrenica massacre of July 1995, where 7,000 Muslim men were killed by
Serbs while unarmed Dutch troops, who served as UN forces in the area
and knew about Mladic's intent to kill the Muslims, stood by. When the
report was released, the Dutch parliament debated its implications. Ultimately, the cabinet resigned, stating that by not intervening on behalf of
the Srebenicans, it, too, bore responsibility for the most horrific slaughter
of the Bosnian war. The UN subsequently also apologized for restricting
those like the Dutch troops to acting only as observers. The Dutch should
have had reinforcements and weapons and authority to use them.

As The Hague tribunal continues its work into 2003 and beyond, the
major ongoing trial is that of Slobodan Milosevic, who is being prosecuted
for crimes in Kosovo and also in Croatia and Bosnia. As of September
2002, only the first phase of Milosevic's prosecution, dealing with crimes
in Kosovo, had been completed. The second phase, which took up war
crimes in Bosnia and Croatia, began in late September and continued only
intermittently due to the accused's chronic heart condition and other ail-
ments. One notable development in fall 2002 was the testimony of Stipe
Mesic, Croatia's president, who accused Milosevic of mass killings in
Bosnia. In July 2003, the prosecutors of the IWCT indicated that they had
begun at last to establish a paper trail from Milosevic to war crimes in
Bosnia. As of late 2003, the proceedings against Milosevic were expected
to go on for at least another year and a half. Other key Serbians were also
scheduled for trial. Prominent among them was Vojislav Seselj, the grizzly
paramilitary leader and political figure who turned himself over to the
tribunal in February 2003. Meanwhile, in early 2003, the court at The
Hague continued to press Serbia for extradition of other wartime leaders.
Serbia's prime minister, Zoran Djindjic, was allegedly preparing to comply
when he was assassinated in mid-March 2003. But fear of terrorist reprisals at home is likely to make Serb officials reluctant to send indictees to
The Hague.

The U.S. administration under George W. Bush, in power since early
2001, may also affect the IWCT's deliberations and even U.S. commitment
to peacekeeping in the former Yugoslavia. The Bush government fears
that the tribunal will adversely judge U.S. actions abroad. The Hague
tribunal had on its agenda an investigation of the 1995 "Operation Storm,"
the blitz action taken by Croat troops that effectively "cleansed" the Krajina of Serbs. The operation was spearheaded by U.S. special forces, a
growing element in the American defense arsenal, whose existence and
identity the U.S. government prefers to keep secret. The Bush administration is also determined to prevent the International Criminal Court (ICC),

newly established in spring 2002, from restricting U.S. activity. The United States boycotted its signing ceremony, although the Clinton administration had been among the 120 nations who met in Rome in 1998 and had pledged to support the court. The ICC, which will also sit in The Hague, became operational in early 2003. Meanwhile, the United States, fearing that its leaders might be prosecuted by such a court, railed against it. And in summer 2002, the United States temporarily vetoed extending the term of the UN peacekeeping force in Bosnia unless the war crimes tribunal exempted U.S. citizens from prosecution. Acting unilaterally, the United States thus irritated and alienated even close allies over this issue.

In January 2003, Bush's State Department, anxious to extract the United States from the Balkans as soon as possible—no doubt in order to concentrate fully on the impending war with Iraq—exerted new pressure on Serbia over war criminals. It offered to drop demands for all indicted suspects if Serbia agreed to extradite the three most notorious, including Ratko Mladic. The United States even suggested that it might help the Serbs round them up, but the assassination of Serbia's prime minister in March 2003 derailed this proposal. Speeding up The Hague's proceedings, focusing on only the most high level criminals, could serve to bury other matters, such as those that may have been committed during "Operation Storm" in Croatia. By late 2003, the prosecution of some lesser figures had been moved from The Hague to local courts in the former Yugoslavia, while some cases were speeded along by allowing the accused to plea-bargain. But, to the chagrin of the United States, the work of the IWCT was far from completed.

In addition to dealing with the prosecution of war crimes, an activity primarily centered at The Hague, at home the human devastation was being dealt with daily on a more immediate and personal level. There were the war dead, numbering close to 250,000, and their survivors, some of whom were physically disabled (about 200,000), while millions suffered the emotional scars of wartime brutalities and loss. During the decade of war, there had also been numerous waves of refugees. In the early stages of each war—while the Serbs were on the offensive—the ones fleeing were Croats (1991–1992), Muslims (1992–1995), or Kosovar Albanians (early 1999). These refugees went to other parts of the former Yugoslavia or to other European states, particularly Germany, Switzerland, and Sweden. Later, the refugees were primarily Serbs, who fled Croatia in summer 1995, left the Bosnian Federation (Muslim-Croat territory after Dayton) in 1995–1996, and Kosovo in 1999. The Serbian refugees have ended up primarily in Serbia, not exactly what the Serbian nationalists of the mid-1980s had in mind when they voiced their dream to unite all Serbs in one state. The nationalists had hoped, of course, to expand the national territory by annexing Serbian lands in neighboring states; instead, the ethnic domain was effectively shrunken to Serbia proper (excluding Kosovo and even Vojvodina to a certain extent).

According to 2002 UNHCR figures, of the nearly 1.3 million persons still classified as refugees or internally displaced persons (IDPs) from the wars in Yugoslavia, the largest number was Serbs, and 657,000 of them lived in Serbia. They were Europe's largest refugee problem, but tended to be "forgotten victims," according to an authority on refugees of the former Yugoslavia. There were also 462,000 refugees and IDPs in Bosnia (232,000 IDPs were probably Serb, since they lived in the "Serbian Republic") awaiting a solution to their situation. Resettlement outside former Yugoslavia is an option that has pretty much dried up; European states have sent refugees home and erected quota barriers against them. Repatriation of refugees, although guaranteed by the Dayton treaty and UN Resolution 1244 (relating to Kosovo), was also seldom possible. It depended on "real" guarantees for personal security, legal and property rights, and assurance of employment, all of which were still rare in the area. The only option available was integration into the community, but in both Serbia and Bosnia the host country was weak, the economy stagnant, and the unemployment rate high. Financial aid for refugees had come mostly from the West, but amounts were diminishing. The picture was bleak, and the refugee problem threatened to be around for a long time.

In 2003 there were five states where there had once been one Yugoslavia: Slovenia, Macedonia (FYROM), Croatia, Bosnia-Hercegovina, and the newly renamed state of Serbia and Montenegro (called the Federal Republic of Yugoslavia between 1992 and 2002). Slovenia, with a population of two million, which escaped all but the initial stages of the war in 1991, fared better than the others during the 1990s and is best compared with the central European and Baltic states that were also freed of communist rule at about the same time. Slovenia's parliamentary government was working well, a third (five-year) presidential term since independence began after national elections in late 2002, and, the country had among the highest per capita income levels of all the CEFTA (Central European Free Trade Association) states, of which it was a member. In fall 2002, Slovenia was invited to join both NATO and the European Union. The induction ceremonies were projected for spring 2004.

The other four states of the former Yugoslavia have not done nearly as well. They are all dealing, to a greater or lesser extent, with the physical and economic destruction of war and its aftermath. Crime and corruption became a way of life for many people and was generally condoned by the political leadership. Success in crime, in fact, led to personal wealth and often naturally paved the way to political power. This phenomenon was particularly so in two of the states: Bosnia-Hercegovina and Serbia and Montenegro. There, only the new elites benefited from the new way of life, which in turn prevented needed economic recovery and development, and perpetuated political instability. It also frightened off foreign investors.

Macedonia, properly known as FYROM (Former Yugoslav Republic of Macedonia), began its independent existence precariously. Its neighbors, Greece (who had insisted on the new state's clumsy official name), Serbia, and perhaps even Bulgaria, had designs on its territory. A poor country, with a $960 per capita annual income, Macedonia had a mixed population. A quarter to a third of its two million inhabitants were Albanians, while most of the remainder were Slavic Macedonians. Yet the state had an enlightened and tolerant leadership that kept Macedonia out of the wars of the 1990s, and it shouldered the enormous burden of providing for 250,000 Albanian refugees from Kosovo who overran the country during the spring of 1999. The cost was $1.5 billion. Its two presidents, Kiro Gligorov, a natural conciliator, who in late 1999, at age 82, resigned from a post he had held throughout the 1990s, and Boris Trajkovski, a Kentucky-educated, Methodist minister, who was elected to succeed Gligorov, worked virtual miracles to keep Macedonia quiet.

The greatest threat to Macedonian stability came in 2001, when from spring until November, it grappled with its own Albanian issues. Fighting erupted in March 2001, in the border areas with Kosovo. It appeared that Kosovo Albanians (perhaps KLA) had embarked on an operation to incorporate Macedonian Albanian territories into Kosovo. It was not immediately known what ties the Kosovars might have had with local Albanians and whether the two were collaborating to undermine the Macedonian state. For months, the Macedonian army fought the rebels, while it negotiated with leading Macedonian Albanians of various political persuasions. Ultimately, President Trajkovski and parliament worked out a deal with Macedonia's Albanians. It became clear that local fighters were not committed to the KLA. Instead, they called themselves the National Liberation Army (NLA) and insisted that their goal was not union with Kosovo but rather more rights and a larger political voice in Macedonia.

Over the summer, meetings with NATO leaders George Robertson and Javier Solana helped work out a formula for accommodating the Albanians. Trajkovski labored tirelessly to defuse Slavic Macedonian objections to a new constitution. It took several months, but in November parliament approved the document with a generous majority. The key gains for Macedonia's Albanians were recognition of Albanian as an official language and as a language of higher education, increased representation on the police force, and amnesty for NLA fighters who, it was stipulated, must surrender their weapons. NATO troops (1,000) agreed to remain in the area for three months—that is, into 2002—to assure the peace. After the September 2002 parliamentary elections, the Albanian wish for greater political representation was also realized. The new prime minister, Branko Crvenkovski, a former communist, who headed the "Together" coalition of parties, included four former NLA members in his cabinet. Stability appeared to have settled in, enough so that in early 2003 the Macedonian government asked the EU to take over the NATO peacekeeping mission in their country. In April 2003, NATO troops were replaced by 320 from the EU. The Macedonians also asked to be considered for membership in the EU; their minds seemed at last to be more on peacetime development than on war and ethnic conflict.

Post-Dayton Croatia was shaped by two factors. One was "Operation Storm," the military victory in August 1995 that quickly reclaimed most of the western lands lost during 1991–1992. (The eastern or Danubian areas, reabsorbed in late 1997, pretty much made Croatia whole again.) In sweeping through the Krajina in the summer of 1995, the U.S.-trained Croatian army of 100,000 performed with astonishing speed, just steps behind 300,000 fleeing Serbs, whose ancestors had settled in the area three or four centuries earlier. "Operation Storm," no doubt named by U.S. special forces, accomplished a virtual ethnic cleansing of the area. Subsequently, villages were recombed for lingering Serbs; many of the stragglers were forced out or killed. It was not a pleasant ending, but it achieved the goal nationalist Croats favored—ethnic homogeneity for Croatia.

The second, and more important, factor molding Croatia after Dayton was Franjo Tudjman, the country's president. The former communist general, later historian, political prisoner, and finally organizer in 1989 of the Croatian Democratic Union (CDU), continued as its authoritarian head. The government during Tudjman's two terms (1991–1999) appeared to have the trappings of democracy but, in fact, was weighted in favor of strong presidential and CDU party power. Tudjman and the CDU ran Croatia and, among other things, were determined to keep Croatia free of Serbs. Hence, although the Dayton treaty provided for the repatriation of refugees and human rights guarantees for them, hardly any Serbs dared return. Human rights organizations and the OSCE regularly chastised Croatia for this, but with little result. Tudjman cronies and police toughs continually made life difficult for non-Croats and political dissenters. The Hercegovinian extremists, Croats whose goal it was to merge Hercegovina into Croatia and whose émigré contingent had helped bankroll Tudjman's

1991 electoral victory, continued to hold major sway in the administration. The émigré community, incidentally, had guaranteed representation in parliament—12 out of 120 seats—while the ethnic minorities in Croatia were allowed only 7 positions. In Tudjman's Croatia the media was controlled, myths about the nation were glorified, ties with the Church and Catholicism were stressed, and Tudjman himself was transformed into a cult figure.

Franjo Tudjman and the CDU also drove the economy into the ground. The president, his relatives, CDU bigwigs—altogether about 250 families—grabbed up the country's wealth in a privatization blitz. While they luxuriated, the economy floundered, operating at 60 percent of what it had been in 1990. Only one million of Croatia's 4.6 million people were employed; and one million were retirees, whose pension checks were often late. The economy was bolstered with artificial support, foreign loans to the tune of $15.1 billion. Many banks were near collapse by the end of the decade.

Tudjman died in December 1999 after a lingering bout with cancer. Although he was mourned by many, the majority of Croatians was grateful for the opportunity to have a new regime. This was demonstrated in elections in early 2000; only weeks after Tudjman's death, the CDU was ousted from power. The Social Democrats formed a government, and Ivica Racan, the new prime minister, whose American wife taught political science in Wooster, Ohio, was in the unenviable position of telling the Croatians that the country was virtually bankrupt. Together with Stipe Mesic, who was elected Croatia's new president (he had been the very last president of the former Yugoslavia before it disintegrated), Racan presented Croatians with the inevitable tasks ahead. Cooperating with The Hague, enforcing human rights for minorities, curbing the Hercegovinian lobby, and dealing with the economy were now on the government's agenda. The regime made a good beginning. War criminals were sent to the Netherlands, although not without strong opposition from some conservative elements at home, who may still cause the new leaders considerable difficulty. The Hercegovinian extremists were reined in; some were arrested. Protection for ethnic minorities improved and persuaded some Serb refugees at least that it was safe to come home. The economy, too, began a slow upswing. Prosecution of the greedy business elites was begun and likely will include Tudjman family members. Also, the war-devastated tourist industry of the 1990s, which had flourished in the Tito era, began to recover. Some estimates have the coastal economy back to 80 percent of prewar levels.

The new regime was also welcomed by the international community. Many had long grown weary of Tudjman, who as late as 1999, during the

Kosovo war, was still talking about annexing Bosnian lands. President Mesic put a stop to such talk, making it clear—especially to the extremists—that Croatia had no designs on territories outside its own Dayton boundaries. This had a stabilizing effect on the area in general. In fall 2002, Mesic also went to The Hague to testify against Milosevic, whom he had not seen in a decade. Mesic charged him with spilling "rivers of blood," and testified that he had witnessed Milosevic conspiring with Tudjman to divide Bosnia. That Mesic implicated Tudjman as well as Milosevic was instructive for Croatians as well as the world. It meant that Croatia's new government clearly would not condone aggressive nationalism, and that it did not approve of what had been done by the previous regime in the name of the nation. The unstated implication, of course, was that Tudjman himself had been a war criminal and merited prosecution by the IWCT. Mesic would have nothing, however, of any talk of collective national war guilt. Croatian archives for the period are being opened and could provide information about individual Croats who should be prosecuted for war crimes.

In late November 2003, with Mesic still serving as president, parliamentary elections brought back the CDU. Although the party did not tally an outright majority, the CDU has regained dominance, and its center-right leadership promises a new era for Croatian politics. The CDU's new leader, Ivo Sanader, has rejected Tudjman's legacy of ultranationalism. The pro-American Sanader hopes to put Croatia on a fast track into the European Union and NATO.

Bosnia-Hercegovina was the republic most associated with the war in former Yugoslavia. The multiethnic state had been the primary object of aggression. It had endured the longest siege (three and one-half years), experienced the greatest number of horrors, and also had the most refugees. In 1995 the peacemakers in Dayton therefore focused most on Bosnia and on writing its new constitution (see chapter 3). Chief among their goals was checking ethnic hatred. At Dayton, many believed—perhaps naively—that the ethnic factor would fade as Bosnians began living together again. The multiethnic ideal, sometimes used to describe prewar Bosnian society, would surely revive. But ethnic hatred, if it was not pronounced before the war, was certainly an important by-product of it. Trust proved difficult to nurture in the postwar period, as the reluctance of refugees to return illustrates. Of the refugees, close to one million Serbs, Croats, and Muslims had returned to Bosnia since 1995, and although 100,000 returned in 2002, the highest number since 1995, it was unlikely that many of the 1.2 million who remain displaced would ever come back. Although there may always be a nostalgia for the homeland—particularly among older Bosnians—many have reconciled to being elsewhere. Bosnia, with its depressed economy, its high unemployment rate, and its residual social tensions, held little appeal.

Seven years after Dayton, the national factor continued to be central, particularly in politics. It was clear from the outcome of numerous elections in the Bosnian state as well as in its two component parts, the Serbian Republic and the Muslim-Croat federation. In the latest balloting, which took place in October 2002, the nationalist candidates were still the voters' favorites. This frustrated representatives from the UN, the OSCE, NATO, and other international agencies—Bosnia's temporary administrators. At Dayton the democratic ideal had been equated with political pluralism and a multiethnic society. Hence voting for a nationalist candidate for town mayor, for example, was regarded as a deviation from the multiethnic model and therefore undemocratic. Conservative critics concluded that introducing democracy in Bosnia was a hopeless cause, one best abandoned. Liberals conversely urged greater intervention by the international community to assure real democratic development.

Bosnia after 1995 was a protectorate of the international community. NATO troops—first IFOR, then SFOR—assured the peace. The number of soldiers by late 2001 was down to 18,000 from the original 34,000, a decrease that was considered an indicator of progress toward durable peace. The OSCE supervised Bosnia's elections, and in order to assure their democratic character, OSCE vetted candidates, decided where people should vote (to balance constituencies ethnically), and controlled the media to assure fair reporting. They also bankrolled new parties, hoping to achieve greater diversity and multiethnicity but succeeding primarily in fragmenting the electorate and spending a lot of money. Even so, nationalists continued to be elected. After the fall 2002 vote, Paddy Ashdown, the British Labour Party leader who served a term as head UN representative in Bosnia, chose to put a favorable spin on the election results. One needed, he said, to look positively at the votes for national candidates. They were based on informed decisions, and they were votes against nonperformance of the nonnational parties.

The United Nations supervised day-to-day developments in Bosnia through its High Representative (HR), an appointed official. In reality, he often acted much like a benevolent despot. Spanish Carlos Westendorp, who succeeded Swedish Carl Bildt as HR in mid-1997, defended his heavy-handed policies, saying that "imposing democracy by force" might "look ugly," but it needed to be done. Westendorp patronized his Bosnian "flock," almost in the manner of a nineteenth-century colonialist. Wolfgang Petritsch, the Austrian who succeeded him, dismissed at will elected officials who acted "undemocratically." He also issued laws giving public television programming commercial advantages over privately owned stations; his reason was to assure multiethnicity. A *New York Times* editorial accused him of censorship, a decidedly undemocratic practice.

Democracy, traditionally and by its very definition, is developed by the people, from the bottom up. In Bosnia it was imposed from above by appointed officials from abroad, using "democratic" standards, ethics, and values that had been established elsewhere. If the standard was not met, the Bosnians were blamed. No one thought to question the activity or motives of the implementors. One analyst has suggested that the international community failed to see its own short-comings because it had become totally wrapped up in the "democratization" process itself.

As Bosnians were marginalized from decision making in their own country, the international representatives knitted together a post–Cold War security commitment for Europe and the United States. High Representative Carl Bildt called Bosnia the cutting edge of transition for European security and stability. Bosnia was, in other words, the testing ground for the world powers who had been left at sea after the collapse of communism, looking for purpose and a new international system. If their mission in Bosnia failed, their credibility in the rest of the world could be in question. As their protectorate over Bosnia continued, the goal of Bosnian democracy became almost secondary to the primary agenda of building a new U.S.-European world order. For some, it was also an experiment, a testing ground for future democratization projects. It was expensive. During the 1990s, the average cost to American taxpayers for U.S. involvement in the Balkans was $500 per person. In 1997, one-third of the total U.S. foreign policy budget—at $1,200 per capita—was allocated for Bosnia. But it was said by HRs Petritsch and Ashdown to be worth it, for success in Bosnia could be applied to other places. In 2002 HR Ashdown mentioned Afghanistan and East Timor in particular. Others have suggested that what was learned in Bosnia might be applied to democratization in the Middle East, perhaps even Iraq.

If Bosnia was to be a successful test case in democratic nation building, above all, something needed to be done about its economy. The ministate was sustained by foreign aid, huge amounts of it. Up to the beginning of 1998, its chief benefactors were the World Bank, the EU, and the United States, whose aid packages to Bosnia accounted for $15 million, $80 million, and $19 million, respectively. In mid-1998, the amounts were renegotiated upward, totaling $1.5 billion annually. In summer 1999, 39 world leaders, including the U.S. president, Bill Clinton, met in Sarajevo, and pledged an additional $700 million in aid, trade programs, and business incentives to generate investment. Yet, with a recovery package many times the amount of the Marshall Plan for European recovery after World War II, Bosnia in 2002 still required outside assistance. In addition to a huge trade deficit, the Bosnian economy was characterized by lack of domestic investment and overblown budgets. Added to that were massive unemployment and a dejected populace. A UN survey in late 1999 found that 62 percent of Bosnian youth would leave if given the opportunity. Potential foreign investors shied away from Bosnia, and those who had established operations there—like Volkswagen, Coca-Cola, DHL World-wide Express, and McDonalds—were reconsidering their commitment. They cited government bureaucracy as a chief impediment to business: privatization moved too slowly; getting the many required business per-mits was a nightmare.

While an open capitalist economy was barely emerging, a clandestine, underground one thrived. It had been developed during the war, partly because of the UN arms embargo, and was expanded to include needed supplies as the war dragged on. Smuggling became a way of life, and smugglers, because their occupation helped sustain the populace, became hero-patriots. Sarajevo, long under siege, especially relied on smugglers. By the time the war ended, Bosnia had a well-developed underground economic infrastructure. After the war, the state remained weak and unable to control crime, so smuggling continued and expanded. Sarajevo, for example, became the center of Europe's used-car market, which flourished from the influx of automobiles stolen across Europe.

Criminal capital was laundered and, after Dayton, criminals eased into the government apparatus. Politicians commonly took bribes, or they en-gaged in the underground economy directly. President Alija Izetbegovic's son, for example, enriched himself through control of Sarajevo's housing bureau, taking $2,000 kickbacks for allocating publicly owned apartments (80,000 of them). Bakir Izetbegovic also owned 15 percent of Bosnia Air, the country's airline. Politicians and their relatives regularly skimmed a share of foreign relief aid, according to some estimates, up to $1 billion by the summer of 1999.

Two UN High Representatives, Petritsch and Ashdown, have com-mented on what the UN might have done better in Bosnia: it should have concentrated on establishing rule of law rather than on holding elections. Law and order would have eased the fears of returning refugees and tamed ethnic hatreds. A lawful Bosnia could also hope to curb smuggling and encourage legal businesses, both foreign and domestic, while collecting taxes from manufacturers and goods sold. Instead, the international com-munity actually assisted in the corruption, sometimes by just being there.

Administration offices and airstrips were rented from Bosnian politicians at exorbitant prices. Services provided for foreign soldiers and as many as 10,000 administrators and nongovernmental organization (NGO) employees thrived on criminal activity. For example, brothels that used women smuggled from former republics of the Soviet Union and catered to the international community derived 70 percent of their profits from foreigners. The largest smuggling center in all Europe, called the "Arizona Market," near Brcko, was originally a NATO-enforced zone of separation, where Western officials promoted local entrepreneurship. The U.S. Defense Department provided some of the start-up financing for what one analyst calls a "smuggler's paradise." It did booming business while the state lost an estimated $30 million in taxes annually. The UN has been unable to control the Arizona Market, but hopes are that it can be made a center of legitimate business. Perhaps the European Union will fare better at this endeavor after it takes over the administration of Bosnia in 2004.

Of the six former Yugoslav republics, the most complex and troubled was Serbia. Technically, in 2003, Kosovo and Vojvodina were still a part of it. Kosovo after June 1999, however, was really a UN protectorate, according to UN Resolution 1244, and Kosovars remained intent on independence. Some analysts believed that the Serbs were resigned to letting Kosovo go, but were holding on to it in order to trade it for something— perhaps Bosnia's Serbian Republic. Meanwhile, stirrings (economic rather than ethnic) in the Vojvodina pointed toward greater autonomy in that relatively prosperous province. In addition, in February 2003 a dramatic change occurred in Serbia's relationship with Montenegro, the coastal state of 650,000 Serbs who had long had a love-hate relationship with Belgrade and had more recently refused to support Serbia in the Kosovo war. "Serbia and Montenegro" became the official new name of Yugoslavia, the rump state that had comprised the two republics since April 1992. The move greatly loosened the ties between the two, each thereafter to have its own economy and currency. (Montenegro had begun using the German mark in 1999, and accepted the Euro in 2002, when the EU adopted it as a common currency.) Many in Montenegro, particularly Milo Djukanovic, its president since 1997, who had made his fortune smuggling tobacco and gasoline, had wanted independence for the state. Pressures from Serbia, but especially from the international community, which opposed further breakups in the Balkans, persuaded the Montenegrins to continue the political association for at least three more years. A referendum on independence could be held in 2006. Most believed that the two states would eventually go their own ways. Serbia's dreams of empire seemed to be over.

The heart of Serbia had major problems of its own, most of them political. Slobodan Milosevic, its president when the wars began, remained in power until fall 2000. He and wartime associates had survived remarkably long after Dayton, without proper reckoning. During those five years, political opposition was dealt with mafia-style: with threats, kidnapping, and assassination. Among the victims were Ivan Stambolic, Milosevic's prewar mentor; Pavle Bulatovic, a Montenegrin who was Yugoslavia's defense minister; Slavko Curuvija, the journalist who turned against Milosevic; and Arkan (Zeljko Raznjatovic), the notorious paramilitary leader, to name just a few. For nearly three months in early 1996, thousands in Belgrade demonstrated daily against Milosevic's regime, but he survived these protests as he had in 1991. Part of the problem was that opposition leaders were ineffectual, unwilling to cooperate with each other, or, in Vuk Draskovic's case, downright silly. (There were two assassination attempts against Draskovic; he was wounded in one, and in the other his brother-in-law was killed.)

In summer 2000, Milosevic succeeded in changing the Yugoslav constitution to allow himself a third presidential term. Then he called for an early election in September. For many Serbs—economically destroyed by war, international embargoes, and unemployment—it was the last straw. The opposition this time took on a new character and was finally effective. New political leaders, like Zoran Djindjic and Vojislav Kostunica, came forward, joined forces in the Democratic Opposition of Serbia (DOS), and stayed united through the September 24 election. A student movement, Otpor (Resistance), whose symbol was a clenched fist and which had as many as 70,000 members, played an important role producing propaganda. The students, who had their own Web site, held rock concerts and made leaflets, badges, and 400,000 posters with the slogan "He's Finished!" on them. They were financed by a $3 million grant from the National Endowment for Democracy, based in Washington, D.C. Other funding came from the U.S. A.I.D., which, in 1999, had earmarked $25 million for the purpose of getting rid of Milosevic.

Everything finally came together after the Yugoslav presidential election. Vojislav Kostunica beat Milosevic in the first round of voting (53.3 percent to 35 percent), a fact that Milosevic refused to accept, and he called for a rerun. After days of indecision in the capital, a takeover was organized. But it was not Belgrade middle classes and intellectuals, nor even the Otpor students who clinched the overthrow of Milosevic. The one-day "revolution" was mounted by workers, miners, and persons generally from provincial towns. Armed with cell phones and organizational skills, they assured the cooperation or at least the neutrality of the Belgrade police and off-duty paratroopers. The hero of the day, October 5, when parliament was finally taken on behalf of the new president, was Velemir Ilic, the mayor of Cacak. Ilic had led a 12-mile-long convoy of vehicles, including tractors and the bulldozer that triumphantly cleared the way into the Belgrade parliament building. He told his compatriots that they were about to show Belgraders how to take over their own town hall and announced that on that day they would be "free or die." The job was accomplished with little bloodshed—two died—and that evening Kostunica was able to address his country on state television. The next day Milosevic resigned, followed by resignations from others in his regime. Milosevic met Kostunica the following day, and Igor Ivanov, the Russian foreign minister, helped smooth the transition to a new era in Serbia. In late December, Serbian parliamentary elections were held, and Zoran Djindjic's party got nearly 65 percent of the vote. In January 2001, Djindjic became prime minister. One observer commented that, if the work of the Solidarity movement in Poland in the early 1980s was the "beginning" of the end of communism in eastern Europe, what occurred in Serbia in the last months of 2000 sealed communism's "end."

Following these events, Serbian politics regressed to their usual fractiousness. Djindjic and Kostunica, the two most prominent figures in DOS, became bitter rivals, built upon an animosity that had roots in the politics of the early 1990s. They differed fundamentally about how to deal with basic problems facing the country. One of these was the decimated economy. In 2001 the gross domestic product was one-half of its 1989 level, unemployment was at 50 percent, and the inflation rate was 70 percent. Even those who had jobs were often superfluous, such as most of the 8,000 Radio Television Serbia (RTS) employees (a number twice that employed by CNN worldwide). They had been kept on, as had many workers of bankrupt companies, partly because that had been the practice under communism but also because the unemployed were not likely to vote for candidates who would drastically reform the economy. (Most feared was "shock therapy" restructuring, an economic policy that was advocated by some Western economists for postcommunist regimes.) Yet there was no denying that the country had been bankrupted. Many individuals had lost their savings by investing in banks that promised quick money based on pyramid schemes. Foreign currency bank accounts had been raided by the Milosevic regime to the tune of $4 billion. At least $1 billion was stowed in Swiss institutions; other monies were deposited in banks in Greece and

Cyprus. As late as the fall of 2000, while the revolution was underway in Belgrade, Serbian/Yugoslav officials transferred 380 pounds of gold to Switzerland.

To get the country back on its feet, Zoran Djindjic, the Serbian prime minister, was willing to plunge into economic reforms that would feature market forces. Yugoslav President Kostunica, however, favored a slower approach. As a legalist, he believed the state was obligated first to fulfill its "social contract" commitments, which included pensions, health insurance, jobs, education, and the like. The international community offered assistance with economic reconstruction. Yugoslavia, which had been welcomed jubilantly into the United Nations already in November 2000, was, in spring 2001, declared eligible for funds from the World Bank and the International Monetary Fund. But money from abroad came at a price. The contingency was that war criminals, particularly Milosevic, be turned over to the IWCT for prosecution. Kostunica adamantly opposed this. He believed that Serbs should be tried at home for crimes committed there. The clash between Djindjic and Kostunica flared in late March 2001 when it came to Milosevic's arrest. The Djindjic people engineered the act, without Kostunica's approval; the immediate reason for it was a U.S. threat to withhold $100 million in foreign aid if Milosevic was not apprehended by the end of the month. At the end of June, under a similar challenge, Milosevic was hustled off in the night to Americans in Tuzla, who flew him from a military air base to the Netherlands. Kostunica was informed of this only after the fact. Djindjic, the prime minister of Serbia, had thus assured another $120 million in aid, while the Yugoslav President Kostunica's back was turned.

For Serbs, it was hard to know who was or should be running things. Kostunica was the more popular figure. He was thought to be honest and a friend of the people, whereas Djindjic was suspected of shady dealings, an opportunist not to be trusted. The dilemma took on a larger significance as Yugoslavia's life as a state was drawing to an end. Given that his position as its president would also be ending at the close of 2002, Kostunica decided to run for president of Serbia. Presidential elections were held three times in the last months of 2002. Kostunica got the most votes each time, but, since less than 50 percent of voters cast ballots in the two runoff contests, none of the elections was deemed legal. An impasse ensued. Consequently, at the end of 2002, the speaker of parliament became Serbia's acting president (the same was true in Montenegro, where voters also turned out in too few numbers). Yugoslavia has since then ceased to exist, and, in mid-March 2003, Zoran Djindjic, Serbia's prime minister, was assassinated. The temporary presidency continued because yet another election in November 2003 also failed to elect a permanent leader. In Serbia the locus of power and its future remained uncertain.

How the Serbian people have been affected by all that has happened in the last 15 years will take time to sort out. Outside observers, who are often quick to simplify, draw broad negative national stereotypes and demand Serbian acceptance of war guilt. Only in accepting responsibility for the Milosevic years and complicity in war crimes, some have argued, can this broken nation be healed. But the story is not so simple; neither is the remedy. Eric Gordy, a thoughtful analyst, has suggested that Serbia's firmly established political culture will be difficult to dislodge. For one, Milosevic's nationalist authoritarian government, which supplanted the communist one in the early 1990s, retained much of its predecessor's elaborate apparatus. The new regime sustained power through control of the media, particularly television, that ironically was far less free than it had been under communism. The state police assisted in silencing whatever opposition developed. The political challengers, as has been seen, were generally disorganized and corrupt, and Serbia did not have a tradition of multiple-party elections. In fact, although Serbs had been accustomed to voting from the old communist days, they did not associate the process with *choosing*. During the 1990s the government also manipulated popular culture, marginalizing rock and roll in favor of "turbofolk" music. The latter promoted ethnic values and made Milosevic a folk hero.

Perhaps most serious were the psychological effects of the last decade and a half. The criminal elite that came to wealth and power adopted a cocky, smug attitude and an immoral lifestyle. It thumbed its collective nose at Serbia's enemies, particularly NATO. For the rest of the Serbs, an overwhelming number, the 1990s brought poverty, scarcity, insecurity, and social isolation. They became self-absorbed, felt unfairly victimized by UN sanctions and NATO actions, and consequently backed their government against foreign foes. What else could they do? They did not think about war crimes and certainly did not consider themselves war criminals. When they thought of the war years, they remembered bread lines, electrical outages, misery, and helplessness. And they blamed mostly the West. They continued to watch the ongoing Milosevic trial in The Hague. Many saw it as a political show, designed to discredit not only their former president, but Serbs in general. That Milosevic has held his own and even elicited compliments from legal experts has made many Serbs feel good. Yet most Serbs believe Milosevic should be tried at home. He needs to account for the economic devastation his regime brought upon the country. As for the wars, many Serbs still believe Milosevic should not be tried for starting them, but rather for not fulfilling his promise to create a greater Serbia.

Presidents of former Yugoslavia's six republics (left to right): Momir Bulatovic (Montenegro), Milan Kucan (Slovenia), Franjo Tudjman (Croatia), Kiro Gligorov (Macedonia), Alija Izetbegovic (Bosnia and Hercegovina), and Slobodan Milosevic (Serbia). The photo was taken before Yugoslavia disintegrated. All six were still in power as heads of state in early 1997. By late 2003, none were in power. Tudjman and Izetbegovic had died, and Milosevic was in prison at The Hague. *Courtesy of DELO.*

Balkan foes sign a peace agreement in Paris, December 14, 1995. Front row (left to right): Serbian President Slobodan Milosevic, Croatian President Franjo Tudjman, and Bosnian President Alija Izetbegovic. At rear (left to right): Spanish Prime Minister Felipe Gonzales, U.S. President Bill Clinton, French President Jacques Chirac, German Chancellor Helmut Kohl, British Prime Minister John Major, and Russian Prime Minister Viktor Chernomyrdin, great power leaders. *Courtesy of Reuters/Charles Platiau/Archive Photos. © Copyright Archive Photos, 530 West 25th Street, New York, NY 10002, (212) 675-0115.*

Ethnic Albanian negotiators at the Kosovo peace talks (left to right, sitting at table): Veton Surroi, Ibrahim Rugova, Hashim Thaci, and Rexhep Qosja sign a draft accord hammered out at Rambouillet chateau at the International Conference Center in Paris, March 18, 1999. The accord called for self-rule for Kosovo, plus the deployment of a NATO-led peacekeeping force. *© AFP/CORBIS.*

Young supporters of the Democratic Opposition of Serbia (DOS) make the three-fingered Serbian nationalist sign and brandish a placard reading "He is finished!" as demonstrators block a street in Belgrade, October 1, 2000, to demand official recognition of opposition federal presidential candidate Vojislav Kostunica's apparent electoral victory over Yugoslav President Slobodan Milosevic. The DOS, a coalition of 18 opposition parties, called for a campaign of mass civil disobedience to start October 2 to force Milosevic to step down. ©AFP/CORBIS.

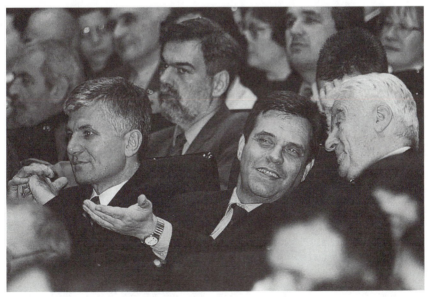

Yugoslav President Vojislav Kostunica (center) is flanked by prime minister candidate Zoran Djindjic (left) and chairman of the lower chamber of the Yugoslav parliament Dragoljub Micunovic (right), December 20, 2000, in Belgrade as they attend the preelectoral meeting of the Democratic Opposition of Serbia (DOS) party. ©AFP/CORBIS.

Within two weeks, more than 120,000 refugees had arrived from Kosovo in the Macedonian border region of Blace. Many were forced to leave their homes within minutes, often with little more than the clothes they wore. *UNHCR/R. LeMoyne.*

The International Committee of the Red Cross (ICRC) is in charge of family tracing. Here, ICRC staff at work at the Stankovac 1 reception site in Brazde, Macedonia. *UNHCR/H.J. Davies.*

Distribution of food to new arrivals in the town of Kukes, northern Albania. *UNHCR/R. Chalasani.*

Biographies: The Personalities behind the Breakup and the Wars

Arkan. *See* **Zeljko Raznjatovic**

Josip Broz (Tito) (1892–1980)

Josip Broz, whose underground name was Tito, was born in 1892 in the village of Kumrovec, then part of the Habsburg Empire (now part of Croatia), to a Croat father and a Slovene mother. One of 15 children, he needed to leave home to make a living, taking on various semiskilled city jobs and developing a social consciousness along the way. He involved himself in workers' organizations and became acquainted with Marxism. As a soldier in the Austro-Hungarian army during World War I, he was sent to the eastern front, experienced the Russian Revolution first hand, and became a Bolshevik. When Josip Broz returned home, Austria no longer existed. His village was now in the newly formed Kingdom of Serbs, Croats, and Slovenes. But economic conditions were, if anything, worse than before the Great War. He took up revolutionary work, came to know other revolutionaries at home and abroad, and studied Marxism in Moscow in the mid-1930s. Like other revolutionaries of the day, he also spent considerable time in prison for his political leanings.

In 1937, Moscow, seat of the Communist International organization, decided that Broz should head the Communist Party of Yugoslavia (CPY). The party had recently been federalized, and its headquarters were moved from Belgrade to Zagreb. The revolution in Yugoslavia, in other words, would not be centralized or Serbian-dominated. Broz, who came to be known by his underground name, Tito, pursued the cause, but only during World War II did the opportunity to seize power present itself. That war came to Yugoslavia relatively late, in April 1941. Yugoslavia was attacked and occupied by the Axis powers and their allies. All of Yugoslavia's neighbors annexed parts of the country. And an independent and enlarged Croatia emerged as a puppet state to Italy and Germany. It was headed by the Ustasha leader, Ante Pavelic.

Tito's communists waited for a sign from Moscow, which was bound to Nazi Germany in a nonaggression pact. When the Soviet Union was attacked by Germany on June 22, 1941, Tito's communists set their resistance movement into operation. A royalist resistance had already been organized by Draza Mihailovic, whose Chetniks sought to restore the Serbian dynasty to power. Tito's Partisans, on the other hand, projected a federal republic for postwar Yugoslavia, thus attracting those elements in the country that opposed monarchy and/or Serbian centralistic rule. The war and the resistance swept Tito to power, due partly to local support, partly to Western support (the Allies stopped backing Mihailovic in 1943 and sent aid to Tito instead), and partly because Tito's communists had already set up a provisional government in occupied territories. It is important to remember that Tito came to power at the expense of the Serbian Chetniks and the Croat Ustasha. Supporters of these elements had been active in events of the mid-1930s.

When Tito and the communists came to power in post–World War II Yugoslavia, they introduced reforms modeled after the Soviet Russian system. But even before the changes had gotten under way, Tito and Stalin, head of the Soviet Union, were locked in head-on confrontation over how communism should develop in Yugoslavia. It was essentially a conflict of personalities. In the end Stalin had Tito and Yugoslavia expelled from the Cominform, the international communist organization, hoping that Tito would then be overthrown. Instead Tito and the Yugoslavs went their own way, developing their own socialist model, which came to be known as Titoism. It featured socialist self-management at home and nonalignment in the international arena. Self-management involved an ever-evolving system of local participation in economic and political decisions. Nonalignment put Yugoslavia outside the East and West blocs, and projected the country into the company of Third World powers, of which Yugoslavia became a leader. Shortly after the Tito-Stalin break in 1948, the West began courting Yugoslavia and extending it financial aid. Russia became friendly after Stalin's death in 1953; in 1955 the Russian leadership even made a trek to Belgrade to get Tito's approval.

Tito ruled Yugoslavia until his death in 1980, balancing the varied national elements by stressing what they had in common, their Yugoslavness. There were troubled periods, especially in the mid-1960s and early 1970s, when the Croats and Slovenes pushed for liberalization and greater autonomy for the republics. But the balance held, although sometimes through repressive means. A by-product of the liberalization move, noted above, was a new constitution in 1974, which made Tito president for life. That constitution also provided for greater decentralization of the government, for example, a rotating presidency that allowed each republic and autonomous province to take its turn at heading the state. From hindsight, it is clear that the decentralization weakened Yugoslavia and contributed to political deadlock and final disintegration in 1991. At the time, however, the constitution was hailed as an enlightened measure; it seemed to indicate that Yugoslavia was evolving democratically. Abroad, Tito's Yugoslavia, in contrast to the Soviet bloc states, received much praise. And Tito, too, was regarded as "a giant among communists." What became apparent after his death, however, was that Tito, a bit like the Habsburg Francis Joseph, to whom he is sometimes compared, was the last remaining integrating force in his country.

Zoran Djindjic (1952–2003)

The son of a Yugoslav army officer, Zoran Djindjic was a Serb born in Bosnia. Early in life he established a pattern of opposition to the communist regime. In high school he was reprimanded for circulating a petition objecting to the fact that Tito had been made president for life. In the 1970s, Djindjic was associated with the Praxis school of philosophers, whose New Left views were in vogue at the time. In 1974 he attempted to recruit Slovene and Croat students to help establish a noncommunist youth organization, an activity that earned him a one-year suspended sentence from the court. After completing a degree at Belgrade University, Djindjic moved to Germany, where he spent most of the 1980s. In Germany, he studied for his Ph.D. with Jurgen Habermas at Heidelberg University, held some temporary teaching jobs, and also started a textile business.

He was back in Yugoslavia in 1989, the year the breakup began, to help start the Democratic Party, which he continued to head for the next 14 years. During the wars in Croatia and Bosnia, he was a staunch opponent of Milosevic, yet Djindjic also held a hawkish position on the Serbian national question. For example, when Milosevic split with Karadzic in 1994, Djindjic continued his support of Karadzic and also backed him in 1996 during elections in the newly created Serbian Republic of Bosnia. In 1996–1997, Djindjic was among the most visible figures associated with mass opposition to Milosevic, leading impressive—but ultimately unsuccessful—daily street demonstrations for nearly three months.

Djindjic came to power only at the end of December 2000, after Milosevic had been defeated by Vojislav Kostunica in the September presidential election. Djindjic's party, which was one of 18 in the Democratic Opposition of Serbia (DOS) movement that helped defeat Milosevic, won the parliamentary election in December 2000. As head of the party, and because of its overwhelming victory, Djindjic became prime minister, a post he continued to hold after Yugoslavia dissolved into two parts in 2003.

Djindjic was a telegenic, urbane, "European" type, which was not necessarily appreciated by the Serbian people. He was not very popular, and many regarded him as shrewd, slick, amoral, and opportunistic. There was evidence to support this characterization. During the Kosovo war in 1999, he fled the country for Montenegro where he sought refuge; it was surely at that time that he strengthened his ties with Montenegro's president, Milo Djukanovic, with whom he collaborated in black marketeering (cigarettes). In fall 2000, Djindjic, back in Serbia, maintained close ties with the security police, and when on October 5 the parliament was being stormed, Djindjic's operatives were taking control of what really mattered—the state bank and the customs office. On the issue of what to do with Milosevic once he had been ousted, Djindjic, ever the pragmatist, favored turning him over to the court at The Hague. In March 2001, when Milosevic was arrested, and in June of the same year, when he was turned over to the West, Djindjic seemed most motivated by money. Many feel Djindjic acted inappropriately—Yugoslavia's then president, Kostunica, a committed legalist, being the chief among Djindjic's critics. That Milosevic's defense was going impressively at The Hague, and continued to be a popular television attraction in Belgrade, irritated Djindjic.

Zoran Djindjic was assassinated in central Belgrade on March 12, 2003, leaving Serbia without a prime minister or a president. The likely assassins were from Serbia's criminal element, who may have had links to the security police and the Serbian paramilitary forces that had ravaged Croatia and Bosnia in 1991–1992. Djindjic had allegedly been in league with this element, but was preparing to rein it in and perhaps even allow members to be extradicted to The Hague. According to some Serb insiders, the assassination was likely the case of the mob taking revenge on one of its own betrayers.

Vuk Draskovic (1946–)

Vuk Draskovic has been Slobodan Milosevic's most persistent political opponent. Draskovic, born in 1946 in the multiethnic Banat area of northeastern Serbia, completed a law degree and was a communist as a young man. His early career was as a journalist for an establishment news agency, Tanjug, where he worked nine years. At first he reported domestic news, then he moved on to foreign reporting, assigned to southern Africa, where he covered Rhodesia and Mozambique. He was also briefly an adviser to Mika Spiljak, the Croat who was president of the rotating collective Yugoslav presidency from 1983 to 1984. In 1985 Draskovic took up a new occupation, that of novelist. He achieved considerable recognition as a writer; one of his books was singled out for a literary prize until it was banned for its excessive Serbian nationalism.

By 1991, when Yugoslavia was about to disintegrate, Draskovic had become Serbia's leading political dissident. The previous year, together with Vojislav Seselj, he had founded the Serbian Renewal Party. That party unsuccessfully challenged Slobodan Milosevic's former communists in Serbia's first multiparty elections, in December 1990. In March 1991 Draskovic led a large demonstration in Belgrade to demand a free press, free broadcasting, and an independent judiciary. The 40,000 demonstrators were at first attacked by local police, and when that failed to subdue them, Milosevic sent army (JNA) tanks against them. Draskovic was arrested and spent several days in prison. By that time he had become a radical nationalist. Apologizing for having once been a communist, which he described as a childhood illness he had overcome, Draskovic espoused the cause of a Greater Serbia. He called for the unification of all lands where Serbs had been in a majority before World War II (post-1945 Yugoslav boundaries were for him only an administrative contrivance). Draskovic also had immersed himself in religion, specifically Serbian Orthodoxy, and he had become a monarchist. He hoped that Alexander Karadjordjevic would become Yugoslavia's Juan Carlos, referring to the king of Spain, who had succeeded the dictator Francisco Franco. His political views were not only far to the right of Milosevic's, but to the right of those of many moderate Serbs as well.

Draskovic was again the center of attention in summer 1993. He had continued to oppose Milosevic, blaming him for the war in the former

Yugoslavia and referring to Serbia's president as a Balkan Saddam Hussein. In June, Milosevic linked up with the Chetnik leader Seselj to oust Dobrica Cosic, the writer who was then president of Yugoslavia. Draskovic, then in parliament, was drawn into the fracas. He and his wife Danica, a devoted associate and militant nationalist in her own right, were arrested and sentenced to 60 days in prison for disturbing the peace. They were both beaten in jail by the police, a fact that brought international criticism of Serbia and visits from concerned foreign dignitaries, including the wife of François Mitterand, president of France. Draskovic, ever the romantic novelist, began a hunger strike, and later said he had planned to die a martyr. He had even selected the precise date: July 17, the anniversary of the killing of Tsar Nicholas II of Russia and the date of the execution of Draza Mihailovic, the Chetnik leader whom Draskovic admired. Together they would be remembered as a trio who had been martyred by the communists.

Draskovic was not martyred in 1993. He surfaced again in 1996, this time as head of the opposition coalition, Together (Zajedno), which ran against Milosevic and the left in the November elections. Because Milosevic refused to acknowledge the victories of the Together parties in more than a dozen municipal elections, Together and its supporters took to the streets to protest. Draskovic, his mane of black hair and black beard still flowing, was among those leading massive demonstrations in Belgrade, which lasted for two months, but failed to oust Milosevic. In subsequent years, Draskovic, whose political base was Belgrade, controlled the powerful Studio B television station and tempered his radicalism. In early 1999, he even accepted Milosevic's offer of a federal cabinet post, a position he held for several months. Draskovic's participation in the opposition camp waned largely because of his bitter hatred of Zoran Djindjic, whose political star was rising. In 1999 and 2000, Draskovic participated half-heartedly in opposition rallies, which, until October 2000, were lackluster and disorganized. In the December 2000 Serbian elections, two months after Milosevic's ouster, Draskovic's party did so poorly that it got no parliamentary seats.

Lawrence Eagleburger (1930–)

Lawrence Eagleburger, as a deputy secretary and later secretary of state and a member of President George Bush's cabinet, was central in formulating U.S. policy toward Yugoslavia in 1991 and 1992. Born in 1930 in Milwaukee, Wisconsin, Eagleburger, with degrees from the University of Wisconsin (B.S., 1952; M.S., 1957), joined the foreign service in 1957.

Among his assignments as a career diplomat were two postings to Yugoslavia, the first as second secretary (1962–1965), and the second as U.S. ambassador (1977–1981). At that time, Eagleburger came to know Slobodan Milosevic, the banker, and he believed Milosevic was someone the United States could trust. (Eagleburger later publicly apologized for misjudging the Serbian leader.) When Eagleburger left the State Department in 1984, he accepted the presidency of Kissinger Associates, an organization that advised governments and foreign corporations in their dealings with the United States. Eagleburger's remuneration was $900,000 a year, and among his clients were several Yugoslav companies (a major bank and the company that made Yugo automobiles) that had subsidiaries in the United States. After Eagleburger returned to the State Department during the Bush administration, he exempted himself from participating in policy decisions on Yugoslavia for one year. During the volatile developments in 1990 and 1991 that resulted in the breakup of Yugoslavia, Eagleburger was in favor of Yugoslav unity and was believed by his critics to be pro-Serbian as well.

The Yugoslav breakup was under way when U.S. foreign policy was chiefly focused on Iraq, its leader, Saddam Hussein, and troubles in the Persian Gulf. Then, in early 1991, the Gulf War consumed the attention of the United States as well as that of the coalition partners who participated in the confrontation. When the war ended in spring of that year, the United States was not anxious to become involved in another overseas venture. Politically, this was not an expedient time. The following year was an election year; George Bush, whose approval rating by the American people was then at its highest, was not about to risk his reputation on a Yugoslavia venture. James Baker was Bush's secretary of state, but his deputy was Lawrence Eagleburger, and Brent Scowcroft, another old Yugoslavia hand, was head of the National Security Council. Yugoslavia was in turmoil during all of that critical election year. Baker, who in late summer 1992 was put in charge of Bush's reelection campaign (Eagleburger replacing him as secretary of state), insisted that the United States "did not have a dog" in the Yugoslav fight. Bush seemed only peripherally interested in Yugoslavia, asking Scowcroft weekly to tell him again what the crisis was all about.

It was against this background that Eagleburger executed policy on Yugoslavia and its successor states. As deputy secretary of state and Yugoslavia expert, he was often called upon by the press to explain the crisis. Whether he truly believed it or not, Eagleburger adhered to the "age-old ethnic hatreds" line. Repeatedly, he described the Yugoslavs as barbarians who needed to fight it out until the fight was out of their system. The implication was that no one, not even the United States, could do anything to stop the war. That the United States had no interest in stopping any war in late 1991, just after the Gulf War, or in 1992, an election year, was not mentioned. When Eagleburger replaced Baker as head of state, the Baker policy was essentially maintained. A number of State Department Yugoslavia experts resigned to protest the Bush administration's wimpy policy. Only after Clinton was elected did Eagleburger venture out a bit on his own. In December, at a meeting in Geneva, he named Milosevic, Karadzic, Mladic, Seselj, Arkan, and others as war criminals, signaling a shift to an anti-Serbian position. However, the only immediate result was that the Serbs rallied behind Milosevic and perhaps helped defeat Milan Panic, the Serbian American pharmaceuticals executive who was running against Milosevic for president that month. It was politics that elected Milosevic and politics that prevented Eagleburger and the United States from becoming more actively involved in the Yugoslav crisis when it might still have been possible to prevent the bloodbath it would become.

Richard Holbrooke (1941–)

Richard Holbrooke, the American diplomat who has been credited with nearly single-handedly bringing peace to the former Yugoslavia, was born in 1941 in New York City. He received a Bachelor's degree in physics from Brown University in 1962 and later attended the Woodrow Wilson School at Princeton University. His career has alternated between diplomacy, generally under Democratic administrations, and journalism and finance. His experience in finance has included the position of managing director of the prestigious Lehman Brothers (1985–1993) and the post of vice chairman of CS First Boston Corporation (after 1996). Holbrooke's career as a diplomat has included various assignments related to Vietnam between 1962 and 1969 (he came to know President Clinton's national security adviser, Anthony Lake, during these years); a stint as Peace Corps director in Morocco (1970–1972); the post of U.S. ambassador to Germany (1993–1994); and the post of assistant secretary of state for European and Canadian affairs (1994–1996).

In his capacity as assistant secretary of state, Holbrooke, a forceful, impatient, and ambitious man, took personal charge of the Bosnian situation in August 1995. Like others in the State Department, he had become increasingly frustrated by the lack of diplomatic progress toward peace; he also had become weary of dealing with Washington's bureaucracy. It also troubled him that in the postcommunist period the United States had not been able to establish a higher profile in Europe, particularly regarding

Bosnia. He decided to take on the peace mission himself. He arrived in Bosnia on August 19 along with Robert Frasure of the State Department, Deputy Assistant Secretary of Defense Joseph Kruzel, and Colonel Nelson Drew of the National Security Council. Because of the "usual Serbian runaround," Holbrooke was unable to secure safe passage into Sarajevo's airport, and the team had to arrive by helicopter, landing on Mt. Igman outside the Bosnian capital. The drive from the mountain proved fatal for Holbrooke's three companions, who were killed when their vehicle slipped off the road. The event, according to observers, was a turning point for Holbrooke, who was devastated by the loss of his colleagues and thereafter pursued the peace mission with unrelenting determination.

Holbrooke pinned his solution to ending the war in Bosnia on Slobodan Milosevic, the Serbian president. The two first met in mid-August 1995, and it became clear to Holbrooke that the United Nations sanctions on Yugoslavia were destroying Milosevic politically. By the end of the month Milosevic had secured the authority to act on behalf of the Bosnian Serbs Mladic and Karadzic, and he passed the information on to Holbrooke. Milosevic's authority was confirmed in a written statement that became known as the "Patriarch document," because even the Serbian Orthodox church leader had endorsed it. Holbrooke took things from there, while NATO assisted by bombing Serbian targets. He used his most characteristic attribute, that of bullying, to bring the Serbs, as well as the Croats and the Muslims, to the peace table. (Early in August Hobrooke had given the Croats approval for their successful anti-Serbian offensive in the Krajina. In September, because the combined Croat and Muslim forces were by then rapidly advancing on Banja Luka in Bosnia, Holbrooke bullied them to stop so as not to jeopardize the peace effort he had gotten under way.) Once the process was started, the road to peace talks in Dayton had been cleared.

The rapport Richard Holbrooke had established with Milosevic in August paid off during the three weeks of peace talks in Dayton (November 1–22, 1995), a story Holbrooke told in his memoir, *To End a War.* In the end Milosevic agreed to give up areas in both Croatia and Bosnia-Hercegovina that Serbs had claimed and, for a time during the war in the former Yugoslavia, controlled. In Dayton, Holbrooke reportedly hammered away, bullied, and plied the Serbian leader with copious amounts of brandy, until an all-night session finally clinched the deal. (Hobrooke even had Secretary of State Warren Christopher shuttling to and from Dayton from locations as remote as Japan in order to impress the Balkan leaders with the seriousness of U.S. intentions.) Milosevic came around, but then clearly he had the authority to do so. The meeting at Dayton proved two things: that Milosevic had the final say over Serbian affairs throughout the former Yugoslav lands, and that Hobrooke was right about singling out Milosevic to nail the peace.

In late summer 1999, Holbrooke became America's ambassador to the UN, 14 months after being nominated for the job. The appointment had been held up due to allegations that Holbrooke had violated federal ethics laws. In fall 1998 and spring 1999, Holbrooke was again engaged in Balkan affairs, meeting one-on-one with Milosevic over Kosovo, a crisis that would not defuse. Holbrooke was unable to prevent the Kosovo war. In November 2000, a month after Milosevic's ouster, Holbrooke, then UN ambassador, welcomed Yugoslavia back into the world organization.

Alija Izetbegovic (1925–2003)

Alija Izetbegovic, the Bosnian Muslim leader and president of Bosnia-Hercegovina after 1990, was born in 1925 in Bosanski Samac but lived in Sarajevo most of his life. He was educated as a lawyer at the University of Sarajevo and became a corporate legal adviser. Izetbegovic was also a devout Muslim intellectual who over the years wrote philosophical works about Islam. In 1973 he authored the *Islamic Declaration,* which in the 1990s was wrongly denounced by Serb and Croat extremists as an Islamic fundamentalist political tract. In fact it was a scholarly document intended for philosophical discourse. Izetbegovic was imprisoned twice in the former Yugoslavia for religious beliefs that were construed as politically connected. Shortly after World War II, when the communists came to power in Yugoslavia, Izetbegovic, as a member of the Young Muslims, was arrested and spent three years in prison; thereafter he was under police surveillance. In 1983 he and a dozen Muslim intellectuals were jailed for plotting against the state. At their trial it is said that Izetbegovic spoke so eloquently and with such quiet power that the court was in awe of him. He was nevertheless sentenced to 14 years in prison, but served only 5. He was released in November 1988 on the eve of revolutionary developments in the former Yugoslavia.

In 1990 Alija Izetbegovic became one of the founding leaders of the Muslim Party of Democratic Action (PDA), which was established just months before Bosnia's first multiparty election in November. The party tallied the most votes of the nationalist parties—the Muslims being the largest national group in Bosnia—and Izetbegovic, who had been chosen party leader, was now also elected president of the presidency of Bosnia-Hercegovina, a position he continued to hold throughout the war in Bosnia.

Of the newly elected presidents of Yugoslavia's republics, Izetbegovic was the only one who had never been a communist.

By the time Izetbegovic became president of Bosnia at the end of 1990, Yugoslavia was already disintegrating. Along with Kiro Gligorov, the president of Macedonia, Izetbegovic tried to sponsor a compromise solution to Yugoslavia's political impasse by proposing a loose confederal reorganization of the country. But by spring 1991 Milosevic and Tudjman were already plotting Bosnia's dismemberment, and in spite of Izetbegovic's entreaties, they refused to tell him of their secret discussions. In July 1991, after the war in Slovenia was already coming to a close, Izetbegovic traveled to Turkey, where he accepted an offer to join the Organization of Islamic Countries. Some regard this move as folly, for it allowed his political enemies thereafter to accuse Izetbegovic of Islamic fundamentalism. In mid-October 1991, Radovan Karadzic issued his mortal threat to Bosnia's Muslims, and Izetbegovic, in what would become characteristically naive fashion, assured the national assembly and the people of Bosnia that there would be no war, that Bosnia was safe.

War began in Bosnia in April 1992, and the Serbian-dominated Yugoslav army, the JNA, quickly overran much of the country and captured part of Sarajevo, including its airport. In early May the JNA also captured Izetbegovic when he returned from an international conference in Lisbon where the Yugoslav situation was being discussed. While army officials debated what to do with him, Izetbegovic was left alone with the airport director, who, when he answered an incoming telephone call, turned the phone over to Izetbegovic when he asked for it. Izetbegovic told the caller—an ordinary citizen of Sarajevo—who he was and asked the caller to notify the presidency and the media that he was being held captive at the airport. In a truly bizarre series of developments, Izetbegovic was freed and continued as president of his newly recognized independent republic. His position would be a sad one, as he helplessly watched his country and its citizenry destroyed. Some would contend that Bosnia's predicament was partly Izetbegovic's fault, for he had trusted too much in the forces of peace, had not prepared or armed for the probability of war, and had not foreseen the voracious political appetites harbored by the Serbs and Croats both within Bosnia and in neighboring republics.

During the course of the war and through the hundreds of meetings and conferences dealing with it, Izetbegovic agonized. Diplomats who observed him found him likeable but enigmatic—a statesman who seemed to be struggling to balance his religious principles with the task of being a secular ruler. He was a very private person, difficult to get to know, and one who was hard to negotiate with because of his inner struggles. The course of the war brought little but pain to Izetbegovic. His country was overrun, but the international community supplied little but humanitarian aid. Bosnia was not allowed to arm; therefore, it could not effectively fight back. The international community in the end colluded with the aggressors and presented Izetbegovic with peace proposals that stipulated Bosnia's dismemberment. The United States had offered some encouragement, as had some Islamic countries (e.g., Iran, which supplied some covert weaponry), but in the end a bitter and sad Izetbegovic was compelled in Dayton in 1995 to agree to Bosnia's division. He could hardly believe that the West had allowed Bosnia to fall, yet he consoled himself with the fact that Bosnia was at least no longer at war.

In fall 1996, Izetbegovic was reelected to the presidency of Bosnia. He quit political office in mid-2000, giving age and ill-health as reasons (he had had two heart attacks). The following year he also resigned his post as head of the PDA. He died on October 19, 2003.

Radovan Karadzic (1944–)

Radovan Karadzic, the future Bosnian Serb leader, was born in 1944, not in Bosnia or even Serbia but in a village in Montenegro. That republic, a part of both the second and third Yugoslavias and a neighbor to both Bosnia and Serbia, has long had a love-hate relationship with Belgrade, for although Montenegro is predominantly ethnically Serbian, many Montenegrins are fiercely individualistic and cherish the long independent tradition of their principality and their rugged mountain culture. When Karadzic moved to Sarajevo in his mid-teens to pursue a medical education, the milieu of his youth and that of the multiethnic, multireligious capital city of Bosnia, with its centuries-long history of urban civilized life, must have stood in stark contrast to each other. Karadzic completed medical school in Sarajevo with a specialty in psychiatry, and was employed at a local hospital (he later also counseled a local soccer team). His wife, whom he met in Sarajevo in the apartment house where he lived, is also a psychiatrist. Karadzic published poetry, which was not highly regarded by the intellectual elite, and he had a reputation for drinking and gambling. He lived in a multiethnic neighborhood a few blocks from Alija Izetbegovic; he socialized with Muslims and Croats and ministered to their health needs. Many of Karadzic's former neighbors attest to his being a genuinely friendly and likeable fellow. Even in the late 1980s there was no hint that Radovan Karadzic might become a Serbian extremist, who would position his men in the hills surrounding Sarajevo (Pale, the Bosnian Serb capital, was located here), and in Montenegrin mountaineer fashion lay siege to the city whose civilized tradition, in his eyes, had become the enemy of Serbianness.

Before 1990 there was little indication that Karadzic would become an important political personage. In 1968 he had made an impassioned speech at the Philosophy Faculty in Sarajevo, after which, Karadzic maintains, he was always under police surveillance. (He later said it was a turning point in his life.) In 1987 he spent 11 months in investigative detention on a matter involving a home loan and perhaps embezzlement. He was cleared of the charges and declared innocent, a rare development in Bosnia. Other than these two run-ins with the law, Karadzic seems to have stayed out of the public light and certainly outside of politics, except that he was briefly associated with the Greens, a party with an ecological agenda. In 1990 Karadzic was chosen president of Bosnia's Serbian Democratic Party (SDP)—because no one else wanted the job, he maintains. (The SDP had been established by Croatian Serbs earlier that year in Knin.) The Bosnian SDP was organized in preparation for republican elections scheduled for November 1990. When the party was officially inaugurated, even Izetbegovic was an honored guest, while Karadzic spoke on behalf of equal rights for religion, culture, and economic advancement for all in Bosnia. In the 1990 election the SDP won 72 seats in parliament (out of 240), with only the Muslim Party winning more (86). In late February 1991, when Bosnia held a referendum on sovereignty and independence, the SDP boycotted the vote, and thereafter started undermining the Bosnian parliament. That spring Karadzic began openly urging that Serbs in all Serbian areas of Yugoslavia, including Bosnia, have their own armed forces. In the early autumn he proclaimed an autonomous republic for the Serbs of Bosnia, a parliament for the Bosnian Serbs, and, for himself, political leadership of the Bosnian Serb community, a position to which he was never elected. Then, in mid-October, Karadzic went on the offensive and issued a death sentence to the Muslims of Bosnia.

For the next four years Radovan Karadzic was the leading spokesman for the Bosnian Serbs. His aim was to hold Yugoslavia together so that Serbs would remain in one state, but as it became apparent that Bosnia would soon be independent, Karadzic insisted on autonomy, then independence, for Bosnia's Serbs. When Bosnian independence was recognized in early April 1992, peace demonstrators were shot at by Serb snipers from Sarajevo's Holiday Inn, where Karadzic had his headquarters, and thus the siege of that city began. Karadzic wanted to make it a Serbian city, or at least a divided one, like Berlin before the wall came down. The war then spread to all of Bosnia and Hercegovina. Karadzic expected rapid success, for he did not believe that the Muslims could defend themselves.

He knew, too, that he had the backing of Milosevic in Belgrade, that Serb troops from the Yugoslav army were being transferred to Bosnia, and that Ratko Mladic would soon be leading the Bosnian Serb forces.

During the four-year war, Karadzic was the Bosnian Serbs' most visible figure. He was on the television news daily, promoting the Serb cause and waging a propaganda war against the Croat "fascists" or the Muslim "fundamentalists." He became a master at psychological warfare, striking terror among the Western powers when he warned of the potential dangers of intervention in civil wars. He taunted them with buzz words like Vietnam, Mogadishu, and body bags. He also lied constantly and with such sincerity that diplomats who dealt with him were completely abashed. He denied that there were detention camps in Bosnia, that ethnic cleansing was happening, that Muslim women were being raped by Serbs. He also changed his stories to suit the circumstances; Croats, for example, ceased to be "fascists" when they too began fighting the Bosnian Muslims. His trademark was a mop of unruly hair styled by solicitous cosmeticians who beamed when they were photographed blow-drying it.

In the Serbian political world, Karadzic's strongest support came primarily from conservative elements. The Orthodox Church stood firmly behind him, as did those who represented the Chetnik tradition. Mladic, Karadzic's able military commander, was not really comfortable with the rightists, for Mladic had come from a Partisan family and the Yugoslav army tradition. Karadzic's profligate life style was also repugnant to the general. The two were allied by the necessity of war. Meanwhile, the Serbs in Yugoslavia, like Milosevic, accepted Karadzic until he was no longer useful. Milosevic distanced himself in mid-1994 when the West promised an easing of the embargo against Yugoslavia; thereafter the Milosevic-controlled media began depicting Karadzic as a drunk and gambler who had accumulated enormous debts at Belgrade casinos while the war raged in Bosnia. As Karadzic became isolated, he grew even more bombastic and full of contempt for the international community, declaring Bosnian Serbs to be alone and embattled, but with God on their side. Diplomats and journalists were disgusted by him. Milosevic, meanwhile, sidled up to the West and landed the job of spokesman for the Bosnian Serbs at the Dayton peace talks in 1995. Karadzic, who by then had been indicted for war crimes by The Hague tribunal, was not even allowed to come to Dayton. During the spring of 1996, Karadzic was ousted from the presidency and replaced by Biljana Plavsic, and was not permitted to run in Bosnian national elections, which were held in September. For a time Karadzic continued to live in Pale, but after apprehension of indicted war criminals was stepped up in Bosnia, Karadzic made himself invisible. The U.S. State

Department has offered $5 million for information that could lead to his arrest, but silence about his whereabouts proves that Bosnian Serb loyalty to him is still strong.

Vojislav Kostunica (1944–)

Born in a village named Kostunici, located in the Serbian heartland, Kostunica came from a middle class, anticommunist family and was educated in the law. He completed Belgrade University Law School in 1966 and got a master's degree in 1970 and a Ph.D. in 1976. His thesis and dissertation titles, respectively, were: "The Political Theory and Practice of the Constitutional Judiciary in Yugoslavia" and "Institutionalized Opposition in Capitalist Political Systems." He taught briefly as a lecturer at the university but was dismissed in 1974 when he supported the criticism of Yugoslavia's new constitution. His objection to it was twofold: that it fragmented the Serbian nation and that the provincial and republican boundaries were an artificial communist invention. These were points that the Serbian Academy developed in the mid-1980s as it assumed a more nationalistic stance. After his dismissal from the university, Kostunica was employed by the Institute for Social Sciences at the Institute for Philosophy and Social Theory, where he wrote widely for academic journals. One publication that endeared him to Western observers, once Kostunica entered politics, was his translation into Serbo-Croatian of the *Federalist Papers.*

Kostunica's political career began as Yugoslavia started to disintegrate. In 1989, together with Zoran Djindjic, he helped found the Democratic Party. When the party split in 1992, Kostunica established his own organization, the Democratic Party of Serbia. Djindjic and Kostunica continued to be at odds for most of the 1990s. Kostunica and his party did not participate in the popular, but ultimately unsuccessful, Together coalition of 1996–1997 that sustained nearly three months of protests against the Milosevic regime. Kostunica, however, held a seat in parliament from 1990 to 1997. In 2000 Kostunica and Djindjic came together in an 18-party coalition, the Democratic Opposition of Serbia, which was challenging Milosevic's bid for a third term as Yugoslav president. On September 24, Kostunica ran against Milosevic and tallied 53.3 percent of the vote to Milosevic's 35 percent. When the latter refused to accept the election's outcome, there was some confusion about how to proceed, but by October 5, Kostunica was firmly established as Milosevic's successor. Within a few months, Djindjic became prime minister of Serbia, and the rivalry between the two resumed. In the second half of 2002, given that Yugoslavia was to cease existing officially, to be replaced by a state called "Serbia and Montenegro," Kostunica decided to run for president of Serbia. Due to a constitutional provision that an election was valid only if 50 percent of the electorate voted, three successive elections in as many months failed to elect Kostunica to the job. In 2003 an acting executive—the president of the parliament—headed the country. The situation favored the Djindic political camp.

Much has been written about Kostunica's philosophical and political views. A popular figure, regarded as an authentic, humble, "normal man," with genuine ethnic roots, the West initially rejoiced at his successful challenge to Milosevic. Kostunica described himself as a Western liberal, championing free speech, an independent media, and rule of law. But the West soon learned that he had no love of the so-called liberal West, just as he had no respect of Soviet Communism. Much like the Russian writer Aleksandr Solzhenitsyn, Kostunica felt that much harm could come from both West and East. He was loathe even to meet with foreign represen-tatives, notably snubbing Madeleine Albright, the U.S. secretary of state, who had requested a meeting with him in Vienna. He trusted in the simple, ethnic values and national goals. He believed Serbia and Montenegro were the heart of the Serbian nation and should act as a magnet drawing other Serbs to it. His political program during the mid-1990s wars was very similar to Radovan Karadzic's, and Kostunica continued to believe that Bosnian Serbs belonged to Serbia. He also felt that Kosovo and Vojvodina should remain a part of Serbia and that their status should be subordinated to Belgrade. Some have referred to him as "Seselj in a frock coat." As for the tribunal at The Hague, Kostunica dismissed it as a political instrument. If it were his choice, no Serb would be extradicted to the war crimes venue: crimes by Serbs should be prosecuted in Serbia.

Ante Markovic (1924–)

Ante Markovic, a Croat born in 1924 in Konjic (Hercegovina), was the Socialist Federal Republic of Yugoslavia's last prime minister from March 1989 until December 1991. He had been a member of the Communist youth organization before World War II, and during the war he engaged in some guerrilla activities on the side of Tito's Partisans. After the war he trained in Zagreb as an electrical engineer. A technocrat and industri-alist, Markovic developed his career in the 1960s and for 25 years managed a large Yugoslav company that built machinery. He was a businessman who favored a market economy, and therefore opposed federal laws and practices restricting free trade. The repressive 1970s and the financial cri-ses of the 1980s were exceedingly bad for business, so Markovic, tired of fighting an immovable federal bureaucracy, decided to enter the political arena in order to help change the laws. In the 1980s Markovic served briefly as prime minister of Croatia. In March 1989 he became the prime minister of all of Yugoslavia.

When Markovic took over the government, Yugoslavia was in very serious economic trouble. The unemployment rate was 20 percent, inflation rates were in the neighborhood of 2,000 percent per year, workers were striking in unprecedented numbers, and the International Monetary Fund (IMF) was insisting upon strict austerity measures. (Markovic's predecessor, Branko Mikulic, had been forced to resign because of the economic crisis.) Markovic, who strongly believed in Yugoslav unity, undertook economic "shock therapy" intended to reform the country's economy radically. Laws were passed to enable the market to operate freely, and other laws encouraged privatization. By the end of the year, there were already promising signs. The Yugoslav monetary unit, the dinar, had been devalued and tied to the German mark; the dinar had also been made convertible. This helped bring the inflation rate down to single digits and earned Markovic a Yugoslav-wide constituency among those who longed for economic stability.

Markovic's nemesis was Yugoslavia's volatile political situation. The leading politicians with vested interests in the republics distrusted Markovic and feared that their own republics would suffer as a result of economic reforms. In 1989 nationalist political undercurrents were already undoing the Yugoslav unity upon which Markovic's reforms were based. He might have saved his program and Yugoslavia if multiparty elections had been held on the federal level in early 1990. However, the republics held their elections first and gave the mandate to local nationalists. In July, midway through the course of the republics' elections (which took place between April and December 1990), Markovic hurried to organize a "Yugoslav" party, calling it the Reform Alliance Party, but he was too late, and the party made little impact.

Markovic continued to be supported by the IMF and the international community, but his domestic base was declining. At home he functioned primarily as a mediator among the republics and eventually presided over the dissolution of the federation. Among his greatest foes were the Serb president, Slobodan Milosevic, and the Croat president, Franjo Tudjman, who were known to have plotted Markovic's demise at a secret meeting in Karadjordjevo in March 1991. Milosevic, however, had virtually sealed Markovic's failure by December 1990 by secretly securing an illegal loan worth $1.7 billion from Serbia's main bank in order to ease his reelection that month. The loan undermined Markovic's economic austerity program, undoing the progress that had been made toward controlling the country's inflation rate.

Markovic stayed on as prime minister as long as he felt there was a possibility of pulling Yugoslavia back together. Described as an eternal optimist, always smiling, he continued to pursue peace and unity. But by the fall of 1991 the war had gone too far. His home republic, Croatia, had fallen into a savage conflict with the JNA (mostly Serbian troops); the JNA even bombed Croat government headquarters while Markovic was there meeting with President Tudjman. Markovic resigned in December 1991, about the time the European Community announced that it would recognize Slovenia and Croatia. A prime minister who believed in Yugoslav unity was no longer needed. Markovic moved to Austria and resumed business activities.

Mirjana Markovic (1942–)

Mirjana Markovic, the wife of Slobodan Milosevic, has often been described as the sinister force behind the Serbian leader. Her mother was a militant communist—a onetime secretary of the Belgrade Communist Party—who was in the hills fighting alongside Tito's Partisan forces during World War II when Mirjana was born in 1942. The child was given to a relative to rear, and the mother was killed by Nazis when Mirjana was one year old. With this heroic revolutionary past in her blood, so to speak, Mirjana always seemed to be intent on fulfilling her mother's communist dreams.

She met Slobodan Milosevic in Pozarevac, where they became high school sweethearts and were inseparable after the age of 16 (they married in 1965 and have a daughter and a son). Like Milosevic, Mirjana studied at the University of Belgrade, where she completed her doctorate in sociology. She accepted a post at that university, and continued to profess a militant Marxist philosophy. Dr. Markovic, as she preferred to be called, also continued her political activity among those who made up what was left of Serbia's Communist Party. She ran for parliament in 1993 but was not elected. In 1994 she helped organize the Yugoslav United Left (YUL), which had 200,000 members; it allied itself with her husband's Serbian Socialist Party in the November 1996 elections. YUL drew to it left-oriented and antinationalist elements in Serbian society, but was only marginally successful with the voters. Mirjana continued to believe that communism would make a comeback; in her view, nationalism, including Serbian nationalism, had clearly gone too far. The dissolution of Yugoslavia and of socialism had brought too much misery to the peoples of that former federation.

It was as her husband's confidante that Mirjana Markovic has made her real mark, many would argue. During the late 1980s and also in the 1990s, when war raged in the former Yugoslavia, Mirjana continued to write a biweekly column for the journal *Duga.* Journalists and political pundits read her articles religiously, looking for signs of what Milosevic's next moves might be. In 1993 Markovic's columns essentially predicted the fall of Dobrica Cosic, Yugoslavia's president; and her negative writings on Radovan Karadzic prepared her readers for Milosevic's break with the leader of the Bosnian Serbs. Her writings have been published in a book entitled *Answers.* The book was translated into Slovene in 1996, and Markovic made a semiofficial state visit to the former Yugoslav republic late that year to promote her book, and perhaps also to promote closer ties between Serbia and Slovenia.

Until the Dayton peace agreement, Mirjana Markovic remained in the political shadows. But afterwards she began to speak out openly. She was especially outspoken against those who demonstrated in Belgrade from November 1996 through January 1997 in support of the Together coalition, which ran opposition candidates against the ruling socialists. A vocal opponent of her husband's political critics, she harbored a particular hatred for Vuk Draskovic's wife, Danica, whose father was an important Chetnik. The two women have fought in public. During the late 1996 street demonstrations, Mirjana Markovic became the butt of jokes and the subject of an unkind pop music hit that was a favorite among the protesters. She came to be called Baba Yula (the old lady/grandmother of YUL). She continued, however, to hold her own, occupying a shabby office in a deteriorating League of Communists headquarters building, ever austere, usually humorless, rather dumpy looking in photographs standing next to her tall husband, the neatly attired bureaucrat. Her only concession to femininity was a plastic rose she often wore in her dyed black hair.

Since her husband's ouster from power in October 2000 and his arrest and imprisonment in 2001, Mirjana Markovic has maintained a low profile. Her political life was over; her party got no seats in the 2000 parliamentary elections in Serbia. She and her daughter, Marija, remained in Belgrade, while her son, Marko, and his family resettled in Russia. In September 2000, Marija received an eight-month suspended sentence for her armed resistance to police who arrested her father; and Marko, whose pet project was building "Bambiland," a theme park in Pozarevac, the family's hometown, has certainly absconded with illegal monies. Mirjana Markovic has traveled numerous times to the Netherlands to visit her incarcerated husband. In April 2003 she was implicated in the assassination of Ivan Stambolic, a political foe of her husband, and reportedly fled to Russia to escape prosecution.

Slobodan Milosevic (1941–)

Slobodan Milosevic, the person most blamed for the breakup of Yugoslavia and the war that followed, was born in 1941 in Pozarevac, in Serbia. His parents were from Montenegro. His father was a former seminarian who became a teacher; his mother also taught school and was an ardent communist. The parents separated, and both were said to have committed suicide, in 1962 and 1974, respectively, although Milosevic denies this. In Pozarevac, a town 40 miles south of Belgrade, Milosevic met his future wife, Mirjana Markovic, while both attended the same secondary school. (His wife and former schoolmates and other associates from Pozarevac would figure prominently in Milosevic's regime after he came to power in Serbia.) He became a member of the League of Communists (LC) in 1959.

Milosevic completed a law degree at the University of Belgrade in 1964, but pursued a career in business and banking rather than law. He worked for a number of manufacturing companies and was director of Tehnogas from 1970 to 1978. Between 1978 and 1982 he headed Beobanka, a leading bank in Serbia, and traveled to the United States on bank business a number of times. (He speaks English quite fluently.) That he was a party member and well connected to important communists no doubt helped Milosevic attain the company directorships. This was common practice in Tito's Yugoslavia, particularly with the return of hard-line communists to power after 1972. In 1982 Milosevic accepted a full-time position with the League of Communists, and in 1984 he succeeded his friend, Ivan Stambolic, as head of its Belgrade branch. Two years later, in 1986, Milosevic became head of the Serbian LC, which put him in the very powerful position of controlling the republic's party and its membership. Some who analyze Milosevic's rise to power compare him to Stalin, who held a similar position in the Russian Communist Party shortly before he eliminated his political opponents and captured power in the USSR. In 1987 Milosevic was elected president of the presidency of the LC of Serbia.

Milosevic's rapid rise to public popularity began in 1987, one year after the Serbian Academy of Science and Arts issued its memorandum encouraging the Serbs to assert themselves. Although Milosevic did not publicly express an opinion on the memorandum, he rode the nationalistic wave it produced. In April 1987 he traveled to Kosovo and spoke passionately to an enthusiastic Serbian crowd about how they should not permit themselves to be beaten (by Albanians, who were in the majority in that autonomous province of Serbia). The response of the cheering audience had a visible effect on the usually dispassionate communist bureaucrat. The media, which were then coming under Milosevic's control, played up the speech, and Milosevic was quickly made into a Serbian hero. He had learned that he could move crowds with his speeches. In November 1988 he addressed a group of 100,000 striking workers gathered outside parliament and persuaded them to return to work. The next day the workers, calling his name, "Slobo," and carrying pictures of Milosevic, shouted support for his ouster of moderate communists from the party in Vojvodina, also an autonomous province of Serbia. On June 28, 1989, Milosevic returned to Kosovo. It was the 600th anniversary of the battle in which Serbs had been defeated by the Turks, and Milosevic used the occasion to promote the Serbian cause and, of course, himself as well. Some estimate that 1 million people attended the event to cheer on the newly anointed leader.

While Milosevic was rousing the masses in Serbia, the rest of Yugoslavia was beginning to worry. It was 1989, the year when all of eastern Europe was ridding itself of communist rule and the governmental and economic apparatus that went with it. The communist parties within Yugoslavia confronted the issue head-on in January 1990, but the League of Communists of Yugoslavia (LCY) was divided over how to proceed. The Slovene communists led the movement to reform the party by decentralizing it. Serbia and its backers, who had lined up behind Milosevic, favored greater centralization. The LCY expired that month, because the Slovenes, defeated in vote after vote at the 14th party congress, walked out. The Croat delegation, after some hesitation, followed. With the Yugoslav Communist Party defunct—it never met again—a new political ballgame began. Multiparty elections were held in Yugoslavia's republics (although not in Yugoslavia as a whole), and Milosevic had to adapt his political strategy to the new reality. He formed the Serbian Socialist Party, which was actually the LC of Serbia renamed. It participated in republic voting in December, and Milosevic, in order to assure its victory (it won 194 of 250 seats in parliament), rigged the elections. He also secretly arranged a $1.7 billion loan from the leading Serbian bank. It bolstered Serbia's economy, but it was an act that undermined the Yugoslav federal government of Ante Markovic and his needed economic reforms.

In early 1991, opposition began to develop against Milosevic within Serbia, comprised of Serbs who felt that he was too nationalistic, others who felt that he was not nationalistic enough, and still others who opposed him because he was a communist. In March 1991, the opposition, led by Vuk Draskovic, staged demonstrations in Belgrade. This time Milosevic found that his words had little effect on the crowd, estimated at 500,000. Local police were used against the demonstrators, and when that did not suffice, Milosevic's man on the Yugoslav presidency, Borisav Jovic, persuaded that body to dispatch JNA tanks against the populace. The demonstrations were eventually dispersed, but Milosevic had had to resort to all means—even police and military force—to preserve his power.

That Slobodan Milosevic was primarily a political animal has been confirmed by the way he acquired and maintained power in Serbia. Ideologies did not sway him; most would maintain that he was neither a true communist nor a real nationalist. His methods remained amoral; neither friendship nor the repulsiveness of political allies diverted him from his Machiavellian pursuit of power. In the 1980s he used his friendship with Ivan Stambolic, the nephew of a prominent Partisan and communist, to advance his career. Stambolic helped him along, as Milosevic succeeded Stambolic in business and then LC posts. When Milosevic reached the top in Serbia, he used his authority to destroy his old friend, who opposed the nationalistic turn of Milosevic's politics. In maintaining his power and later orchestrating the war in Croatia and Bosnia-Hercegovina, Milosevic embraced the help of the unsavory war lords Vojislav Seselj and Zeljko Raznjatovic (Arkan). He allotted them money and power, and even allowed them to run for parliamentary positions. He turned against them, especially Seselj, when it was no longer to his political advantage. Milan Panic, the Serbian American pharmaceuticals executive who was briefly prime minister of Yugoslavia in 1992, also experienced the devious strategy of Milosevic, who called on bureaucratic cronies and the media, which he controlled, to do in Panic during the December 1992 elections. Even Dobrica Cosic, the once-eminent Serbian writer and author of the Academy memorandum that outlined the Greater Serbia program, could not survive in the face of Milosevic's ill will. In 1993 Milosevic, using his alliance with Seselj at the time, had Cosic, then president of Yugoslavia, removed.

Slobodan Milosevic consolidated power in Serbia first. This included not only Serbia proper, but its autonomous provinces of Kosovo and Vojvodina, where the populations were 10 percent and 57 percent Serbian, respectively. He stripped the provinces of their autonomy—Vojvodina in October 1988 and Kosovo in March 1989—and then put his own people in as party and government officials. He was determined that the provinces remain firmly under Belgrade's control in spite of their sizeable non-Serbian populations. Milosevic then looked to the neighboring republics of Yugoslavia. In January 1989 he co-opted Montenegro for his cause, and through its president, Momir Bulatovic, was assured solid support. (The population of Montenegro was essentially Serbian.) In 1990 Milosevic extended his grasp in the direction of Croatia and Bosnia-Hercegovina, where there were Serbian communities. In these two republics he could peddle his message of Serbian unity, and did so by supporting—financially and militarily—those elements that opposed Zagreb and Sarajevo. Serbian nationalist parties were also established in these republics.

Hence, by 1991 Milosevic was well positioned to challenge the federal government in Belgrade for control of Yugoslavia. That government was headed by a collective presidency, comprised of eight representatives from the republics and the two provinces. Milosevic had the votes of four of the eight in his pocket, and in early 1991 the president of the presidency was a Milosevic coconspirator, Borisav Jovic. Together they blocked the normal rotation to a new president (the Croat Stipe Mesic), and effectively brought the Yugoslav government to a standstill in May 1991. This development convinced the Slovenes and the Croats that they must go ahead with declarations of independence the following month. The scene was set for war, and Milosevic was prepared, for he had also begun undermining the Yugoslavism of the army.

The war began in late June 1991. In Slovenia it was over quickly. The Slovenes won their independence, although Milosevic claims that he was not interested in winning Slovenia and that he counseled the army to let that republic go. The war in Croatia was another matter. It quickly turned very brutal, thanks to Milosevic's thugs, Arkan and Seselj, who engaged in terrorist acts against the civilian population. This enabled the JNA—which by the fall of 1991 was essentially a Serbian army—to occupy one-third of Croatia. In January 1992 Milosevic could act peace-loving and magnanimous when Cyrus Vance proposed a truce to be enforced by UN forces. Milosevic knew that the plan was to his advantage: the JNA had gone as far as it could, and the UN forces could act as enforcers of the new boundaries while the JNA prepared for the onslaught in Bosnia.

Milosevic, with renewed confidence, turned to promoting war in the former Yugoslavia's most diverse republic. He bolstered his Serbian nationalist clients there, among them Radovan Karadzic. Even before the war began, Milosevic had Serbian troops in the JNA transferred to Bosnia, and he gave the Serbian warlords Arkan and Seselj license to initiate their campaign of terror in eastern Bosnia. Shortly after the war began there in April 1992, Serbia and Montenegro, at Milosevic's wish, became a third Yugoslavia. That state then aided the Serb forces in Bosnia with financial, military, and moral support. However, as Milosevic often reminded diplomats and his critics, Serbia/Yugoslavia itself was never at war. As the war continued and diplomatic efforts produced plan after plan to end the fighting, Milosevic usually went along with the proposals, in general because they were to his political advantage. The later plans were, in effect, cosponsored by him and Tudjman. The so-called Vance-Owen plan under discussion in spring 1993 was a turning point for Milosevic. He agreed to accept it (albeit as leader of a state that was itself not actually engaged in war) and promised to persuade the Bosnian Serbs to go along. In May 1993 it was clear that Milosevic had lost control over his clients. Although Radovan Karadzic was eventually brought around, the Bosnian Serb parliament in Pale refused to accede to the plan.

By the following year the rift between Milosevic and the Bosnian Serbs grew greater, and the Contact Group powers (the United States, Great Britain, France, Germany, and Russia) took advantage of the situation. In June 1994 they offered Milosevic a partial lifting of the international embargo against Serbia, where the local population was experiencing dire shortages, in return for his closing of the border to Bosnia. Milosevic complied and embarked on a media smear campaign against the Bosnian Serbs, who were depicted as murderous, profiteering lowlife led by Karadzic, a profligate gambler and drunkard. The Contact Group was encouraged by the negative press, but Milosevic did not entirely stop supplying the Bosnian Serbs. He wanted them defeated and Karadzic destroyed, but politically rather than militarily.

The rift between Milosevic and the Bosnian Serbs developed as the war between the Croats and the Bosnian Muslims was coming to an end. The United States had taken the initiative, promising Croatia's President Tudjman massive financial assistance if he persuaded his Croatian clients in Bosnia-Hercegovina to stop their fighting. The agreement, known as the Washington Accords, was signed in the U.S. capital in March 1994. Milosevic saw that it was time to dump Karadzic and company and to shift into gear on the Tudjman-Milosevic agreement, dating back to Karadjordjevo (March 1991), which proposed to divide Bosnia-Hercegovina between Croatia and Serbia. Thus Milosevic, and Tudjman, too, went to Dayton, Ohio, as peacemakers and came home heroes. Milosevic, whose country had never been officially at war and who himself had never acknowledged assisting the Bosnian Serbs, became the spokesman for the Pale government. Karadzic and the Bosnian Serbs, many of them accused of war crimes and fearing arrest, were not even present during the deliberations in Ohio.

Milosevic, the former banker and party bureaucrat, who had lived a fairly modest life until the end of the 1980s, went through many incarnations. In the late 1980s he became the demagogue whose passion sparked the embers of the ancient Serbian soul. When the war began, he was widely depicted as "the Butcher of Belgrade," or another Saddam Hussein preying on helpless people. In late 1992 Lawrence Eagleburger, the U.S. secretary of state under George Bush, branded him a war criminal and called for his prosecution. But during the war, diplomats, as they came to know him, described him more charitably. He was not a racist or a nationalist, nor was he paranoid, according to David Owen. Those who dealt with Milosevic at Dayton were even more favorably disposed toward him. He was said to be perfectly at home in the Wright-Patterson Air Force Base quarters outside Dayton, enjoyed lunching at the officers' club, and became one of the drinking buddies of Richard Holbrooke, the U.S. peace broker. Journalists in Dayton reported that Milosevic was infinitely more agreeable than the elusive Tudjman, who jetted to and from Zagreb, and the brooding Alija Izetbegovic, who was lamenting the carving up of his country. Milosevic seemed, in other words, to belong.

During the war Milosevic was still master of the former Yugoslavia's political world. But after the end of hostilities and an ostensible return to peace, Milosevic found himself on shaky ground in Serbia. The November 1996 elections produced victories for Milosevic's opponents, a coalition of parties calling themselves Together (Zajedno). Together captured majorities in 14 municipal council elections. Milosevic refused to accept the voting results. Months of street demonstrations followed; as many as 250,000 participated in some protest marches during the Christmas holidays. Milosevic adopted the technique of stonewalling the opposition as well as the representatives of the European Union who investigated the election results. He survived the demonstrations, and things calmed down briefly until conflict developed on another front. This time the challenge came from Kosovo.

During 1998, KLA terrorism against symbols of Serbian authority increased in Kosovo. Belgrade met the attacks with police and brute force, not only against the KLA operatives but also against civilians. Sometimes whole villages were targeted. Albanians began to flee the Serb reprisals. Richard Holbrooke, the overseer of Dayton, traveled to Belgrade several times to bargain with Milosevic, but to no avail. Milosevic held firm, put in his hard-line generals, and prepared for war with NATO. The war lasted nearly three months in spring 1999, and culminated in Milosevic's capitulation. Milosevic and four of his closest aides were indicted by the tribunal at The Hague, while Kosovo was put under a UN protectorate. In spite of these developments, Milosevic survived. Demonstrations were organized from time to time in 1999 and 2000, but most petered out after a few days. No doubt Milosevic believed he had once again escaped ouster, so he had the courts alter the Yugoslav constitution to allow him a third term as president Then he called for early elections. The voting, which took place September 24, brought electoral defeat; Vojislav Kostunica had beaten Milosevic in the first round. Milosevic refused to step down, and was ousted on October 5 by a mass uprising of Belgraders, Otpor students, and demonstrators from the provinces who came to the capital for the specific purpose of overthrowing the president. It was done in one day.

Milosevic conceded, but stayed on in Belgrade. His party even ran candidates—although with limited success—in Serbia's December elections. But Milosevic's luck was running out. Serbia's new prime minister, Zoran Djindjic, was vulnerable; threatened with the withdrawal of foreign aid from the United States, Djindjic had Milosevic arrested at the end of March 2000. At the end of June, under a similar threat, the "butcher of Belgrade" was turned over to U.S. authorities, who flew him to The Hague. Milosevic appeared before the war crimes tribunal for the first time in early July, declared the court illegal, and refused to enter a plea. The judge entered a not-guilty plea on his behalf. Since then Milosevic, the lawyer, has been very busy handling his own defense—charged with crimes against humanity, including genocide.

The Hague divided the proceedings into two parts: crimes in Kosovo and crimes in the wars in Croatia and Bosnia. The Kosovo phase of the procedure against Milosevic began on February 14, 2002, and lasted until September 12. There were 95 days of testimony and 124 witnesses. No direct link, however, was established between Milosevic and events in Kosovo, although much evidence pointed to Milosevic knowing about an ethnic cleansing campaign in that province. The second phase, dealing with crimes in Croatia and Bosnia, began on September 22, 2002, but has been interrupted many times because of Milosevic's health. Nevertheless, Milosevic proposes to continue his own defense, assisted by several Serbian lawyers who help sort through and evaluate the mountains of paper assembled by the court. Since fall 2002 he has seemed less disrespectful of the court. Legal experts have given him high marks for his handling of the accusations against him, and Serbs at home watch the proceedings with interest, some with sympathy. In summer 2003, the court's prosecutors announced that they were just beginning to uncover a paper trail between Milosevic and war crimes in Bosnia. The trial is expected to go on for at least another year and a half. Meanwhile, in April 2003, in Serbia, Milosevic and his followers were charged with plots to assassinate Ivan Stambolic and Vuk Draskovic. Milosevic is likely to be tried for these crimes in absentia.

Ratko Mladic (1943–)

Ratko Mladic, a Serb, was born in 1943 in the village Bozinovici in southeastern Bosnia-Hercegovina, about fifty kilometers south of the capital, Sarajevo. Mladic's father was killed by Croats in 1945; both he and his wife had been Partisans who had fought against the Nazis and their Croat Ustasha allies during World War II. Hercegovina, where the Mladic family lived, was an Ustasha stronghold. Ratko, who was born during the war and named Ratimir ("war and peace"), recalls the murder of his father by Croats as a defining factor in his life.

Mladic attended high school near Belgrade, in Serbia, and then went on to Yugoslavia's military academy. He completed his studies there in 1965 and also became a member of the League of Communists the same year. (In November 1995, on the thirtieth anniversary of his graduation from the academy, Mladic donned civilian clothes—white shirt and bow tie—to attend his class reunion in Belgrade, out of reach of Richard Goldstone, head of the war crimes tribunal at The Hague, who was then pressing for Mladic to be apprehended for war crimes prosecution.) As a military officer Mladic had been trained as a Yugoslav. After all, the army (the JNA) was—and remained—the defender of all of Yugoslavia, disintegrating only after the war began in 1991. Over the years Mladic held various posts in diverse parts of the country, and, no doubt because of his loyalty to the state and the army, he was sent to the Command Staff Academy, where he completed his studies in 1978. When the war began in 1991, Mladic was a deputy commander in Kosovo, the troublesome autonomous province within Serbia where Albanian-Serbian tensions had brewed for a decade.

The war in Yugoslavia brought Ratko Mladic to military prominence. In June 1991, when fighting began in Croatia, Mladic was transferred to its Krajina area, where the Serbo-Croat conflict first erupted around the Croatian Serb stronghold of Knin. Here the JNA became involved against Croat special forces and the local police, ostensibly on behalf of Yugoslav unity. In the end, the army essentially helped the Greater Serbian cause, and because of this, Mladic's exploits against Croatia came to the attention of Greater Serbs elsewhere. Specifically, the Bosnian Serbs, then preparing for their grab for power and territory, recognized him as "the man we need." In May 1992, a month after war began in Bosnia-Hercegovina, Mladic was transferred at the personal request of Milosevic to the newly formed Bosnian Serb army. He was raised to the rank of lieutenant colonel general that May; in June 1994 he became a colonel general.

Mladic thus became commander-in-chief of the Bosnian Serb army. From this position he directed an all-out war against the Bosnian Serbs' opponents. Sometimes this included Bosnian Croats, but mostly he fought successfully against the army of Bosnia-Hercegovina (sometimes erroneously called the "Muslim" army) and against Bosnia's civilian population. The operation was ruthless. Ethnic cleansing, rape, slaughter of prisoners of war, and bombing of civilian populations (the siege of Sarajevo being the most intense) were so many features of the Mladic effort. It also included treating outside forces—NATO, the United Nations, and other international organizations—cavalierly and with contempt. Mladic's forces were stopped only in the second half of 1995, when the Croat lightning war in August and NATO air strikes in September reduced Bosnian Serb holdings to half of the republic's territory.

Mladic, as a main player in the war in the former Yugoslavia, was many things. A soldier's soldier to his men, he led an ascetic life, slept on a simple cot, and slogged through the mud with his troops. A warrior prince to the Serb believers, he was and is adored as one of a long line of Serbian heroes stretching back into the medieval past. For those civilians who were promised safety in the towns he took—like Srebrenica, where in summer 1995 7,000 or more Muslim men were executed—Mladic is the epitome of evil. He had promised (recorded on film) that no ill would come to those under his care, but Bosnian Serb forces under Mladic's command wreaked havoc on them instead. The war crimes tribunal sitting at The Hague has called for his prosecution. For the tribunal, Mladic, as commander of the military, bears heavy responsibility for war crimes. In the Serbian political world, Mladic has been close to Milosevic, although the latter betrayed him at the Dayton peace conference by giving away Bosnian Serb territorial gains. For Radovan Karadzic, his political counterpart among the Bosnian Serbs, he feels little amity. In Mladic's eyes, Karadzic, the profligate gambler and show-off who threw a lavish wedding for his daughter—although invited, Mladic did not attend—while Serbs were dying in war, lacks dignity and honor. Mladic, a son of his Partisan parents, openly rejected the Chetnik tradition, which Karadzic and other more traditional Serbs embraced. He continues to mourn the death of his daughter, a medical student in Belgrade who committed suicide in 1993, perhaps out of despair over her father's activities. He continues to have strong support among Bosnian Serbs, although—and perhaps it is just another Serbian political attempt at deception—he was dismissed from his post as head of Republika Srpska's army in fall 1996. He reportedly continues to live in Serbia, near Belgrade, where he is sighted from time to time. Both Zoran Djindjic and Vojislav Kostunica, Milosevic's successors refused to turn Mladic over to the Hague court.

David Owen (1938–)

Lord David Owen, the British politician who served as peace negotiator in the former Yugoslavia for three years, was born in 1938 in Plymouth, England. Owen studied at Cambridge, earned a medical degree, and practiced medicine before settling into politics in the British Labour Party. He has been a member of parliament (1966–1992), and under Labour Party governments has served as minister of the navy (1968–1970), minister of health (1974–1976), and foreign secretary (1977–1979). After Margaret Thatcher and the Conservatives came to power in 1979, Owen split with the Labour Party, concluding that it had become too leftist. In 1981 he founded the Social Democratic Party, but split from it six years later to become an Independent Social Democrat. In the 1980s Owen served on the Olaf Palme Commission on European Disarmament and Security. He was made an honorary peer (baron) by Queen Elizabeth II.

In late summer 1992, David Owen became a peace negotiator in the former Yugoslavia, representing the European Union (EU). He replaced Lord Peter Carrington, who had helped oversee the EU negotiations between Belgrade and Slovenia and Croatia in 1991. Owen worked with two different United Nations mediators: initially Cyrus Vance, a former U.S. secretary of state, and then Thorvald Stoltenberg, a former foreign minister of Norway. The envoys shuttled extensively around the Balkans and to European capitals, but held most of their official meetings in Geneva, Switzerland. They produced two peace plans—dealing primarily with Bosnia-Hercegovina—both of which were rejected.

The Vance-Owen Peace Plan (VOPP), made public in January 1993, retained the territorial integrity of Bosnia-Hercegovina, but proposed that it be divided into ethnic enclaves. There would be 10 cantons, divided among the Muslims, Serbs, and Croats, while Sarajevo was to be jointly administered. The Croats were very pleased, and adopted the slogan "Thanks, Vance Owen." The Serbs were initially approving, but changed their minds by spring. The Muslims, especially President Izetbegovic, could not be brought around to the ethnic division of their republic. Vance resigned in May, shortly before the plan was rejected. Owen continued the mission with Thorvald Stoltenberg, and the two produced a new proposal in August 1993. This plan provided for a more explicit partition of Bosnia. Their aim was to gain Serbian approval, but this time the Muslims could not be persuaded to consent. The Owen-Stoltenberg plan, with its bizarre division of the territory, was described as ridiculous by many. The Bosnians said that they would not even consider adopting it unless Bosnia was assured a port on the Adriatic. This unequivocal demand doomed the plan. Thereafter the peace negotiations, although Lord Owen continued to take part, became more and more the domain of the United States, the Russians, and what came to be called the Contact Group. David Owen resigned from the mission in May 1995, saying that he was fatigued and that the peace talks had not made significant progress.

The Bosnians as well as journalists covering the war in Bosnia have been critical of Owen's role as a negotiator. Owen's tack seemed to have been to treat all warring parties equally. His position was that the war in Bosnia was not a simple matter. One was not dealing primarily with a victim and an aggressor; all sides were somewhat guilty and should be treated accordingly. Consequently, Owen, in negotiations in Geneva, avoided interjecting moral principles into the deliberations. Owen and Stoltenberg, for example, treated Tudjman, Milosevic, and Karadzic as if all were legitimate rulers, even though war crimes investigators had named them as possible criminals. David Owen was especially singled out for his cold, dispassionate approach to the negotiations. It was a *realpolitik* approach, where only power and control of territory mattered. Whether wrongs had been committed seemed to be of little or no concern. For his stone-heartedness, Owen was depicted by many as an appeaser, a Neville Chamberlain (who, under Nazi German pressure, had agreed to the division of Czechoslovakia in 1938) for the 1990s. Others credited him with doing British Prime Minister John Major's dirty work for him. Alija Izetbegovic, Bosnia's president, was a bit more charitable, although very cynical. He said, "If David Owen did not exist, the Europeans would find another David Owen."

Owen for his part claimed that in all his years in public life he had never had to operate in such a "climate of dishonour, propaganda, and dissembling." He found that the Balkan leaders with whom he dealt had no sense of what truth was. The British envoy further maintained that he tried to be impartial, not neutral, especially in matters relating to human rights violations, such as ethnic cleansing. Lord Owen has presented his account of the complex diplomatic story involving the war in the former Yugoslavia in a memoir entitled *Balkan Odyssey* (1995).

Milan Panic (1929–)

Milan Panic, born in 1929 in Belgrade, defected from Yugoslavia in 1956 while representing his country in a bicycle race in the Netherlands. He immigrated to the United States. There he became a naturalized citizen in 1963 and settled in Costa Mesa, California, where he developed a highly successful pharmaceuticals business. Established in 1960, International

Chemical and Nuclear (ICN) became a half billion dollar industry. Its subsidiary Galenika was based in the former Yugoslavia, specifically Serbia, and in the early 1990s John Scanlon, a former U.S. ambassador to Yugoslavia, was one of ICN's directors. ICN, however, had a rocky history and was for a long time in legal difficulties with the Food and Drug Administration and the Securities and Exchange Commission. The company was charged with defaulting on an $8.4 million loan and also with misrepresenting one of its products, Virazole, for which ICN paid a $600,000 fine.

During the second half of 1992 Milan Panic became a political personage in Yugoslavia (Serbia and Montenegro). On July 2, 1992, Panic was named the country's prime minister and was formally elected by parliament to that position 12 days later. He was backed by Serbs like Dobrica Cosic, who hoped to minimize Milosevic's influence, and he had to be given express permission by the U.S. Treasury Department to travel to Yugoslavia because it was then under United Nations sanctions. Although an American citizen, Panic was allowed by the Bush administration to head Yugoslavia, a foreign government that was much maligned in the United States at the time. John Scanlon served as his special adviser. It was no doubt the wish of both Panic's Serbian and American supporters that he would disentangle Yugoslavia from the mess it was in and perhaps effect peace. But Panic failed to work miracles.

Prime Minister Panic was out of his depth. He spoke English with a Serbian accent, Serbian with an American accent, and both languages often incoherently. Many were puzzled about what his powers and functions were, as he, too, seemed to have been. Without getting at the political root of Yugoslavia's problems and those of the war then raging in neighboring Bosnia, Panic embarked on a flurry of ill-prepared and disorganized peace activities. He met, for example, with Croat negotiators—Western diplomats were present—to discuss territorial settlements, and nearly gave away Kotor Bay, an extremely vital strategic objective, because he was unaware of its importance. He seemed to bumble from one such encounter to another, until his supporters lost hope. Milosevic, who could not abide Panic, patiently waited for him to self-destruct. This occurred in December 1992, when Serbian presidential elections gave Milosevic 56 percent of the vote to Panic's 34 percent. Milosevic's support, at a low point in summer, had rallied among constituents who blamed the West for economic sanctions and the ensuing economic woes. That Milosevic had recently been branded a war criminal by the West and that Panic was thought by some to be an American agent factored into Panic's defeat. The following month he was ousted from the premiership. With his mission ended, Panic returned to California and a troubled business, which had also suffered because of United Nations sanctions against Yugoslavia. Panic's company's woes made news intermittently in the later 1990s, largely because of huge debts of its Serbian subsidiary.

Biljana Plavsic (1930–)

Biljana Plavsic was born in 1930 near Tuzla in Bosnia to a wealthy merchant family, and like her father became a biologist. Her father was director of natural sciences at a museum in Sarajevo, where Plavsic lived most of her life. Biljana studied botany and plant viruses at Zagreb University, where she received her doctorate. In the early 1970s she spent some time in New York on a Fulbright fellowship. She soon settled into a professorial post at Sarajevo University where she taught biology and was remembered for her stunning wardrobe and her toughness and aloofness as a teacher. In 1990 she aspired to be head of the biology faculty, but lost to another candidate. Instead Plavsic went into politics.

Plavsic claimed that her university colleague, Nikola Koljevic, an ardent proponent of the Bosnian Serb cause who died in 1996—probably a suicide—persuaded her to become politically active. In 1990, after Bosnian elections late that year, she found herself a member of that republic's presidency. In April 1992, when Bosnia was declared independent, Plavsic moved to the presidency of the self-proclaimed Bosnian Republic of Serbia. As a member of the Serbian Democratic Party (SDP), she often boasted that she had never been a Communist Party member although she had belonged to the Socialist Alliance of Working People, a small distinction. As a leading SDP member, she soon became vice president of Radovan Karadzic's government.

During the war in Bosnia, Plavsic revealed her ardent and bellicose Serbian nationalism. She was a regular visitor to the front lines where troops greeted her as "the empress." Normally cool and reserved, Plavsic was all emotion in her embraces and praise of Arkan, the paramilitary leader who killed mercilessly for the cause of Greater Serbia. Arkan returned the favor by naming a coffee shop after her. Plavsic's militancy during the war placed her into conflict with Slobodan Milosevic, then president of the FRY.

After the war, Biljana Plavsic became president of the Serbian Republic of Bosnia, a position she held until 1998, when she lost her bid for reelection to a Serb hard-liner. The United States was disappointed by her loss. In early 2001, Plavsic flew voluntarily to The Hague to face war crimes charges, including genocide, to which she initially pled not guilty.

In fall 2002 she changed her plea, admitting to planning and carrying out persecution of non-Serbs during the war. At her trial at the end of 2002, high-profile witnesses, including Madeleine Albright, urged the court's consideration of the indictee's remorse. All charges but one were dropped. In late February 2003, Plavsic was sentenced to 11 years in prison. Tribunal watchers feel Plavsic may be an important witness in future trials.

Plavsic, or the "Iron Lady," as she was known, remains an enigmatic figure. Although she claimed to be a democrat, she regularly expressed a wish to restore the Serbian monarchy. She was known to have close contacts with Prince Tomislav. Her Serbian nationalism, however militant, was always intensely nostalgic. For years, she took flowers and lit candles at a monument to Gavrilo Princip, the assassin of Archduke Francis Ferdinand, on the anniversary of that Bosnian Serb's death.

Zeljko Raznjatovic (Arkan) (1953–2000)

Zeljko Raznjatovic, the son of a Serb who was a Yugoslav army colonel, was born in 1953 in Slovenia. A tall, swashbuckling type, he was for a time a major figure on Belgrade's Red Star soccer team. Otherwise, his activities were less public. He became an agent of the Yugoslav secret police, presumably with the mission of liquidating Croat Ustasha elements living abroad. His assignment involved him in various criminal activities in western Europe, where Raznjatovic was marked by Interpol and wanted by foreign governments for bank robberies and jail breaks. In Sweden he was wanted for murder. When the war broke out in the former Yugoslavia, Raznjatovic-Arkan was formally the owner of a fashionable ice cream parlor in Belgrade.

The war in Yugoslavia was made to order for those like Arkan. Thugs, criminals, and those used to operating lawlessly thrived in the chaotic environment. Arkan became an agent of the Greater Serbian cause, organizing his band of Tigers and using terrorist methods to intimidate and execute Croats and Muslims who stood in the way of Serbian unity. Arkan and his Tigers plunged into the fray in the fall of 1991 in eastern Slavonia. He himself moved into Vukovar and threatened to take the city. When Bosnia was on the verge of war in early April 1992, Arkan and his men crossed the border from Croatia into eastern Bosnia. First they hit Bijelina, a multiethnic city, where they harassed its Muslim population, positioned snipers, and quickly eliminated resistance developing inside the city. Within days the opposition was broken (Muslim institutions, including centuries-old mosques, were destroyed, and Muslims cowered before the terrorists). By the second week of April, Arkan's units moved on Zvornik in eastern Bosnia, demanding that Muslims, who comprised 60 percent of the population, move out; when they failed to do so, Arkan took the town.

If Arkan was not the initiator of the war's ethnic cleansing policies, as some claim, he and the Tigers were certainly responsible for some of its most bloody atrocities. Although Slobodan Milosevic initially claimed not to know him, Arkan's activities clearly aided Milosevic and the Greater Serbian cause. Isolated Serbia, under economic boycott, depended on smugglers and drug traffickers such as Arkan. Arkan's handiwork was also appreciated by the Bosnian Serb authorities—Biljana Plavsic, Radovan Karadzic's sidekick and president of the Serb Republic of Bosnia since the summer of 1996, greeted Arkan with a big kiss after his 1992 exploits in Zvornik. The war made Arkan enormously wealthy. In February 1995 a twice divorced Arkan, father of seven children, married a 21-year-old turbofolk pop singer in what was billed as the "wedding of the century." The event was an extravaganza that reportedly cost $500,000 and included a pageantry of costumes ranging from medieval Serbian folk dress, to royal military uniforms, to a Scarlett O'Hara dress purchased in Rome for the bride. The Tigers constituted an honor guard for the newlyweds, and Milosevic, who was trying to distance himself from the likes of Arkan, could not snub the warlord whose smuggling had kept Serbia afloat financially: he brought a wedding present wrapped in shiny paper.

Arkan billed himself as a defender of Serbdom. He extolled the virtues of family, Orthodoxy, and patriotism. As such, he also ran for parliament as head of the Party of Serbian Unity. He was elected in 1992, but lost his seat in the next election. When the Dayton Accords were signed in 1995, Arkan's people were obliged to remove themselves from eastern Slavonia, leaving behind coveted control of the area's oil production assets. In 1997, Arkan was secretly indicted for war crimes in Bosnia and Vukovar, Croatia. He was assassinated in a Belgrade hotel in January 2000. Although the regime denied it, many suspected Milosevic and the state police were behind the killing. After the assassination of Zoran Djindjic in March 2002, Arkan's pop-singer wife was arrested for harboring suspects in the killing.

Ibrahim Rugova (1944–)

Born in the village of Crnce, and raised by an uncle after his father was killed in World War II, Ibrahim Rugova was a shy Albanian child who did not participate in sports, but rather passed his time reading. He was educated in Pristina University and at the Sorbonne in Paris, where he completed a Ph.D. in Albanian literature. Once back in Kosovo, he pursued his specialty, editing a journal, doing research, writing literary criticism, and publishing books—10 of them.

He was drawn into political life in the late 1980s, as Kosovo came under pressure from Belgrade. In 1989 he was among those who organized the Democratic League of Kosovo (LDK); he was soon chosen its head. LDK became a mass movement with virtually all Albanian adults in Kosovo professing membership. When Belgrade ended Kosovan autonomy, the LDK declared Kosovo an independent republic (1992), and Rugova formulated a pacifist policy for his conationals. The slogan he promoted was "independence through peaceful means," and while most of the rest of Yugoslavia was at war, the Albanians of Kosovo went about their lives largely unaffected. They established a shadow government, operated schools and hospitals, and collected taxes to pay for all these functions.

The Kosovars expected to be provided for after the war ended in Bosnia. Yet the Dayton Accords did not address their concerns. Kosovo, treated as a Serbian domain, was off bounds at the conference. For some Kosovars, this was confirmation that Rugova's pacifism had failed, and this gave way to support for a militant movement, the Kosovo Liberation Army. Serb retaliation against the KLA's attacks against Serb authority, led in February 1999 to the Rambouillet meeting where Serbs and Kosovars were pressed to agree to a détente. The Kosovar delegation was made up of Albanians of various persuasions, but it was indicative that Rugova's pacifism had been eclipsed when Hashim Thaci, the KLA leader, was chosen to head the delegation. After NATO's war against the Serbs, Kosovo was made a UN protectorate, with Rugova as president and Thaci as prime minister of the provisional government. Within the protectorate, Kosovars have achieved some measure of autonomy. In spring 2002, in Kosovo's first free election, Ibrahim Rugova was chosen Kosovo's president. Kosovars, wary and apprehensive of the KLA and the criminal element associated with it (Mafiosi from Albania), preferred their popular leader of the 1990s. Independence for Kosovo remains on Rugova's agenda for the future.

Vojislav Seselj (1956–)

Vojislav Seselj, the future ultranationalist Serb warlord, was born in 1956 in eastern Hercegovina, a region that has spawned extremists among all of its ethnic groups. Seselj, who for a time was a professor of political science at the University of Sarajevo, was imprisoned in 1984 after being tried for conspiring to overthrow the Yugoslav state. His eight-year prison sentence was reduced; in the end he served two years, six months of which were in solitary confinement, where he was probably tortured. Seselj has been described as a psychopath. A tall man with a heavy, potbellied frame, crude and brash, Seselj enjoys shocking and taunting those he comes into contact with. He shouts and fights in parliament, charges foreign journalists huge sums for interviews, and regularly spouts bloodcurdling remarks about Croats and Muslims. He played a pivotal role in Serbia during the breakup of Yugoslavia and in the ensuing wars in Croatia and Bosnia-Hercegovina.

In 1989, as the Yugoslav republics prepared for multiparty elections, Seselj helped Vuk Draskovic found the Serbian Renewal Party in order to challenge the former communists for control of Serbia. He soon broke with Draskovic and formed the Radical Party, an organization that espoused ultrapatriotic symbols and goals. It linked itself with mythical medieval Serbian heroes, with Serbian saints, and particularly with Draza Mihailovic, the World War II Serbian general who fought Tito's communists with the aim of restoring a Serbian monarchy. Mihailovic and his Chetniks were beaten; Mihailovic was tried and executed after the war, and the Chetniks were outlawed. The breakup of Yugoslavia, however, helped resurrect the Chetniks, this time a band of paramilitaries organized and led by Seselj.

Vojislav Seselj and the Chetniks served as a special Serbian force in the wars in Croatia and in Bosnia-Hercegovina. They raped, tortured, pillaged, and engaged in ethnic cleansing in both republics. Their activities, often directed toward civilians, helped escalate the atmosphere of fear and terror that swept the area in 1991 and 1992. And although Milosevic has denied any complicity in the Chetnik operations, Seselj has explicitly implicated Milosevic in them. He has asserted that many of the operations were, in fact, planned, directed, and paid for by Belgrade. Milosevic courted Seselj, for the latter was useful in furthering the Greater Serbian goals and rallying the rightists and Serbian patriots. He used Seselj against political enemies, including Milan Panic in late 1992 and the writer and Yugoslav president Dobrica Cosic in 1993. But Seselj was not merely, or even, Milosevic's henchman. By the middle of 1993 Seselj had become the second most powerful figure in Serbia, for his party held the second largest number of seats in parliament. In fall 1993, Milosevic, his other political enemies eliminated, purged the military and moved against Seselj and his forces. Although Seselj was jailed briefly by Milosevic, the latter was not successful in displacing the ultranationalist.

Seselj remained politically strong in post-Dayton Serbia. He continued to be a member of parliament, and in the December 1996 election was also elected mayor of Zemun, a city on the Danube north of Belgrade with a population of 200,000. His Radical Party captured 18 percent of the popular vote in the 1996 election. In September 1997, Seselj emerged as one of two leading candidates for the presidency of Serbia, and in the presidential election of September 2002, Seselj received 22 percent of the vote. In February 2003, Seselj decided to surrender to the war crimes tribunal, telling a rally of 10,000 supporters the day before his departure that he intended to use the venue at The Hague to put the Americans and NATO on trial. In December 2003, Seselj's party got the largest number of votes—one-third—in Serbia's parliamentary election. Seselj, from his cell in The Hague, headed the party list.

Haris Silajdzic (1945–)

Haris Silajdzic, a leading Muslim—or, as he later preferred to call himself, "Bosniak"—political figure, was born in 1945 in Sarajevo. He studied in Libya, graduating from Benghazi University's Faculty of Arabic and Islamic Studies in 1971. He also spent one year in Washington, D.C., while preparing his doctoral work on U.S.-Albanian relations. Silajdzic's training was strongly Islamic in character. He published articles in the field and acted as adviser to the head Muslim religious leader in Yugoslavia. One would therefore expect that once Silajdzic became politically prominent in the early 1990s, he would promote a Muslim religious, or at least a (Bosnian) Muslim national, agenda. Silajdzic, however, became and remained the leading spokesman for a multicultural, multireligious, and united Bosnia.

When war broke out in Bosnia-Hercegovina, Haris Silajdzic was its foreign minister. Together with Alija Izetbegovic and other Bosnian officials, he led the diplomatic effort to bring international pressure to bear on the Bosnian Serbs and on Belgrade, which supported the war. When it was clear that the fighting would not be stopped, Silajdzic implored the West at least to allow the Bosnian government to arm itself against its attacker. He traveled abroad, speaking eloquently—his command of English is superior—about the moral responsibility to aid the victims of aggression. His pleas were taken up by liberal journalists. Yet he failed to evoke a show of unity and force against the Serbs from the European powers and the United States. By fall 1993, the cosmopolitan Silajdzic, bitter and worn down by disappointment, told a reporter who interviewed him that the Western powers considered the Bosnians a nuisance that they wished would simply go away. Bosnia, he said, was an embarrassment for the West, whose conscience understood its moral obligation but would not or could not do the right thing. During the course of the war the West never permitted the Bosnian government to buy weapons legally.

Toward the end of 1993 Silajdzic was named prime minister of Bosnia-Hercegovina. It was not a post he welcomed, but he accepted the appointment with the understanding that he could use his authority to crack down on the Muslim mafia. That element, which was particularly strong in Sarajevo, was made up of thugs and war profiteers who added extortion and street crimes to the daily burden of the war-weary Bosnians. Silajdzic dealt with these criminals swiftly and effectively. He also continued trying to get the world's attention regarding the plight of his country. When the Sarajevo marketplace was bombed yet again in February 1994, resulting in many deaths and injuries, Silajdzic used the presence of ABC Television's Peter Jennings to broadcast worldwide about Bosnia's troubles.

During the course of the war, Silajdzic grew apart from the other Muslims in the government. He did not get on well with Mohammed Sacirbey, who succeeded him as foreign minister, and he and Izetbegovic became less close. The war in some cases had made Muslim leaders more committed nationalists or drew them toward Islamism. At the Dayton peace talks, where his country was being divided by Western diplomats in November 1995, Silajdzic was more melancholic than ever. Yet he persisted in his goal of preserving a united, multinational Bosnia. In spring 1996 he established the Party of Bosnia and Hercegovina and became its presidential candidate in Bosnia's postwar elections (September 1996). During the campaign in the town of Cazin, Silajdzic was beaten up by agents of the then more extreme Muslim-dominated government. In the election itself, Silajdzic, the democrat and champion of multicultural unity, lost. He received about one-fifth the number of votes Izetbegovic got, and even Serb and Croat presidential candidates tallied more votes than he. Although multinationalism had thus far been rejected by the electorate, Silajdzic continued to promote it and also the reunification of Bosnia during elections in October 2001.

Hashim Thaci (1969–)

A Kosovar Albanian, one of eight children, who grew up in the village of Boja, Hashim Thaci studied history at Pristina University. As a student leader, he ran afoul of the Serb authorities and was expelled. He was also tried in absentia and sentenced to 22 years as a terrorist. He fled first to Germany, then to Switzerland, where he did postgraduate work in political science at the Universities of Lucerne and of Zurich. He was in and out of Kosovo in the early 1990s, hiding from authorities but also organizing what would become an alternative to Ibrahim Rugova's LDK party. Thaci maintained that the Kosovo Liberation Army had its roots in the National

Movement for the Liberation of Kosovo (LPK) founded in 1993. Few Albanians, not even Rugova, were aware of the LPK, but after Dayton and especially after 1998, more and more Kosovars became acquainted with the LPK and its military arm, the KLA, through its well-publicized terrorist attacks on Serbian authorities in Kosovo. When in 1999 the West became concerned that war was about to break out again in Yugoslavia, it summoned the Serbs and Albanians to a meeting in Rambouillet. There Thaci emerged as the Kosovar leader. The Albanian delegation, made up of various political factions, meeting at Rambouillet, chose Thaci as its spokesman, a symbolic development signifying a rejection of Rugova's pacifist policies.

At Rambouillet, Thaci at first refused to sign the agreement. He feared that KLA forces at home would oppose it. After a trip home to consult with KLA ranks, he became confident that there was support for Rambouillet. He returned to France and signed on March 15, 1999. The NATO war against the Serbs ensued. In 1999, the Kosovar provisional government included Thaci as prime minister, with Rugova as president. In March 2002, Kosovo had its first ever free election, and though Thaci's party did well, Thaci would no longer be premier. Rugova, however, proved to be a popular vote getter; he was elected president. Public esteem for the KLA and Thaci had diminished after the war. Many blamed the KLA for increasing local crime, attributed to mafia activities linked to Albania proper. Thaci himself remained an enigmatic figure, as he had been in the mid-1990s; KLA operatives referred to him as "the snake."

Tito. See Josip Broz

Franjo Tudjman (1922–1999)

Franjo Tudjman, the nationalist president of Croatia after 1990, was born in 1922 in Veliko Trgovisce, Croatia. He became a military man during World War II, joining Tito's Partisans in 1941, and fought against Ante Pavelic's Ustasha units, the Axis powers' Croat fascist ally. (During the war a younger brother of Tudjman was killed by either Nazis or Ustasha.) Franjo Tudjman, who rose through the army ranks, was a major general in the JNA and a member of the League of Communists when he left the military in 1960 to become a historian.

In the 1960s Tudjman was director of Croatia's Institute for the History of the Workers Movement; he was also on the executive committee of the

Matica Hrvaska, the leading Croat cultural society. In the mid-1960s Tudjman and the historical institute became a dissident organization. It reexamined and reevaluated Croatian history on the basis of new data. The official Communist Party history was challenged, particularly as it stressed Croatia's negative role in World War II. Institute historians concluded that Croats were not all fascists, that they were not chiefly responsible for the breakup of the first Yugoslavia, and that they were not inherently bloodthirsty killers of Serbs. Tudjman's own study of wartime deaths in the territory of the Socialist Republic of Croatia concluded that the number of deaths was about 60,000, many fewer than was commonly believed, and that many of the dead were liberal Croats, whom the Ustasha regarded as national traitors. In other words, Serbs were not the only victims in World War II Croatia.

In 1967, on the eve of the cultural-political upheaval known as the Croatian Spring, Tudjman was associated with the "Declaration Concerning the Name and Position of the Croatian Literary Language"; with it, Tudjman had clearly moved toward a politically nationalistic stance, which was in conflict with the Yugoslavism of the federal government in Belgrade. He was asked to resign his posts and was subsequently expelled from the League of Communists. In the early 1970s, after the Croatian Spring was suppressed by Belgrade, Tudjman was imprisoned. He spent two years in jail for engaging in "hostile propaganda" and for his role in the Croatian reform movement. In 1981 he was also stripped of his military rank by the communist government.

When by 1987 the Serbian Academy of Science and Arts and the Serbian political leadership, especially Slobodan Milosevic, began engaging in anti-Croatian rhetoric, the Croats had real cause to worry. They had been uncharacteristically quiet since the early 1970s crackdown against their reform movement. Now they were again being accused of Ustashaism and stereotyped as anti-Serb, fascist sympathizers. In this charged atmosphere, Franjo Tudjman came to the political forefront. He became head of the Croatian Democratic Union (CDU), organized in early 1990. In April of that year, the first multiparty elections in Croatia since World War II gave the CDU control of parliament. That body then appointed Tudjman as Croatia's president. Tudjman's party was the most nationalistic of the major parties contending for office in 1990; the Croat electorate seemed to be matching the Serbs' nationalism with a similar version of its own.

Croatia's new president, with a strong CDU majority in parliament, was able to establish near authoritarian control in the republic. He seemed to have forgotten his Partisan past, when he was committed to a united Yugoslavia. Instead, he promoted Croatian national ends. Nationalistic symbols, like the red and white checkerboard design for the Croatian flag, were introduced. These were interpreted as a revival of the Ustasha past, particularly among the Serbs, who constituted 12 percent of the population of the Croat republic. Croatian Serbs, goaded on by rhetoric from Serbia, began to fear that they would be brutally killed, as many had been during World War II. In general, Tudjman failed, or refused, to see that the new flag, the renaming of streets, the purging of government administrative offices (often it was Serbs who lost their jobs), and the like would escalate nationalism and fear on all sides.

In 1991, the year Yugoslavia disintegrated and the war began, President Tudjman played the Machiavellian politician. He prepared, along with the Slovenes, to declare independence in the event the federal government was not transformed into a loose confederation. (Analysts agree that this preparation for independence was poorly planned and executed; Tudjman, a former army general, did not even put his military in order.) Meanwhile, in March 1991, Tudjman also secretly met and plotted in Karadjordjevo with the Serbian leader Slobodan Milosevic. Although the substance of their talks is not known, it can be assumed that the two discussed re-drawing the map of soon-to-be former Yugoslavia. Tudjman very likely proposed that Croatia be expanded to include a large portion of Bosnia-Hercegovina, and he probably agreed that the Serbs, in addition to annex-ing the other Bosnian territories, should be allowed to take parts of eastern Croatia—perhaps even Vukovar. Statesmen and diplomats, among them Lord David Owen, who negotiated with Tudjman and Milosevic during the course of the war, would later confirm that the two had an agreed-upon agenda for the division of Bosnia. (Borisav Jovic, the last Serb president of the rotating Yugoslav presidency and a close Milosevic col-laborator, candidly described the Tudjman-Milosevic agreement in mem-oirs published in 1995.)

In late May 1991 Croatia held a referendum on independence. The result was positive, and the following month, on June 25, Croatia declared independence. Shortly thereafter, Tudjman's Croatia was at war. By the end of the year, one-third of the country was occupied by the JNA (mostly Serbian troops); Vukovar had been destroyed; and Dubrovnik, a Venice on the eastern shores of the Adriatic Sea, was under siege. A truce ar-ranged by Cyrus Vance in early January 1992 brought United Nations forces (UNPROFOR) into the area to monitor the cease-fire lines. And on January 15, 1992, the European Community recognized Croatian inde-pendence. But in the end, this still left Tudjman with only two-thirds of his country. As a politician, he needed to rally domestic support in spite of military losses, and he needed to figure out a way to get the rest of Croatia back.

Tudjman's position between 1992 and 1995 was unenviable. In spring 1992, after calling a snap election, he did manage to be reelected to the presidency (this time by popular vote). He and the CDU won again because the war was (at least temporarily) over, and because Tudjman controlled the media, which promoted his candidacy. Nevertheless, the Serbs occupied significant portions of his country and soon came to control large areas of Bosnia-Hercegovina as well. They also continued to threaten other Croatian territories (e.g., by destroying a strategic bridge in the Zadar area, the north of Croatia was severed from the wealthy tourist areas of Croatian Dalmatia). Only in 1995 did Tudjman's fortunes improve. He was helped partly by Germany, which from the start of the Yugoslav crisis had backed Croatia, and by the United States after the Clinton administration decided to deal with the Balkan problem by bolstering Croatia. Military advisers were sent to Croatia, loans were promised, and a sympathetic Peter Galbraith became the U.S. envoy to Tudjman's state.

In early 1995 President Tudjman unilaterally broke what had become a stalemate regarding the status of Croatian frontiers. He announced that the United Nations mandate in occupied Croatian lands would be terminated on March 31, 1995. With this challenge he was able to negotiate a new status for Croatia that undercut Serbian claims to the occupied areas. Soon thereafter Croatian forces began their retaliation against the Serbs. Their major offensive came on August 4, 1995, in the Krajina area, where within two days they managed to effect the evacuation of virtually all Serbs left in the area. About 150,000 left Croatia and resettled in Serbia. Milosevic, the Serbian president of Yugoslavia, probably advised them not to resist the Croats, and Radovan Karadzic, the Bosnian Serb leader, also did not urge resistance. In the end Croatia had, in a weekend, been "cleansed" of all but about 150,000 of its ethnic Serbian population, and Tudjman was able to claim national laurels. That the Croatian forces then continued their operations, moving into adjacent Bosnia to drive back the Serbs, promised only to enhance Tudjman's image. He was now being perceived as the winner in the Balkans. Tudjman could now dictate the redrawing of the former Yugoslavia's frontiers.

Tudjman went to Dayton in a strong position. His Croatia was essentially restored, and the bargaining power of his protégés in Croat areas of Bosnia-Hercegovina was favorable as well. (Tudjman had throughout the war backed the Bosnian Croats. The Bosnian CDU was essentially an adjunct of Croatia's party, and Bosnian Croat troops were perceived as belonging to Croatia. They wore the same uniforms and the same insignias, and they carried the same types of weapons.) The Dayton Accord provided for a two-part Bosnia, one of which would be a Muslim-Croat federation that was to be confederally allied with Croatia. Tudjman was in his element. Yet during the Dayton meeting in November 1995, Tudjman's world began to crumble.

With the war over, Tudjman's opponents at home became more vocal, and that November the political opposition made an impressive showing in local elections. Many urban centers, including Zagreb, voted decisively for non-CDU candidates. Prominent moderate CDU politicians had split from the party. Resentment had grown over Tudjman's authoritarian rule, his censorship of the media (respected newspapers like *Danas* and *Slobodna Dalmacija* had been silenced), and the nepotism that had placed Tudjman's relatives and cronies in politically and economically powerful positions. Many Croats had also come to regard Tudjman's imperial and imperious style as excessively pretentious. His offices were furnished in French-inspired old regime period pieces, and his honor guard wore anachronistic red tunics with gold braid, more befitting a Lehar operetta than a modern European state.

Tudjman also has not been well regarded by foreign statesmen and diplomats who came to know him during the war in Yugoslavia. The European Union representative from Britain, David Owen, who met with him on numerous occasions, wrote that he never trusted Tudjman. Owen regarded him as vain and opportunistic, like a Partisan general "waiting, acting, deceiving, harrying, feinting, and kicking whenever there was an opening." Tudjman also lost potential sympathy among world leaders due to his tactlessness and his racist and anti-Semitic remarks. During his 1990 campaign he boasted that he was happy that his wife was neither a Serb nor a Jew. More significantly, in 1988 Tudjman published a book in which he asserted that the Holocaust was greatly overstated, that only 900,000 rather than 6 million Jews died during that time. When the Holocaust Museum was dedicated in Washington, D.C., in April 1993, world leaders objected that Tudjman had been invited to the ceremony. After Dayton, the OSCE regularly admonished Tudjman for human rights violations of Croatia's Serb minority.

Though elected twice to the presidency (1992, 1997), Tudjman's support became increasingly limited. His strongest backers were in the countryside and among ultranationalist Croat émigrés who lived abroad in the United States, Canada, Australia, and Germany (where they constitute a temporary labor force). The émigré community strongly endorsed Tudjman during the war, showering him with millions of dollars to sustain his mission. Tudjman had reciprocated by upping his nationalist rhetoric and by including prominent émigré Croats in his administration—one of the most notable was the Hercegovinian Gojko Susak, a pizza parlor titan from Ottawa, Canada, who became Tudjman's defense minister. When Tudjman died of cancer in late 1999, the opposition acceded to power easily. Since 2000, Tudjman's successors have been grappling with the economic devastation of his rule. They have also begun releasing documentation, including taped records, of the Tudjman era, which is likely to reveal that Tudjman and Milosevic were coconspirators in the plot to divide Bosnia.

Cyrus Vance (1917–2002)

Cyrus Vance, acting on behalf of the United Nations, was a major negotiator between the warring factions in former Yugoslavia from 1991 until 1995. Born in 1917 in Clarksburg, West Virginia, he received both an undergraduate (1939) and a law degree (1942) from Yale University. He practiced law except when he was in the public service, first in 1957, and then again during the Democratic administrations of Presidents Kennedy, Johnson, and Carter. Under Kennedy he held the post of secretary of the army (1961–1964) and, continuing into the Johnson presidency, that of deputy secretary of defense (1964–1967); during the Carter administration he was secretary of state (1977–1980). During his entire career he has been noted for his negotiating skills. He was U.S. negotiator at the Paris Peace Conference with North Vietnam (1967), he mediated between Greece and Turkey during the Cyprus crisis (1967), and he played an important role in the Camp David negotiations between Egypt and Israel, to name just a few of his major assignments.

In October 1991, United Nations Secretary-General Javier Perez de Cuellar asked Cyrus Vance to help mediate the Yugoslav crisis. At first Vance worked along with Lord Peter Carrington, the European Community (EC) representative, to bring a stop to the fighting between Croatia and the Yugoslav army (JNA). Vance completed the job after Carrington's resignation, attaining a signed truce on January 2, 1992. According to the agreement, the territories of Croatia, occupied by Serbian troops (a.k.a. the JNA) would be monitored by UNPROFOR (UN Protection Force). Vance's efforts, in other words, effectively ended the war in Croatia.

His next assignment, also for the UN—by this time headed by an old friend, the Egyptian Boutros Boutros-Ghali—was to bring some accommodation to affairs in Bosnia-Hercegovina. In this endeavor Vance was teamed up with Lord David Owen, who represented the European Union (EU) after Carrington's exit. Vance and Owen worked in tandem for more than a year. They traveled extensively among Balkan capitals and Geneva, Switzerland, working out a plan that they hoped would be acceptable to the three warring groups in Bosnia. (It should be noted that Vance, in early 1992, had strongly opposed the EU's recognition of independence for Slovenia and Croatia, believing that it would precipitate war in Bosnia. War, in fact, came within three months of the recognition, in spite of the fact that both the EU and the United States had by then also recognized Bosnian independence.) The Vance-Owen Peace Plan was prepared and fine-tuned for four months before it was presented to the Muslim, Croat, and Serbian representatives in Geneva in January 1993. It provided for a division of Bosnia-Hercegovina into 10 autonomous provinces (3 Serb, 3 Muslim, 2 Croat, and 1 that would be Muslim and Croat; the capital, Sarajevo, was to be jointly administered). The immediate result was that the Serbs opened a new offensive, while the Croats began fighting against the Muslims. The motive in both cases was to acquire more territory, since the apparent criterion for VOPP's division of Bosnia was to legitimize ethnic rule over those areas where the ethnic group was already in control. Deliberations on the VOPP lasted nearly six months, while the fighting continued and the diplomats talked endlessly to Balkan leaders. Vance and Owen achieved a breakthrough of sorts when they persuaded Slobodan Milosevic to go along with the plan. However, neither Milosevic nor Vance and Owen were able to get the Bosnian Serb parliament in Pale to agree. In the end, in June 1993, the plan was rejected. The Vance-Owen diplomatic effort had failed.

Even before the outcome of the VOPP was known, Vance resigned from his UN assignment. He had just turned 76. He was replaced by the former Norwegian foreign minister Thorvald Stoltenberg. But in spite of his resignation, Vance continued to be involved in the affairs of the former Yugoslavia. In September 1995, after concluding a relatively unpublicized negotiating assignment, Vance was able to announce an accommodation in Macedonian-Greek relations. (The former Yugoslavia's Macedonian republic's independence had been recognized in 1993, but Greece had opposed its name and the new republic's flag. Greece insisted that Macedonia be called the Former Yugoslav Republic of Macedonia—known as FYROM in the United Nations Assembly—and imposed an embargo on commerce into and out of Macedonia.) In 1995 Vance succeeded in bringing the two parties to an agreement. Greece agreed to lift its embargo in return for Macedonia's removing the star of Vergina from its national flag (which the Greeks insisted implied a claim to rule over all of Macedonia, a large part of which was in Greece). Vance's career was capped that same month, in 1995, with an honorary knighthood bestowed upon him at the Embassy of Great Britain in Washington, D.C. He died in New York City in January 2002.

Warren Zimmermann (1934–)

Warren Zimmermann, the last U.S. ambassador to the former Yugoslavia, was born in 1934 in Philadelphia. He received a B.A. from Yale in 1956 and a B.A. and an M.A. from Cambridge University (England) in 1958. He joined the foreign service in 1961 and served there until 1994, when he resigned in protest over the Clinton administration's unwillingness to use force against the Serbs in Bosnia. During his diplomatic career, Zimmermann's primary assignments dealt with the Soviet Union and with overall European security. He spent parts of the 1970s and 1980s in the Soviet Union, as political secretary and deputy chief of mission, respectively. In the area of security in Europe, Zimmermann was deputy chairman of the U.S. delegation to the Madrid Conference on Security and Cooperation in Europe (CSCE) (1980–1981) and the U.S. representative (ambassadorial rank) to the CSCE in Vienna from 1986 to 1989. In Yugoslavia, he was political officer in 1964–1965, and, nearly a quarter century later, in 1989, was named ambassador to that country. He remained in Yugoslavia until 1992, when he was recalled to Washington to protest Serbia's aggression in Bosnia-Hercegovina.

As ambassador to Yugoslavia after 1989, Warren Zimmermann stood by (and helped formulate) the U.S. position that Yugoslavia should remain a unified state. He supported the affable Ante Markovic, the new Yugoslav federal prime minister, who had recently introduced far-reaching economic reforms demanded by the IMF and the World Bank, organizations that worried about the viability of their loans to that country. Zimmermann opposed the nationalist leaders of Yugoslavia's republics, whom he described as the destroyers of that state. He particularly disliked Slobodan Milosevic, the opportunistic Serbian leader, who would not even receive the U.S. ambassador until 10 months after he had arrived in Belgrade. For Zimmermann, Milosevic was by far the chief destroyer of Yugoslavia. His opinion of Franjo Tudjman, the Croatian president, was also negative. On January 14, 1992, the day before the European Community recognized Croatia and Slovenia, Tudjman lectured Zimmermann for more than an hour on the desirability of dividing Bosnia between Croatia and Serbia (Tudjman also admitted that he had discussed the matter with Milosevic). Zimmermann described this exchange with Tudjman as "the most astonishing single discussion of my years in Yugoslavia."

Once the independence of Slovenia and Croatia, former republics of Yugoslavia, was recognized—something the United States and Zimmermann opposed—a new policy was formulated. It involved a growing support for independence for Bosnia-Hercegovina, of which the United States became a chief proponent. To that effect, Zimmermann gave encouragement to the Bosnian government, which may have persuaded Alija Izetbegovic that independence could avert a war in his republic. It certainly persuaded the Bosnians that the United States was on their side, and furthermore it implied U.S. support in the event of war in that republic. (Zimmermann's discussion with Izetbegovic upon his return from the Lisbon conference in February 1992 was important in establishing a new U.S.-Bosnian understanding.) U.S. and European recognition came in April, but war was not averted. Not long after, Ambassador Zimmermann, who opposed American military involvement in the Yugoslav war in 1991 (during the Bush administration), became more convinced that Serbian aggression needed to be punished. He was called home in May 1992 (the former Yugoslavia had formally ceased to exist and had been replaced in late April 1992 by the "third" Yugoslavia, comprised of Serbia and Montenegro only), as an act of U.S. protest to Serbian aggression against Bosnia. Zimmermann eventually regretted that as ambassador he had not advised his government to adopt a harsher response to Serbia. When the Clinton administration, too, seemed to be avoiding military action against the Serbs, Zimmermann resigned from the State Department, where he had been heading its bureau dealing with refugee problems since his return from the Balkans.

Zimmermann has written a book about his ambassadorship to Yugoslavia, entitled *Origins of a Catastrophe* (1996). Since 1996 he has been affiliated with Columbia University, where he held a chair in the practice of international diplomacy until his recent retirement.

Primary Documents of the Breakup and the Wars

SERB INTELLECTUALS TAKE UP THE NATIONALIST CAUSE

Serbian nationalism was suppressed after World War II, as were the nationalisms of the other Yugoslav peoples, by the new Yugoslavism (and internationalism) that was being fostered by Tito's communist regime. Although Serbia had its own republic after 1945, it was not independent, and many Serbs now lived in Croatia or in Bosnia-Hercegovina. Moveover, two ethnically mixed areas of the Serbian republic—Kosovo and Vojvodina—had been given some autonomy within Serbia proper. To a Serb nationalist, the postwar arrangement might appear to be part of a deliberate plan to curb Serb power and influence in Yugoslavia. Little was said or written about this during Tito's lifetime.

After Tito's death in 1980, Serb nationalism began to swell within many social circles. Not the least was the nationalism of important intellectuals, members of the Serbian Academy of Science and Arts (SANU), who produced a 76-page memorandum on the status of their nation in May 1985 (it was leaked to the press in September 1986). The intellectuals focused on what they regarded as federal government discrimination against the Serbs. They cited the 1974 federal constitution, which had awarded greater autonomy to Kosovo and Vojvodina, granting each a status that was virtually equal with that of Serbia. In their view, the 1974 constitution had divided Serbia into three parts. The federal government, they felt, had clearly adopted the position of "a weak Serbia, a strong Yugoslavia." Tito (part Croat, part Slovene) and Edvard Kardelj (a Slovene), who was responsible for the new constitution, were blamed for the anti-Serbian policy.

The May 1985 memorandum asserted Serbia's right to preserve its state intact. Kosovo was especially important to the Serbs, because it was the heart of Serb culture and its moral values. The memorandum, however, went on to assert the right of all Serbs "to establish fully national and cultural integrity independently, *regardless of the republic or province in which they live*" (emphasis added). This was clearly a reference to the Serbs of Croatia and Bosnia-Hercegovina. In other words, the Serb intellectuals were probably proposing to extend Serbia's influence into neighboring republics. Non-Serbs were understandably alarmed when the document became public in fall 1986, while Serb nationalists were elated and encouraged by the academy's words.

The rise to power of Slobodan Milosevic coincided with the Serbs' new patriotism. It is no wonder, then, that recapturing control of Kosovo and Vojvodina was among Milosevic's first acts after coming to power. Part of the memorandum's program had been fulfilled. Whether Milosevic would move against Croatia and Bosnia on behalf of Serbs in those republics was on everyone's mind by 1990.

Document 1
MEMORANDUM OF THE SERBIAN ACADEMY OF SCIENCE AND ARTS (SANU)

Many of the misfortunes suffered by the Serb nation originate in circumstances that are common to all the Yugoslav nations. However, other calamities also burden the Serb nation. The long-term lagging-behind in the development of the economy of Serbia, undefined state and legal relations with Yugoslavia and the provinces [Kosovo and Vojvodina], and also genocide in Kosovo have appeared on the political scene with a combined force which have created a tense if not also explosive situation. The crucial nature of these three tortured questions, which derive from a long-term policy toward Serbia, threaten not only the Serb nation but also the stability of Yugoslavia as a whole. They must therefore be given central attention.

* * *

The economic subordination of Serbia cannot be fully understood without [understanding] its politically inferior position, which also determined all relations. For the CPY [Communist Party of Yugoslavia] the economic hegemony of the Serbian nation between the wars was not disputable, although the industrialization of Serbia was slower than the Yugoslav average. Thinking and behavior with a dominant influence on later political events and internationality [sic] relations were formed on the basis of that ideological platform. Slovenes and Croats created their national Communist parties before the war and achieved decisive influence in the CC [Central Committee] of the CPY. Their political leaders became the arbiters of all political questions during and after the war. These two neighboring republics shared a similar history, had the same religion and desire for ever-greater independence, and, as the most developed, had common economic interests, all of which supplied sufficient reason for permanent coalition in an attempt to realize political domination. This coalition was solidified by the long-lasting cooperation of [Josip Broz] Tito and [Edvard] Kardelj [respectively, a Croat and a Slovene], the two most prominent personalities of postwar Yugoslavia, who enjoyed unlimited authority in centers of power. A cadre monopoly allowed them essential influence over the composition of the political apex of Yugoslavia and all the republics and provinces. The exceptionally great contribution of Edvard Kardelj in preparing and carrying out the decisions of AVNOJ [Anti-Fascist Council for the National Liberation of Yugoslavia] and of all postwar constitutions is well known to all. He was in a position to build his personal views, which could not realistically be opposed, into the foundation of the social order. The determination with which Slovenia and Croatia today oppose any constitutional change shows how much the Constitution of 1974 suits them. Views concerning the social order had no chance of being accepted if they were different from the conceptions of [those] two political authorities, and it was not possible to do anything even after their deaths, given that the Constitution insured against any such change by granting [each republic and autonomous region] the possibility of a veto. In view of all of this, it is indisputable that Slovenia and Croatia established a political and economic domination through which to realize their national programs and economic aspirations.

* * *

The Serbian people have a historic and democratic right to establish fully national and cultural integrity independently, regardless of the republic or province in which they live. The acquisition of equality and independent development have a deeper historic meaning for the Serbian people. In less than fifty years, within two consecutive generations, twice exposed to physical annihilation, forceful assimilation, religious conversion, cultural genocide, ideological indoctrination, invalidation, and denunciation of their own tradition under the imposed complex of guilt, intellectually and politically disarmed, the Serbian people were exposed to temptations that were too great not to leave deep scars on their spirit. We cannot allow ourselves to forget these facts at the end of this century of great technological achievements of the human mind. If the Serbian people see their future in the family of cultured and civilized nations of the world, they must find themselves anew and become a historical subject; they must once again acquire a consciousness of their historic and cultural being; they must put forth a modern societal and national program, which will inspire contemporary and future generations.

Source: Peter Sugar, ed., *Eastern European Nationalism in the Twentieth Century* (Lanham, MD: American University Press, 1995), pp. 332–44. Translated by Dennison Rusinow.

THE CROAT NATIONAL AGENDA

Bosnia and Hercegovina had been part of an independent Croatian state during World War II. The state had been governed by the Croat fascist (Ustasha) Ante Pavelic, a puppet of Italy and Germany; it was dismembered and discredited by the victorious Allies after 1945. Croatia and Bosnia-Hercegovina were separated, and each became an individual republic of the new Yugoslav state governed by the communists. Whether Croats believed the two states belonged together or not was not discussed publicly while Tito, who died in 1980, was still alive.

In 1981 Franjo Tudjman, the future president of independent Croatia (1991), wrote about Croatia's neighboring republic in a book that was published in the United States. The book was probably not widely read—it was written in English in a dreary and pedantic style—and was probably not taken too seriously at home or abroad, for Tudjman had been relegated to political limbo in the early 1970s. Tudjman, who had been a JNA general and fought the fascists (including Croat Ustasha), had evolved in his thinking in the post–World War II years. (See biographic sketch of Tudjman.) By 1981 he had clearly adopted a strong Croat nationalist position, one many of his critics equated with the Croat fascist one. His political views on Bosnia-Hercegovina had become clearly imperialistic. Although he did not then call for an independent state for Croatia, he unequivocally urged that Croatia and Bosnia-Hercegovina be united in one republic for historical, geo-political, and economic reasons.

Document 2
FRANJO TUDJMAN ON BOSNIA AND HERCEGOVINA

Bosnia and Hercegovina . . . should have been made a part of the Croatian federal unit. Bosnia and Hercegovina was declared a separate federal republic within the borders established during the Turkish occupation. But large parts of Croatia had been incorporated into Bosnia by the Turks. Furthermore Bosnia and Hercegovina were historically linked with Croatia and they together comprise an indivisible geographic and economic entity. Bosnia and Hercegovina occupy the central part of this whole, separating southern (Dalmatian) from northern (Pannonian) Croatia. The creation of a separate Bosnia and Hercegovina makes the territorial and geographic position of Croatia extremely unnatural in the economic sense and, therefore, in the broadest national-political sense, very unfavorable for life and development and in the narrower administrative sense unsuitable and disadvantageous.

*   *   *

There is little doubt that the main reasons for declaring Bosnia and Hercegovina a separate federal state was [*sic*] the mixed composition of its population and the fact that since the last century the greatest controversy between Croatian and Serbian political leaders concerned the ownership of Bosnia and Hercegovina. The decision, therefore, to make Bosnia and Hercegovina [a] separate federal unit was purportedly taken as an unbiased standpoint. Croatia laid claim to Bosnia and Hercegovina on the basis of a common history and the fact that they constituted a geo-political whole. Serbia's claim was based on "natural right" as the Serbian, Orthodox population constituted a plurality (about 44 percent) while the Croatian, Catholic [people] made up about 23 percent of the population and the Moslems 33 percent. Though the Orthodox population was in the minority as compared with the ethnically largely identical Catholic and Moslem population, which together comprised a majority of 56 percent (which has now grown to 62 percent) the Serbian side overly stressed the "right of the sword" since Serbia had entered World War I because of Bosnia and Hercegovina and had been a victor in the conflict.

An objective examination of the numerical composition of the population of Bosnia and Hercegovina cannot ignore that the majority of the Moslems is in its ethnic character and speech incontrovertibly of Croatian origin. Despite religious and cultural distinctions created by history, the vast majority of the Moslems declared themselves Croats whenever an opportunity arose. This was done in 1920 by the Moslem representatives in the Constituent Assembly. It was done by the Moslem intelligentsia and masses during the Banovina Hrvatska and the Independent State of Croatia, which all Moslems and Catholics of Bosnia and Hercegovina at first accepted as their own state. The historical fact regarding the attitude in World War II of the Moslem population is bolstered by many examples in the war memoirs of Milovan Djilas, a member of the CPY leadership. The fact that the Moslem population was largely of Croatian persuasion was recognized between the two wars by Svetozar Pribicevic, who was one of the most uncompromising champions of greater Serbian unitarianism. About the "Bosnian Moslems" he wrote: "Their intellectuals are in the vast majority of Croatian orientat[ion]; and the masses blindly follow the intellectuals in all political actions. There should be no mistake about this. The hegemonistic system in particular . . . has meant that the Bosnian Moslems in their aspirations and their views on the future completely identify themselves with the Croats. Any Serbian statesman who fails to take this fact into account cannot be considered seriously." On the basis of these facts we arrive at the conclusion that a majority of the population of Bosnia and Hercegovina is Croatian. On the other hand the geoeconomic connection of Bosnia with the other Croatian lands is such that neither Croatia in its present boundaries nor the separate Bosnia and Hercegovina possess the conditions for a separate, normal development.

Source: Franjo Tudjman, *Nationalism in Contemporary Europe* (Boulder: East European Monographs, 1981), pp. 113–14.

THE U.S. AMBASSADOR'S FAREWELL TO YUGOSLAVIA

The war began in Bosnia in early April 1992, and later that month Slobodan Milosevic announced the debut of a third Yugoslavia (the FRY), composed of just two republics, Serbia and Montenegro. The U.S. ambassador, Warren Zimmermann, who had taken up his post in 1989, witnessed the destruction of Tito's Yugoslavia. He would leave Belgrade in mid-May 1992, having been recalled by his government to protest Serbia's aggression against Bosnia-Hercegovina. Before Zimmermann left the former Yugoslavia, he sent a final official message home. He included it in the appendix to his book, *Origins of a Catastrophe* (1996).

In his last cable, Zimmermann stressed that, in his view, Yugoslavia was not destroyed by ancient ethnic or religious hatreds, nor by the collapse of communism, nor even because of the failure of the Western states to act. Yugoslavia was murdered by local political villains who dismantled it from the top down. He offered a scathing attack on Slobodan Milosevic, had little good to say about Franjo Tudjman, the Croat president, and concluded with a wistful and nostalgic assessment of the former Yugoslavia—all of this curiously punctuated by stanzas from children's verse. Zimmermann acknowledged that, as an ambassador, he also had been a policy maker regarding the former Yugoslavia. He had agreed with President George Bush's policy of emphasizing "unity and democracy" for Yugoslavia—a policy that Zimmermann later wrote had been a mistake. He also had urged the United States to refrain from intervening in the Yugoslav crisis, maintaining that it would not have saved Yugoslavia. After Bosnia was attacked in 1992, Zimmermann changed his position and began urging NATO air strikes. He continues to believe that judicious use of force in the summer of 1992 could have ended the war.

Document 3
THE LAST CABLE

12 May 92
FM AMEMBASSY BELGRADE
TO SECSTATE WASHDC IMMEDIATE
FROM WARREN ZIMMERMANN
SUBJ.: WHO KILLED YUGOSLAVIA?

* * *

"Who killed Cock Robin?"
"I," said the sparrow,
"With my bow and arrow.
I killed Cock Robin."

It was nationalism that put an arrow in the heart of Yugoslavia. While the antecedents go back centuries, the nationalism that spawned the process of Yugoslavia's destruction began in 1987 in Kosovo, when Slobodan Milosevic, the young leader of the League of Communists of Serbia, listened throughout one long night to the stories Serbs told him of mistreatment by Albanians. That experience gave Milosevic the issue that brought him his power and charisma. Brandishing the issue of Serbian nationalism, he abolished the autonomy of Kosovo, then of Vojvodina, purged all opposition in Serbia itself, and finally turned his nationalist aggressions on his neighbors.

Ironically, it was Slovenia, the only republic containing no Serbian minority, which Milosevic first attacked. Serbia and Slovenia have always been natural allies, and Milosevic's enmity toward Slovenia was ideological rather than ethnic. What Slovenia, even back in the late 1980s, stood for was democracy, a decentralized Yugoslavia, and a freer market—just the kind of Yugoslavia Milosevic despised and feared. In December 1989 Milosevic tried to displace the Slovenian government by a hostile mass rally of Serbs in Ljubljana, then followed that failure by declaring an economic boycott against Slovenia. These were the first shots in the nationalist war that led to the destruction of Yugoslavia. Croatia became Milosevic's next target, a fat one. Franjo Tudjman's victory in the May 1990 Croatian elections brought to power a narrow-minded, crypto-racist regime hostile to Serbia and to the Yugoslavia that it erroneously believed Serbia controlled. Both Milosevic and Tudjman had a strong interest in Satanizing each other; given their characters, the job was not difficult. With the ancient enmities of Serbian and Croatian nationalism now pitted against each other, the odds of preserving and developing a Yugoslavia along the progressive Hungarian or Czechoslovak model plummeted. Violence became probable. As Vladimir Seks, a prominent militant in Tudjman's party, said of one of the ethnically mixed areas of Croatia: "If we win, there will be no more Serbs; if they win, no more Croatians." With people like that in charge, there could no longer be much hope for a country whose very name—"Land of the South Slavs"—symbolized ethnic tolerance. As Milovan Djilas, the last great Yugoslav, said to me the other day, Yugoslavia could not survive conflict between Serbs and Croats for they are its defining nations.

*   *   *

"Who'll dig the grave?"
"I," said the owl,
"With my little trowel,
I'll dig the grave."

There were many gravediggers of Yugoslavia, including the unusual suspects Slovenia, Croatia, and Serbia. But there is one who stands out. Slobodan Milosevic, one of the most duplicitous politicians the Balkans have ever produced, is duplicitous in this as well. Milosevic poses as the protector and savior of Yugoslavia. Just two weeks ago he wrapped himself in the Yugoslav flag (with the red star cut out, of course) and renewed the Yugoslav national anthem. "Yugoslavia exists" has been his war cry ever since the secessionist rumblings began. It's all bunk. Milosevic is not a Yugoslav; he is a Serbian imperialist. His maximum aim of three years ago was to dominate all of Yugoslavia; hence his effort to overthrow the democratic-leaning government of Slovenia and bring the Croats to heel. When that failed, he gave up on Slovenia and went to war to keep Croatia in Yugoslavia. Thwarted again, he tried to force Bosnia and Macedonia into a "Little Yugoslavia" controlled by Serbia. Finally he has fallen back on the "Federal Republic of Yugoslavia" which disclaims territorial pretensions but has a provision in its constitution for admitting parts of other states. He is currently pursuing actively a civil war in Bosnia designed to deliver two-thirds of its territory to the Serb minority there and is collaborating in the expulsion of non-Serbs in mixed areas of Croatia with the aim of making those areas ethnically clean.

* * *

There have been two Yugoslavias so far—the pre-war Yugoslavia of the Karadjordjevic's [sic] and the post-war Yugoslavia of Tito. Just created is a third Yugoslavia—Milosevic's. As noted, it is no more than a disguised Serbia and a platform for Milosevic's claims on other states containing Serbs. It is surrounded by unstable neighbors whose trust Milosevic has lost, and it is eaten from within by minorities whose hatred Milosevic has earned. Thanks to Milosevic, Serbia—with a stronger democratic tradition than most other Balkan republics—is now consumed by nationalist frenzy; and the many decent, talented Serbs, appalled by the bloodletting, are marginalized. Instability has become a cliche and a permanent condition in and around Milosevic's Yugoslavia. I fear that the crisis now visited upon the fragments of Yugoslavia may last a whole generation—a 20-years' crisis. Nationalism, the Balkan killer, will have to run its span. During this process, one can hope, people will begin to realize that their national passions haven't brought them welfare, or peace, or happiness. They may remember that they once lived together, and pretty well, and that their relations with each other were marked by civility and tolerance. They may also recall that the Yugoslavia they lived in, while not free, was certainly freer than the internecine jungle they inherited, and that it had a more civilized and broad-minded view of the world outside as well. One day they might talk about restoring economic ties and then gradually about creating a political framework. It will all make perfectly good sense since, after all, most of their mini-states are not really viable on their own, their ethnic groups are still inextricably mixed together, and they're condemned by geography to be neighbors forever. Somebody—it will take a great democratic leader, probably from Bosnia—might suggest forming a state. It won't be called Yugoslavia, but it will have historical antecedents. As part of its inauguration ceremonies, I would like to imagine that somebody will leave a rose, just one, on the tomb of the Yugoslavia that has just perished.

> All the birds in the air
> Fell a-sighin' and a-sobbin'
> When they heard of the death
> Of poor Cock Robin,
> When they heard of the death
> Of poor Cock Robin.

Source: Warren Zimmermann, *Origins of a Catastrophe* (New York: Times Books, 1996), pp. 245–54.

THE UNITED NATIONS AND THE YUGOSLAVIA CRISIS

The United Nations first became involved in the Yugoslav crisis in September 1991, when, at the request of the federal government of Yugoslavia, it issued a resolution that established an embargo against the sale of weapons to all Yugoslav republics. That embargo ultimately favored the Serb forces who came to control the JNA, and it seriously impaired the abilities of the government of Bosnia-Hercegovina to defend its territory. Thereafter, as the UN became more and more involved in the war in the former Yugoslavia, it issued dozens of Security Council resolutions condemning the evils being perpetrated in the area and established forces (e.g., UNPROFOR) and institutions (e.g., The Hague war crimes tribunal) intended to deal with the area's problems. The UN condemned ethnic cleansing, dropped the Federal Republic of Yugoslavia (Serbia and Montenegro) from UN membership, established a no-fly zone over Bosnia, and created six "safe havens" for the victims of war. It did little, however, to provide muscle to implement those resolutions.

The UN recognized Bosnia-Hercegovina as an independent state in May 1992 and granted the Republic of Bosnia and Hercegovina membership in the UN General Assembly. However, the UN was unable or unwilling—largely because of disagreements among UN members—to do much to safeguard Bosnia's sovereignty and integrity. Thus, during the course of the war in the former Yugoslavia, the UN's authority was seriously undermined. Many became cynical about the UN's impotence and its empty pronouncements on behalf of peace and human rights for the former Yugoslavia. The reputations of Boutros Boutros-Ghali, the UN Secretary-General, and of Yasushi Akashi, the Secretary-General's special envoy for Yugoslavia, were especially damaged.

Document 4
SELECTED UNITED NATIONS SECURITY COUNCIL
RESOLUTIONS

Resolution 713 (September 25, 1991)

The Council fully supports the collective efforts for peace and dialogue in Yugoslavia under the auspices of the member States of the European Community (EC) with the support of the States participating in the Conference on Security and Cooperation in Europe (CSCE), invites the Secretary-General to offer his assistance without delay and to report as soon as possible to the Security Council, and decides under Chapter VII of the Charter of the United Nations that all States immediately implement a general and complete embargo on all deliveries of weapons and military equipment to Yugoslavia.

Resolution 724 (December 15, 1991)

The Council endorses the view expressed in the Secretary-General's report that the conditions for establishing a peacekeeping operation in Yugoslavia still do not exist, endorses his offer to send to Yugoslavia a small group of personnel, including military personnel, to prepare for possible deployment of a peacekeeping operation, decides to establish a committee to ensure that the general and complete embargo imposed by Resolution 713 (1991) is effectively applied, and encourages the Secretary-General to pursue his humanitarian efforts in Yugoslavia.

Resolution 755 (May 20, 1992)

The Council recommends to the General Assembly that the Republic of Bosnia and Herzegovina be admitted to membership in the United Nations.

Resolution 771 (August 13, 1992)

The Council strongly condemns violations of international humanitarian law, including those involved in the process of "ethnic cleansing," demands that all parties in the former Yugoslavia and all military forces in Bosnia immediately desist from such violations, demands that relevant international humanitarian organizations be granted immediate, unimpeded, and continued access to prison camps, calls on all parties to do all in their power to facilitate such access, and calls on States and international humanitarian organizations to collate substantiated information relating to breaches of humanitarian law.

Resolution 777 (September 19, 1992)

The Council considers that the Federal Republic of Yugoslavia cannot continue automatically the membership of the former Socialist Federal Republic of Yugoslavia in the United Nations, and therefore recommends to the General Assembly that it decide that the Federal Republic of Yugoslavia (Serbia and Montenegro) should apply for membership in the United Nations and that it shall not participate in the work of the General Assembly.

Resolution 781 (October 9, 1992)

The Council decides to establish a ban on military flights in the airspace of Bosnia and Herzegovina, and undertakes to examine without delay all the information brought to its attention concerning the implementation of the ban, and the case of violations, to consider urgently the further measures necessary to enforce it.

Resolution 824 (May 6, 1993)

The Council demands that any taking of territory by force cease immediately; declares that Sarajevo, Tuzla, Zepa, Gorazde, Bihac and Srebrenica and their surrounds should be treated as safe areas by all the parties concerned and should be free from armed attacks and from any other hostile act; and declares its readiness, in the event of the failure by any party to comply with the present Resolution, to consider additional measures necessary with a view to its full implementation, including to ensure respect for the safety of UN personnel.

Resolution 827 (May 25, 1993)

The Council establishes an international tribunal for the purpose of prosecuting persons responsible for serious violations of international humanitarian law committed in the former Yugoslavia beginning January 1, 1991. The Council urges states, intergovernmental and nongovernmental organizations to contribute funds, equipment, and services to the international tribunal. The work of the tribunal will be carried out without prejudice to the right of the victims to seek compensation for damages incurred as a result of the violations.

Resolution 836 (June 4, 1993)

The Council decides to extend the mandate of UNPROFOR to enable it to protect the safe areas of Sarajevo, Tuzla, Zepa, Gorazde, Bihac, and Srebrenica, and to use force in self-defense or in deterring attacks against the safe areas. The Council also authorizes Member States to take all necessary measures, through the use of air power, to support UNPROFOR. UNPROFOR forces are to monitor the cease-fire, promote the withdrawal of military and paramilitary units other than those of the Government of Bosnia-Herzegovina, occupy some key points on the ground, and participate in the delivery of humanitarian aid.

Source: Texts of Security Council Resolutions from Susan L. Woodward, *Balkan Tragedy* (Washington, DC: Brookings Institution, 1995), pp. 401–24.

THE SERBIAN TERMINATORS

In September 1992, *Duga,* a Belgrade (Serbia) biweekly, interviewed Sonja Karadzic, the daughter of Radovan Karadzic, political leader of the Bosnian Serbs. At the time Sonja was a budding young rock star who had recorded her first album just before the war began. The interviewer, mocking in his description of Ms. Karadzic, noted her attire—a leather motorcycle jacket, a black cap with the double eagle insignia of the Serb Chetniks (monarchist supporters of Draza Mihailovic during World War II whose popularity had risen during the 1990s), and a lady's Beretta pistol, which Sonja confessed was "as important to me as my makeup." In the latter stages of the war in Bosnia, Sonja was married in Pale, the Bosnian Serb capital, amid lavish celebration and self-indulgence that embarrassed the Bosnian Serb military head, Ratko Mladic.

In the 1992 Belgrade interview, Sonja was acting as her father's top propagandist for the Serb cause in Bosnia. She urged all Serbs in Serbia to support their brethren in the newly proclaimed Bosnian Serb state with its headquarters in Pale, outside Sarajevo. She also encouraged Serbian Serbs (in cities like Belgrade, Nis, Kraljevo, and Novi Sad) to shun Bosnian Serbs who had fled military service and were now residing, and probably looking for employment and sympathy, in Serbia. True Serbs, she said, would be in Bosnia defending Grbavica and Ilidza (primarily Serbian-populated suburbs of Sarajevo).

Sonja and her cohorts represented a nationalist youth culture—

reminiscent of the Nazi or fascist youth of the 1930s—that came into vogue among Serbian city youth in the 1990s. They appropriated their ethics from American Rambo types and claimed that they were creating a new civilization.

Document 5
AMERICA'S INFLUENCE ON THE BOSNIAN SERBS

If the Americans come to Bosnia, they'll see that our soldiers look at the world like theirs do. We aren't Vietnamese or Iraqis, we are fighters who think in terms of the same images and music as their soldiers do. The Serbian chetnik fighters have grown up with a Coke in their hand and watching the same TV spots as someone their own age in Alabama, and we're into the latest styles just the way guys or girls from Florida are. Together we got our battle ethics from the movies about Mad Max and Terminator, Rambo and Young Guns. And what happened when the war began—we started identifying with the media images and heroes. Our fighters got camo battle dress, short Rambo boots and modern weapons of destruction. They call themselves chetniks—but Mad Max Chetniks, Serbian Terminators. And most important, it doesn't matter which sex you are. Nobody is dirty or sloppy or smelly or unshaven—we're still into good cigarettes and Coca-Cola, nice perfume and makeup, and we're up on the latest movies and music. And we still like a good laugh—not the Moslem nonsense down in town. We're building a new lifestyle in a new country.

Fortunately for us only the best fighters, the real ones have stayed. The others have helped us perform a natural selection by running away from the homeland they weren't prepared to defend and build up. Now they're here in Belgrade with you in your civilian state, and I doubt they will defend you if the need arises. Yet you pamper them and take care of them. If I were a native of Belgrade, Nis, Kraljevo, or Novi Sad I would never allow someone who wasn't prepared to defend Serbia in Grbavica or Ilidza to get a job ahead of me or occupy my space so aggressively and threaten my security in every respect.

For us the Serbian chetniks . . . will always be our heroes, our Serbian Terminators. With fighters like them we are already the victors in this war and leaders in the creation of a new civilization.

Source: Interview with Sonja Karadzic, an official of the Ministry of Information of the Serb Republic [of Bosnia], from "Computer and Cockade atop Great Serbian Salad," by Nenad Stefanovic. *Duga* (Belgrade), September 12–26, 1992; excerpted and translated by Ann Clymer Bigelow.

BARBARIANS AT THE CITY GATES

During the course of the war in the former Yugoslavia, there was massive and often wanton destruction of cultural monuments. Many were of a religious nature—Catholic and Orthodox churches and Muslim mosques. Others, including the National Library and the School of Oriental Studies in Sarajevo, were important repositories of the people's historical records. The structures destroyed were generally located in towns and cities: for example, in Bijelina, five architecturally unique, centuries-old mosques were leveled during one weekend of Serbian rampage in 1992. Among other casualties of the war were Osijek and Vukovar in Slavonia; Mostar, which was attacked first by the Serbs and later by the Croats, who finished off the graceful medieval bridge that had long stood for unity and civilization in the Balkans; and, of course, Sarajevo, which had symbolized international accord as recently as 1984, when it hosted the Winter Olympic Games.

Bogdan Bogdanovic, an architect and Serb, and a former mayor of Belgrade (1982–1986), characterized this destruction as an attack on civilization by latter-day barbarians. He lamented that the bearers of new ideologies, who generally came from the countryside, usually brought ruin upon cities, the centers of civilization. Bogdanovic also worried about the spiritual death of cities. He feared that the new "Huns" would have a negative impact on his own city, Belgrade. For even though his capital had not been in the war, it was being inundated by people from the countryside, many of them refugees, who could undermine its civilization. At the end of his letter to the *New York Review of Books,* he took a swipe at the cultural forefather of the Serbs, Vuk Karadzic, who in the early nineteenth century rejected the existing literary language of the Serbs (used mostly in ecclesiastical writing) in favor of the peasant idiom; in pointing to Karadzic, Bogdanovic found a historical precedent for the Serbs' aversion to cities and the civilization they represent.

Document 6
MURDER OF THE CITY

Much as I ponder the abnormalities of our current civil war, I cannot comprehend why military strategy should make the destruction of cities a main—if not the main—goal. Sooner or later the civilized world will dismiss our internecine butchery with a shrug of the shoulders. How else can it react? But it will never forget the way we destroyed our cities. We—we Serbs—shall be remembered as despoilers of cities, latter-day Huns.

The horror felt by the West is understandable: for centuries it has linked the concepts "city" and "civilization," associating them even on an etymological level. It therefore has no choice but to view the destruction of cities as flagrant, wanton opposition to the highest values of civilization.

What makes the situation even more monstrous is that the cities involved are beautiful, magnificent cities: Osijek, Vukovar, Zadar, with Mostar and Sarajevo waiting their turn. The strike on Dubrovnik—I shudder to say it, but say it I must—was intentionally aimed at an object of extraordinary, even symbolic beauty. It was the attack of a madman who throws acid in a beautiful woman's face and promises her a beautiful face in return.

* * *

The fates of Vukovar, Mostar, and Sarjevo's Bas-carsija—the old Turkish center of the town—bode ill for the future of Belgrade. No, I do not fear foreign hordes beneath the walls of Kalemegdan [the Turkish fortress overlooking Belgrade]; sad to say, what I fear are our home-grown masters of destruction. Cities fall not only physically, as a result of outside pressure; they fall spiritually, from within. The latter is in fact the more common variant. The new conquerors will make us recognize them at gunpoint. Accustomed as Balkan history is to mass migrations, the danger is clear. The National Liberation movement at the end of World War II was at least in part a mass migration, a gunpoint migration of the rural populace to the city, a kind of forced urbanization. Many people still recall the devastating consequences of that "invigorating renewal of our cities," and a similar scenario is not hard to imagine today.

If the brave defenders of Serb villages and the abortive conquerors of Croat towns do in fact force us to recognize them as fellow citizens, if they move in and take over, we know what to expect. The Partisans condemned the decadence of the city and promised its social regeneration; the new Nazi-Partisans promise to cleanse our Serb Sodom and Gomorrah and all national renegades. Once again cities are being destroyed in the name of the highest, the most noble goals. Before long someone will surely decide that Belgrade too could do with a bit of ethnic cleansing, and a theory for momentous national undertakings of the sort—provided our new *Kulturtrager* [upholders of culture] feel the need for one—can always be found. For did not the great father of our nation, Vuk Karadzic, who codified the Serb language in the nineteenth century, teach us that Serbs prefer not to live in cities . . . ?

Source: Bogdan Bogdanovic, "Murder of the City," translated by Michael Henry Heim, *New York Review of Books,* May 27, 1993.

MARGARET THATCHER ADVISES CLINTON
TO USE AIR POWER

When Margaret Thatcher, the Conservative prime minister of Great Britain from 1979 to 1991, visited William Clinton in September 1993, she presented the president with a letter urging him to lead a Western coalition in using air power to bring an end to Serbian aggression in Bosnia-Hercegovina. Clinton, who had campaigned against President George Bush the previous year, had been a stern critic of the latter's policy of noninvolvement in the war. By September, Clinton had been in power more than half a year but had done relatively little to alter U.S. government policy toward the former Yugoslavia. If anything, the United States was supporting the UN and the EU in urging Bosnia to agree to a Serbian-designed settlement, even threatening to cut off humanitarian aid unless Bosnia complied. Meanwhile, the Bosnian Serbs had rejected the Vance-Owen peace plan, Milosevic and Serbia were still strongly backing their protégés in Bosnia, and things were going from bad to worse for the war victims, many of whom had fled to central and western Europe as refugees.

Thatcher, never fuzzy on any issue, stated unequivocally that the war in Bosnia was one of aggression caused by Serbia. She equated it with the 1991 Iraqi invasion of Kuwait. Thatcher urged the West to unite against Serbia, as it had against Iraq. Western democracies needed to act against aggressors. History would judge them harshly if they did not. Failing to act would also lead to future problems in the region. She also let slip the ultimate scare, that caving in to bullies in the Balkans could result in bullies running rampant in the former Soviet Union, too. Empty threats, which the powers had used regularly against the Serbs, stated Thatcher, would produce only contempt for the West. Judicious use of air power was her answer to the Serbs. She urged that it be used against Bosnian Serbs as well as against Serbia proper. She was perfectly clear that Milosevic, like Saddam Hussein of Iraq, was the villain to be dealt with.

Thatcher's letter was cosigned by an impressive array of political and cultural personages, including prominent figures from former Democratic and Republican U.S. administrations and Nobel laureates from central Europe.

Document 7
WHAT THE WEST MUST DO IN BOSNIA

In Bosnia, the situation goes from bad to worse. The people there are in despair about their future. They are victims of brutal aggression. But they are also the victims of the failure of the democracies to act.

Instead of opposing the acquisition of territory by force, the United Nations and the democracies have dispatched humanitarian assistance to Bosnia. But welcome as it is, this will not stop the massacres or halt the ethnic cleansing. Humanitarian aid will not protect the besieged children of Bosnia from being herded into Muslim ghettos or orphaned or maimed or slaughtered.

These could have been our children.

If we do not act, immediately and decisively, history will record that in the last decade of this century the democracies failed to heed its most unforgiving lesson: that unopposed aggression will be enlarged and repeated, that a failure of will by the democracies will strengthen and encourage those who gain territory and rule by force.

*   *   *

1. Humanitarian Aid and Future Ethnic Cleansing

In Bosnia the democracies have used the need to deliver humanitarian aid both to excuse their own inaction and to keep the recognized multi-ethnic state of Bosnia outgunned and therefore itself unable to protect its civilian centers from slaughter by a dictator bent on making a Greater Serbia. Western governments now vying publicly to save several hundred maimed Bosnian children will not escape the responsibility they assumed for the slaughter of hundreds of thousands of other children and their parents, when they refused to let an independent Bosnia defend itself.

Recently, the U.N. and EC mediators, with U.S. support, threatened to withdraw humanitarian aid in order to coerce the Bosnian government into accepting violent changes in its borders and a partition into ethnically pure states, with Bosnia a set of widely dispersed, unarmed Muslim ghettos. But the U.N., the EC and the U.S. have continually condemned such changes and that partition as totally unacceptable. Such a partition, they've said, is unstable: It will mean still more killing, broken families, and the expulsion of millions at a time when Europe is closing its doors to refugees. If the fall of Sarajevo is a preface to a partition creating unarmed Muslim ghettos, it will be a preface also to further disasters, ethnic cleansing and instability—in Sarajevo itself and other Bosnian "safe havens" protected only by the U.N., in the rest of the Balkans, and beyond.

Bosnia, unlike Somalia, was no civil war. Like Kuwait, it was a case of clearcut aggression against a member of the U.N.—a member whose independence the U.S., Europe and the international community have recognized for at least 16 months.

When the Baath dictatorship seized all of Kuwait in August 1990, it tried to erase Kuwaiti identity using rape, torture, the seizure of Kuwaiti passports and the forging of a new identity of Kuwait as a province of Iraq. A coalition of several NATO powers and some non-NATO countries joined the U.S. in demanding and then, in January 1991, compelling Iraq's withdrawal by using first air power throughout Iraq and then ground forces in Kuwait and southern Iraq. The coalition was exercising the right of individual and collective self-defense of each of its members and of Kuwait. It aimed at more than mitigating Kuwait's suffering. The U.N. endorsed the coalition's aim to get Iraq out of Kuwait, and the aims beyond Kuwait to reduce Iraq's power to terrorize its neighbors. But the U.N. exercised no authority over the coalition.

In the same way, the U.S. should now lead a coalition of Western governments that exercises the right of each to individual and collective self-defense. The U.N. Charter does not confer that right; it acknowledges it to be "inherent." Nor is that right conditioned on the secretary-general's approval.

The West's air-to-air fighters overflying Bosnia needed no further preparations to shoot down the command helicopters and helicopter gunships that the Serbs, in yet another blatant violation of their promises, used to drive the Bosnian army from their defenses of Sarajevo on Mounts Igman and Bjelasnica. The West could have done this without elaborate plans to coordinate air strikes against ground targets, without endangering U.N. forces on the ground, and without the permission of the secretary-general, Europe's Council of Ministers, the 16 NATO ambassadors and a variety of U.N. commanders—procedures that appear designed to make the fall of Sarajevo a fait accompli. A disaster not only for the Bosnians, but for the relevance of the U.N., Europe, NATO—and the U.S.

* * *

Western governments should act now substantially to reduce Serbia's immediate and future power of aggression and ultimately to put the Bosnians in a position where they won't have to rely indefinitely on the protection of the international community.

With this limited political aim, Western air power would play a much larger role, and the U.S. and other Western ground forces a much smaller and more transient role, than in U.N.-directed options that look toward an indefinite future of protecting on the ground helpless Muslim ghettos and besieged corridors of supply to them. The ghettos and corridors to them would be subject to continuing artillery, armor and sniper attacks so long as the source of these attacks in Serbia is left intact.

Air power directed against the present and future potential sources of such attack can be used selectively and discriminately. The no-fly zone could be enforced and defenses suppressed over Serbia as well as Bosnia. And a very high percentage of the military aircraft on the large airfields in Serbia could be destroyed, with minimal danger to Serbian civilians or to UNPROFOR (U.N. Protective Force) troops.

The U.N. alternatives mean a future of ethnic cleansing and endless military protection by the international community.

* * *

2. Bosnia Is Not History

What the West says and does now in Bosnia will affect the future in Bosnia itself; in the rest of the Balkans; and in other newly independent countries that, having gained their freedom when a communist dictatorship fell apart, now find that freedom threatened by former rulers who would, like Milosevic, use the pretext of protecting minorities to retake strategic facilities and territory that their pan-national military has never been reconciled to giving up.

Even now, after 16 months of a perverse Western policy piously condemning the pan-Serbian aggressors while doing nothing to stop the massacres, the West can use military force substantially and discriminately to reduce the power of the poorly motivated and ill-disciplined Serbian Army in Bosnia and its source of support in Serbia itself. And the West can help arm the larger, highly motivated Bosnian Army that still maintains a precarious control of the towns containing most of Bosnia's industry, including its weapons industry. In this way the West can improve the odds for the survival of a free multiethnic Bosnia.

On the other hand, if Western mediators and UNPROFOR confine unarmed Bosnian Muslims to small, purified remnants of Bosnia, the public will watch with horror as these ghettos disappear before its eyes on television while Serbs violate this ceasefire—as they have all the others for 23 months in Croatia and Bosnia. A spectacular display, at the same time, of the unshakably naive faith in Serbian promises that underlies Western cynicism. Realpolitik revealed as fantasy in real time.

Even if, like Kuwait in August 1990, all Bosnia (and not just Sarajevo) were seized, it would be essential for the democracies to make clear, as they did in the case of Kuwait, that violent border changes and ethnic cleansing will not stand, whether by Serbia in Croatia and Bosnia, or by Croatia in Bosnia.

If the West does not make that clear, it will have nothing persuasive to say to the Croats and the Serbs who have already renewed the conflict Serbia started two years ago when it used the Yugoslavian Army to seize territory in Croatia and then turned to invading Bosnia. Nor will the West be able to stop Serbian ethnic cleansing of Albanians in Kosovo and of Hungarians in Vojvodina. In Macedonia (unrecognized by either the U.S. or Europe because the Greeks object), where the U.S. and Sweden have deployed ground forces with no clear purpose, Western policy seems even murkier than for the other former Yugoslavian republics. There the West will have nothing coherent to say to resolve potential conflicts among Greeks, Serbs, Albanians, Bulgarians, Turks, and frustrated Macedonian nationalists who may topple the moderate Grigorov [*sic*]. Finally, the West will have nothing to say to discourage the now serious threat presented by pan-nationalists in the former Soviet Union and elsewhere.

* * *

3. The Role of Force and of Empty Threats

Empty threats have a perverse effect.

Against a dictator who will yield only to superior force the West can threaten most ferociously in the hope that threats alone will be enough to stop aggression—that its threats and endless preparations will "send a message." But if the West doesn't use force at all or if it uses it symbolically rather than substantially to reduce Milosevic's power, or if it uses force to coerce Bosnian capitulation, "the message" received will only bring American and Western resolve into contempt.

Source: "What the West Must Do in Bosnia," *Wall Street Journal,* September 2, 1993.

BOSNIA'S SAFE HAVENS UNDER ATTACK

As Bosnia disintegrated into war in spring and summer 1992, thousands of Muslim civilians found themselves under attack. They fled from the army of the Bosnian Serbs, and also from Serbian paramilitary units that operated with terrifying efficiency, particularly in eastern Bosnia. Some Muslims were able to flee abroad, but many went to larger towns, where they hoped to find protection. In late summer 1992, the UN began studying what could be done about the human rights abuses committed against Bosnian civilians, and in May 1993 it established six safe havens—Bihac, Gorazde, Srebrenica, Sarajevo, Tuzla, and Zepa. All but Bihac were located in eastern Bosnia, in areas where ethnic cleansing policies were being vigorously applied. The population of the six centers quickly doubled and tripled, taxing the resources of the local communities. In spring 1993, the United States initiated unilateral airdrops of food—mostly MREs (Meals Ready to Eat) left over from the Persian Gulf War—to ease the food shortages. Critically, the UN did not define the safe zones, nor did it demilitarize them, nor, most important, did it provide for their defense by UN or other troops. The safe havens became sitting targets for potential aggressors.

In July 1995 Srebrenica and the handful of Dutch UN forces assigned to it were overtaken by Ratko Mladic's Bosnian Serb forces, who would thereafter move on to yet another safe haven, Zepa. The army separated Srebrenica's men and women from one another. Women and children were transported to nearby towns, while the men—7,000 of them, according to reliable reports—were sent to their execution. Tadeusz Mazowiecki, the first noncommunist prime minister of Poland since World War II (installed in August 1989), headed the UN commission that investigated human rights abuses in the former Yugoslavia. He had been a strong advocate for establishing the safe havens as early as August 1992, and continually worked to influence UN policy to make the centers truly safe. In summer 1995 the Serb attack on Srebrenica and Zepa, and the pro forma acceptance of events by the major powers in London, led Mazowiecki to resign his post.

Document 8
TADEUSZ MAZOWIECKI RESIGNS AS UN HUMAN RIGHTS ADVOCATE

27 July 1995

His Excellency
Mr. Boutros Boutros-Ghali
Secretary-General
The United Nations
New York

Dear Mr. Secretary-General,

Events in recent weeks in Bosnia and Herzegovina, and above all the fact that the United Nations has allowed Srebrenica and Zepa to fall, along with the horrendous tragedy which has beset the population of those "safe havens" guaranteed by international agreements, oblige me to state that I do not see any possibility of continuing the mandate of Special Rapporteur entrusted to me by the Commission on Human Rights.

On accepting the mandate which was given to me for the first time in August 1992, I declared unequivocally that my goal would not simply be writing reports but helping the people themselves. The creation of "safe havens" was from the very beginning a central recommendation in my reports. The recent decisions of the London conference which accepted the fall of Srebrenica and resigned itself to the fate of Zepa are unacceptable to me. Those decisions did not create the conditions necessary for the defence of all "safe havens."

These events constitute a turning point in the development of the situation in Bosnia. At one and the same time, we are dealing with the struggle of a State, a member of the United Nations, for its survival and multiethnic character, and with the endeavor to protect principles of international order. One cannot speak about the protection of human rights with credibility when one is confronted with the lack of consistency and courage displayed by the international community and its leaders. The reality of the human rights situation today is illustrated by the tragedy of the people of Srebrenica and Zepa.

Human rights violations continue blatantly. There are constant blockades of the delivery of humanitarian aid. The civilian population is shelled remorselessly and the "blue helmets" and representatives of humanitarian organizations are dying. Crimes have been committed with swiftness and brutality and by contrast the response of the international community has been slow and ineffectual.

The character of my mandate only allows me to further describe crimes and violations of human rights. But the present *critical* moment forces us to realize the true character of those crimes and the responsibility of Europe and the international community for their own helplessness in addressing them. We have been fighting in Poland against a totalitarian system with a vision for the Europe of tomorrow. How can we believe in a Europe of tomorrow created by children of people who are abandoned today?

I would like to believe that the present moment will be a turning point in the relationship between Europe and the world towards Bosnia. The very stability of international order and the principle of civilization is at stake over the question of Bosnia. I am not convinced that the turning point hoped for will happen and cannot continue to participate in the pretence of the protection of human rights.

Mr. Secretary-General, please understand the motives behind my decision. Please accept, Excellency, the assurances of my highest consideration.

Tadeusz Mazowiecki

Special Rapporteur
on the situation of human rights
in the territory of the former
Yugoslavia

Source: Tadeusz Mazowiecki, "A Letter of Resignation," *New York Review of Books,*
September 21, 1995.

THE BOSNIAN PEOPLE CHARGE GENOCIDE

In late March 1993, Francis Boyle, an American professor of international law at the University of Illinois at Champaign-Urbana, representing the Bosnian government, brought a case on its behalf before
the International Court of Justice (ICJ) at The Hague, a standing court
that has dealt with disputes between states since the 1940s. In that
case, the Republic of Bosnia charged rump Yugoslavia (Serbia and
Montenegro) and its agents, its surrogates (e.g., the self-declared Serbian state in Bosnia-Hercegovina), its paramilitary groups, and other
related parties with genocide. The genocide, or ethnic cleansing, was
alleged to have been directed against the Muslim population of Bosnia-
Hercegovina, and the accused were charged with violating the 1948
Geneva Convention against genocide. Boyle won two World Court
orders (April 8, 1993, and September 13, 1993) that supported Bosnia's case against rump Yugoslavia, which was then ordered to cease
and desist its violation of the 1948 Geneva Convention.

The two excerpts that follow testify to the anti-Muslim character
of the Serb attack on Bosnia in spring 1992. The testimonies, both
by women, also attest to the deliberate use of rape as part of the
genocidal policy of the aggressor. An estimated 20,000 women were
raped by Serb fighters between 1991 and 1995.

The International War Crimes Tribunal (IWCT), an ad hoc body
established by the United Nations Security Council in May 1993, also
has been investigating war crimes in the former Yugoslavia, also at
The Hague. Since June 1996, it has indicted a number of men, charging
them with sexual assault. The first convictions came nearly four years
later, in early 2000. The IWCT first needed to establish the precedent
that rape was to be considered torture and therefore a war crime.
(Unlike the ICJ, the IWCT deals only with cases against individuals).

Francis Boyle has been an adviser to Alija Izetbegovic, president of
Bosnia-Hercegovina since 1993. A strong advocate of Bosnian unity
and independence, Boyle vociferously opposed the Owen-Stoltenberg plan (1994), which proposed dividing Bosnia into three ethnic

sectors; the confederation between Bosnia and Croatia (1994), because it set up part of Bosnia for possible annexation by the Croatian
Republic; and also the 1995 Dayton Accords—all of which Boyle felt
essentially betrayed Bosnia and violated its sovereignty and independence. For him, it was not unlike what the European powers did to
Czechoslovakia at Munich in 1938.

Document 9
THE TESTIMONY OF TWO
REPRESENTATIVE VICTIMS

44C . . . a Muslim woman identified as AD 010 described an attack on
her village by Serbian forces (Chetnicks).

(a) "On the 25th of May the Chetnicks attacked our village, which was
a Muslim village, and by the 31st of May all the men from the village
were taken to a concentration camp. In the first attack they shelled the
village. The people out of fear were fleeing their homes. I saw many of
them fall, their bodies and limbs flying into the air. Bodies of men, women,
children, and all that just because they were Muslims. They killed en
masse, pillaged and burnt our houses, detained women, elderly and children and burnt them alive. They took the young men from 20–30 years
of age [and] brought them to a school to torture them. . . . One of my
uncles was taken. He survived a firing squad. Two of his brothers and four
of his nephews, together with 170 friends, cousins, neighbors. He laid
hiding with three wounds. He managed to escape because the Chetnicks
thought everyone was dead. We took him to a forest after a few days, but
he could not go home, knowing that they would be looking for him since
he witnessed a genocide of 180 Muslims. He's been hiding for two months
and finally they found him one day and since then we have not heard from
him."

(b) "They have been torturing us all in different manners. Every village
had a Chetnicks' headquarters where they spent most of the time. They
would take our food, our gold and jewelry [and] money. They took [my
neighbor's] son away and they threaten[ed] to kill him unless she brings
some money. She and her husband were collecting money through the
village . . . and finally when they brought the money the Chetnicks let her
son go, but they killed her husband. First they mutilated his body with
knives, engraving a cross on his body, [leaving] him to bleed, and finally
killing him only at night. In that same manner they killed another of my

neighbors, it kept going on; and all this for one simple reason: They wanted to cleanse everything Muslim."

(c) "They raped my neighbor, a 65-year-old woman, and then killed her. They killed her husband as well, who was a totally handicapped and helpless person. When we got the permission to bury them, we found them mutilated. We had to pick up his head and the brain with a shovel."

(d) "A friend of mine was kept in captivity because her husband was fighting on the Bihac front. They were threatening her with killing her and her three children if her husband [did] not come back and give himself up. After they took our husbands away we [did] not hear of them for almost two months. They sent us messages from the detention camps letting us know that they were alive. We women were at the mercy of the Chetnicks, being ourselves kept in some kind of a detention camp. The whole village was under their occupation and we were let to do only what they decided we could do. We lived in fear because every day they could kill someone, and we were waiting for the same thing to happen to us." (Information Coordinator on War Crimes in Former Yugoslavia, Statement of victim AD 010.)

44E . . . a young Muslim female identified as JK 001 reported the details of expulsion by Serbian forces.

(a) "Every day they entered houses in which there were only women and children remaining. They plundered, killed and raped even the 5-year-old girls and old women. So our own house was a prison camp to us for they could come in and kill us at any time of day or night. When they were searching my home we were taken into the backyard and made to stand in a row. They threatened to shoot us if they found weapons in the house. There were no weapons, they plundered the house and took the gold and told us they would come back again and kill us because we were Muslims. . . ."

(b) "I and my old mother together with our neighbors joined those people. We stayed in the houses that had been plundered and the owners of which had been killed or taken to camps. It was horrible. There were about fifty of us in one house, we slept on top of each other, and the odor of the dead bodies, which were in the garages [and] in the gardens, was everywhere. They killed the men and the women had to bury their husband, or son, or father with their own hands and to the best of their abilities. There was blood, blood of an innocent son, child, woman, or man on the walls of the house. We slept there and waited for our departure, and they were standing on guard outside, singing, drinking, and listening to the Tchetnik songs and even shooting the houses."

(c) "After a few days 9 trailers and several buses came. . . . On [the way to] Vlasic, 160 men, old and young, were taken from that first convoy that had left before mine, and killed. That information frightened us, so we became upset and started to leave, but they made a circle around us and said that we would get what we deserved, and that was death, death to all Muslims or "Bulaks" as they were calling us. They loaded us onto the trailers and we left, not knowing ourselves whether we were going to death or to freedom. . . . When we came to Vlasic they gave us three minutes to get off the trailer. We were falling down like sacks out of the trailer and it was hardest for the old women and children. When we got out they started to separate girls and women. Fortunately I had a scarf on my head and my aunt's child in my arms. They set apart about thirty girls. They separated an old woman from her two daughters; she protested, cried, went down on her knees and begged, but there was no mercy, she got a bullet in the head. The girls were taken to an unknown destination and even today it is not known. In a line, we started walking towards Travnik; the men went separately and the Tchetniks were shooting after them and many of them got killed because they had been at the back of the line. They told us to follow the road and we would get to our "balijas" [derogatory word for Muslim], and to tell them they should be grateful that they did not kill us all. The journey was long and strenuous; many old women were carried in blankets or in wheelbarrows, and some sons carried their mothers on their backs until finally we reached Travnik, which was hard to believe after so many dead bodies of our Muslims had been left lying on the road and everywhere where the Tchetnik's foot was set. And the only reason for that all is that we are Muslim." (Information Coordinator on War Crimes in Former Yugoslavia, Statement of victim JK 001.)

Source: Francis A. Boyle, *The Bosnian People Charge Genocide.* Proceedings at the International Court of Justice Concerning *Bosnia v. Serbia* on the Prevention and Punishment of the Crime of Genocide (Amherst, MA: Aletheia Press, 1996), pp. 18–19, 24–25.

PRESIDENT CLINTON SPEAKS ON THE DAYTON ACCORDS (NOVEMBER 27, 1995)

Several days after the Dayton Accords were initialed, President Clinton addressed the American public. It was, in some ways, the first major post–Cold War foreign policy speech by a U.S. president, particularly as it related to Europe. He credited U.S. initiative—assisted by European and Russian partners—with achieving a peace agreement for Bosnia. American involvement in the area, he noted, was important for two reasons: it served U.S. strategic interests, and it was consistent with American values and principles.

He went on to say that the Dayton Peace Accords now had to be implemented and that the United States needed to be a major player in their implementation. In appealing for public support, Clinton assured his listeners that the U.S. mission to Bosnia would be limited, that it would be restricted to one year, and that the number of troops would be minimal. Americans were not being sent to Bosnia to fight a war, but to secure peace. (Harm to Americans, he promised, would result in swift retaliation.) The troops would be part of a NATO contingent, and without the United States, NATO would not be there.

Clinton's portrayal of how the peace came about was shamelessly inaccurate. He glossed over the fact that the world powers, including the United States, had tried for four years to avoid getting involved in the Bosnian crisis. Instead of defending the victims and championing a multiethnic society in Bosnia, the United States chose repeatedly to pressure the Bosnian government to give in to Serb aggression. Those who charged the major powers with appeasement were not far off the mark. In many ways, in the end, the powers were shamed into doing something about Bosnia, for their reputation and honor had been seriously damaged by their glaring lack of principle. Once the West found its bearings, sometime in 1995, it finally put an end to the fighting by sending in NATO planes and bullying diplomats (e.g., Richard Holbrooke). The result nevertheless was a divided country and an end to a multiethnic Bosnia.

Clinton also failed to mention that the U.S. Congress had been pressuring him to lift the arms embargo against Bosnia. The argument was that Bosnians should be allowed to arm themselves and fight their own war against Serbia. This could make it unnecessary to send American troops into Bosnia, which Clinton had promised the Europeans he would do when their troops began to withdraw from the area (something that had been discussed since late 1994). Clinton faced a political dilemma: the Europeans opposed a lifting of the arms embargo (they had troops on the ground in Bosnia who might be endangered), while Congress opposed sending American troops to Bosnia. Clinton's decision to press for the Dayton Accords package was thus a political compromise, not a noble gesture.

Document 10
DOING THE RIGHT THING IN BOSNIA

Good evening. Last week the warring factions in Bosnia reached a peace agreement as a result of our efforts in Dayton, Ohio, and the support of our European and Russian partners. Tonight I want to speak with you about implementing the Bosnian peace agreement and why our values and interest as Americans require that we participate.

Let me say at the outset America's role will not be about fighting a war. It will be about helping the people of Bosnia to secure their own peace agreement. Our mission will be limited, focused and under the command of an American general.

In fulfilling this mission, we will have the chance to help stop the killing of innocent civilians, especially children, and at the same time to bring stability to Central Europe, a region of the world that is vital to our national interests. It is the right thing to do.

From our birth, America has always been more than just a place. America has embodied an idea that has become the ideal for billions of people throughout the world. Our Founders said it best: America is about life, liberty and the pursuit of happiness. . . .

[President Clinton then elaborated on U.S. principles and why the country had fought in two world wars. He reminded Americans how peace had faltered when the United States became isolationist after World War I, and how the world really needed American leadership. He acknowledged that the United States could not involve itself everywhere that crises erupted, but, he said, it could make a difference in some places. Strategic interests would guide the president in deciding which areas merited U.S. attention.]

. . . . Nowhere today is the need for American leadership more stark or more immediate than in Bosnia. For nearly 4 years a terrible war has torn Bosnia apart. Horrors we prayed had been banished from Europe forever have been seared into our minds again: skeletal prisoners caged behind barbed-wire fences, women and girls raped as a tool of war, defenseless men and boys shot down in the mass graves, evoking visions of World War II concentration camps, and endless lines of refugees marching toward a future of despair.

* * *

Finally, just 3 weeks ago, the Muslims, Croats and Serbs came to Dayton, Ohio, in America's heartland, to negotiate a settlement. There, exhausted by war, they made a commitment to peace. They agreed to put down their guns, to preserve Bosnia as a single state, to investigate and prosecute war criminals, to protect the human right of all citizens, to try to build a peaceful, democratic future. And they asked for America's help as they implement this peace agreement.

America has a responsibility to answer that request, to help to turn this moment of hope into an enduring reality. To do that, troops from our country and around the world would go into Bosnia to give them the confidence and support they need to implement their peace plan. I refuse to send American troops to fight a war in Bosnia, but I believe we must help to secure the Bosnian peace.

* * *

The only force capable of getting this job done is NATO, the powerful military alliance of democracies that has guaranteed our security for a half century now. And as NATO's leader and the primary broker of the peace agreement, the United States must be an essential part of the mission. If we're not there, NATO will not be there. The peace will collapse, the war will reignite, the slaughter of innocents will begin again. A conflict that already has claimed so many victims could spread like poison through the region, eat away at Europe's stability and erode our partnership with our European allies.

* * *

As President my most difficult duty is to put the men and women who volunteered to serve our nation in harm's way when our interest and values demand it. I assume full responsibility for any harm that may come to them. But anyone contemplating any action that would endanger our troops should know this: America protects its own. Anyone—anyone— who takes on our troops will suffer the consequences. We will fight fire with fire, and then some.

After so much bloodshed and loss, after so many outrageous acts of inhuman brutality, it will take an extraordinary effort of will for the people of Bosnia to pull themselves from their past and start building a future of peace. But with our leadership and the commitment of our allies the people of Bosnia can have the chance to decide their future in peace. They have a chance to remind the world that just a few short years ago the mosques and churches of Sarajevo were a shining symbol of multi-ethnic tolerance, that Bosnia once found unity in its diversity. Indeed, the cemetery in the center of the city was just a few short years ago the magnificent stadium which hosted the Olympics, our universal symbol of peace and harmony. Bosnia can be that kind of place again. We must not turn our backs on Bosnia now.

Source: "Address to the Nation on Implementation of the Peace Agreement in Bosnia-Herzegovina, November 17, 1995," *Weekly Compilation of Presidential Documents* 31, no. 47 (November 27, 1995), pp. 2060–64.

SLAVENKA DRAKULIC: APPREHENSIONS ABOUT THE DAYTON PEACE

Slavenka Drakulic is a Croatian journalist and fiction writer who is well known in the West. Several of her books, among them *How We Survived Communism and Even Laughed* (1992) and *The Balkan Express* (1993), have been translated into English. *The Balkan Express,* a collection of personal essay–short stories—some of which the author wrote in English—was subtitled *Fragments from the Other Side of the War.* She has been a regular contributor to the *New Republic,* the *Nation,* and other Western journals.

As the war raged in Yugoslavia, Drakulic contemplated and wrote about the human dimension of the conflict. For her, the psychological effect of the war, the impact on the inner self, was an insidious and unexpected development. It crept almost imperceptibly into one's being, transforming one's thinking and one's identity. Everything, even if one was not actually involved in the fighting, was defined by the war. Everything was measured in "before the war" and "during the war" time-frames. Everyone, even Drakulic, a Croat who was once married to a Serb and who has a Croat-Serb or Serb-Croat daughter, was grouped into national categories. (Drakulic's *Balkan Express* is dedicated to her multiethnic daughter.) Everyone was touched by death, not only those who died, but also those who did the killing. For among the murderers, most were not psychopaths, and for them having to kill or rape might have been psychologically even worse than being the victim.

Slavenka Drakulic also was appalled by the psychology of the West toward her country as it disintegrated into war. The West's portrayal of the war as an ethnic conflict told the Yugoslavs: "You are not Europeans, not even Eastern Europeans. You are Balkans, mythological, wild, dangerous Balkans. Kill yourselves, if that is your pleasure. We don't understand what is going on there, nor do we have clear political interests to protect" (*The Balkan Express,* p. 3). In the letter that follows, written days after the Dayton peace agreement was reached, Drakulic vented some of her anger toward the war's senseless suffering, death, and destruction. Drakulic, in her rage, demands punishment for those responsible, for without it, healing cannot begin.

Document 11
"NO TEARS OF JOY"

So the day has come, I think as I look at the photograph of Franjo Tudjman, Slobodan Milosevic and Alija Izetbegovic on the front pages of all the newspapers in Zagreb, Croatia's capital. The three presidents stand there and applaud.

For whom, I wonder? Themselves? The Americans, who have been twisting their arms?

One has to take only a superficial glance at the sly, sleazy smile on Milosevic's face, and the painful cramp on Tudjman's, to understand these people have been literally forced to sign the peace treaty. This is why I can't trust them.

During these past four years, whenever I would dare to think of peace, I never imagined it like this.

First of all, it was hard to imagine it at all. But if I secretly indulged in such thoughts, I believed peace was going to be something more solemn, more serious.

A kind of catharsis, a consequence of deep understanding that the war had to stop because it made absolutely no sense.

In short, I naively believed peace would not be imposed from outside but would come from inside. This would be a real chance for a lasting peace.

Now I am frustrated by the Pax Americana [American Peace], and yet am grateful to the Americans who forced it on the Balkans. Instead of shedding tears of joy, I am worried, afraid, uneasy. Since I cannot trust the people who signed the treaty, whom can I trust? Only the Americans, who will have to police this peace if it is to work.

This peace will be extremely artificial and very fragile. One wonders if even 60,000 soldiers will be enough to keep peace going. There are too many open questions to guarantee a lasting solution: Will the Croats really give up Eastern Slavonia? Can a deal be done over the Posavina corridor in northern Bosnia?

And there are already too many calculations of the type: "When the Americans withdraw, we'll interpret the conditions the way we want."

Therefore, the peace depends on the Americans keeping a firm grip.

The other reason not to trust Milosevic and Tudjman is they do not have much of a chance of remaining in power for long if there is a real peace. Last month's election in Croatia shows Tudjman is losing the trust of some voters. Milosevic will regain some power by the sanctions on Serbia being lifted and the normality that will follow, but for how long? If peace has come to stay, they both have hard times ahead.

As for Izetbegovic, he said it best himself: "This is perhaps an unjust peace, but it is better than war." These are words of a desperate man, a loser. Half of Bosnia-Herzegovina's population are refugees, and 200,000 have been killed.

These numbers are precisely what makes me angry. Anger is the strongest feeling I have at this moment. Not joy, not happiness, not even satisfaction—but an overwhelming rage.

I guess that, while the war went on, nobody had time to ask: Why? The question sinks in now, at the chance of peace. Why all the immense suffering? Why Sarajevo? Why Mostar? Why the horrors of Srebrenica? To have ethnically cleansed territories and then to applaud each other? The price for that has been too high; too many have died a useless death.

The worst fear I have, though, is that all of this will soon be forgotten. For this not to happen, to remember what this war was all about, someone should hang first. And I really mean it.

Then, perhaps, I would be convinced that the long and painful process of reconciliation has finally begun.

Source: Slavenka Drakulic, "Instead of Tears of Joy, Croatian Writer Expresses Fear and Worry about Peace," *Columbus Dispatch,* November 29, 1995, p. 11A.

THE NEED FOR A KOSOVO LIBERATION ARMY

In Tito's Yugoslav federation Kosovo (Kosova, in Albanian) was an autonomous province located inside the Serbian republic. Serbs regarded Kosovo as Serbian because it was historically associated with an era of political and cultural greatness in the 1300s. By the 1980s, however, Albanians, who made up 90 percent of Kosovo's population, were demanding greater autonomy on the basis of ethnic and human rights. Beginning in 1981, one year after Tito's death, Kosovars came under what has been described as Serbian apartheid rule. Serbs ultimately revoked Kosovo's autonomy. During the war in Bosnia, Kosovo remained remarkably quiet, undisturbed by fighting. This was due partly to Ibrahim Rugova, head of Kosovo's shadow government, who was a pacifist. The Kosovo Albanians, however, expected to be rewarded for their good behavior. This was not to happen.

In the document below, Hashim Thaci (Thaqi, in Albanian) explains why the Kosovars turned to a more militant approach after 1996. Thaci, who headed the Kosovo Liberation Army after the mid-90s, initially had strong backing from the Kosovar diaspora. By 1997 Rugova's supporters at home began to back Thaci and the KLA. (See biographical sketch of Thaci.)

Document 12
"KOSOVA"

The Kosova Albanians were subjected to Serb violence for a long time, always treated as second-class citizens and always living under the efficient control of the Serb police. Although the issue of Kosova had been addressed in the international arena for years, mainly because of human rights violations, there was no change or improvement in either human rights or any other issue in Kosova's overall situation. Human rights and civil rights were constantly being violated. However, it was not merely an issue of a strict government violating the human rights and freedoms of its citizens; rather, the core problem was the repressing of the political will of a people—the will to freedom and independence. It was the primary rights that were violated in order to repress the collective being of the Albanian people.

Unfortunately, the Dayton Peace Agreement's exclusion of the Kosova issue from its agenda, and its recognition of the FRY (Federal Republics of Yugoslavia, i.e., Serbia and Montenegro), gave a clear signal to the people of Kosova that peaceful policies are not the way to achieve political objectives in this part of the Balkans. Politics should achieve these goals as an "art of the possible." . . . The primary task of politics is the elimination of violence so that bloody conflicts are replaced with other means, a milder way of war, so politics is war, but at the same time it is limiting war through force." These were some of the reasons for the creation of a new force [the KLA or Kosovo Liberation Army], which would choose a less political means for the realization of its aims, but would again use politics to meet its objectives.

Since the creation of the KLA in 1992, its political and command structures embraced the modern theory of international relations: that strength is not only in military force but also in other political, diplomatic, and economic means . . . The KLA's coming onto the scene began to raise the hopes of Albanians for liberation from the Serb occupying forces. Since its creation, the KLA has been pro-Western, especially pro-American. It has been aware that the people of Kosova belong to that world, and that Western support would be of vital importance for the war effort and for victory.

The KLA needed a political platform but not a political wing. So that is how we proceeded. The platform for a free and independent Kosova was supported with no party or ideological colorings. The only objective of the KLA was the withdrawal of Serb occupying forces from Kosova and the achievement of freedom and equality for all its citizens. After a long and difficult war, and with the help of our international allies and NATO, we achieved this objective.

Source: Hashim Thaqi, "Kosovo," in William Joseph Buckley, ed., *Kosovo: Contending Voices on Balkan Interventions* (Cambridge, UK: William B. Eerdmans Publishing Company, 2000), pp. 189–90.

A KOSOVAR SPEAKS OUT
ON BEHALF OF THE SERBS

The selection below was published by Veton Surroi, the publisher of *Koha Ditore,* Kosovo's largest and best-known Albanian language newspaper. Surroi, the son of a former Yugoslav diplomat who died in a mysterious automobile accident in Spain, was educated in schools in Bolivia and Mexico City. A political independent, he has been critical of both the major Kosovar parties. In the aftermath of the Dayton Accords, when the Kosovo Liberation Army began its guerrilla activity against Serb authority in Kosovo, Surroi became a mediator between the activist and pacifist (Rugova) factions. He continued that role at the Rambouillet conference in France in February 1999, just before NATO's war against Serbia started. Surroi returned to Kosovo in time for the war's beginning, and remained in hiding in Pristina, Kosovo's capital, while the bombs fell. He felt it was morally required of him, as one of the signers of Rambouillet, to be with his people during the war.

After the Serbs' defeat by NATO, many Serbs fled Kosovo. Life for those who remained was often marked by the kind of pressures and fears that Albanians had experienced from their Serb oppressors. Surroi, regarded by many admirers in the West as the voice of reason in a chaotic part of Europe, wrote eloquently about why the Albanians must not persecute Serbs in Kosovo. The editor of *Koha Ditore,* who was publicly denounced at home for writing the article reproduced below, continued to urge tolerance among his conationals. In 2000 he traveled to Washington, D.C., to receive a National Endowment for Democracy award. He continued to promote the introduction of a constitution for Kosovo in hopes that tolerance and the creation of a civil society would ensue.

Document 13
"VICTIMS OF THE VICTIMS"

An old woman killed after being beaten in her bathroom; a two-year-old child wounded when her mother was killed by a bullet; two young people killed in a mortar attack; a woman who dares not speak her name for fear that those who attempted to rape her will come back to her door. These things happened to Serbs during the past couple of weeks.

There are the silent residents also, locked up in their homes scared to death by an atmosphere in which every sound seems threatening and every vehicle that stops might carry people with enough hatred inside them to put an end to their lives. The old couple, left to starve because they fear going to the market, unable to speak Albanian, while their Albanian neighbors cannot give them food since they have been warned not to feed Serbs.

I know how these Serbs feel because I, along with nearly two million other Albanians, was in the same situation. Not to mention the Roma, who are persecuted here on an openly racist basis.

I know these sounds: every vehicle that stopped at our doorstep carried potential risk, every sound was a threat of death that was certain to come, and little or nothing could be expected from my Serb neighbors in the way of help. I heard from the Serbian media how the regime gave its forces the automatic right to kill whoever they pleased, including women and children.

I am ashamed to hear, for the first time in Kosovan history, that Kosovo's Albanians themselves are capable of such monstrous acts. I cannot stop myself from stating my concern that our moral code, according to which women, children, and the elderly should be left unharmed, has been violated. I know everyone can automatically excuse this by the fact that we have just been through a barbaric war, where Serbs were responsible for the most barbaric crimes, and that the intensity of the violence has left much desire for vengeance in a large part of the Albanian population. This, however, is not an excuse.

We saw how those Serbs who had cooperated with the regime fled, how those who had participated in the violence against Albanians left. We saw how Serbs who feared the emotional revenge of returning Albanian refugees—who were to discover family members in mass graves—also fled.

Now, two months after NATO troops arrived, we are dealing with more than just an emotional reaction. We are dealing with a most vicious, organized system of violence against Serbs. And we are also dealing with a conviction that lurks behind such violence, that every Serb should be condemned for what happened in Kosovo.

This system, based on such a conviction, is called fascism. It is exactly the same conviction-based system that the people of Kosovo stood up against in their ten-year struggle with Slobodan Milosevic. It was this system that led to the inevitable creation of the Kosovo Liberation Army, to show that the Kosovo Albanians were prepared to fight with guns in their hands.

Today's Serb victims, their lives measured out in collective danger and fear, represent not just the shame of a minority. The shame must be shared collectively, we are all responsible, all those who filled so many television screens with scenes of our own pain. The shame must also be shared by the victims, the hundreds of women, children, and elderly who were massacred simply for being Albanian.

The Europeans and Americans will not blame us for not maintaining a multiethnic Kosovo. Kosovo was a multiethnic Slovenia—no one mentions a multiethnic Slovenia now. But they will point their fingers at the Albanians and accuse the victims of the greatest persecution at the end of the century for turning to persecute others in Kosovo, for allowing fascism to be repeated.

They will be right. And those who think these actions will end once the last Serbs have left Kosovo will be wrong. It will be the Albanians' turn once more, only this time at the hands of other Albanians. We fought for this?

Source: Veton Surroi, "Victims of the Victims," *New York Review of Books,* October 7, 1999, p. 21.

Glossary of Selected Terms

CDU (Croatian Democratic Union): the nationalist Croatian party, led by Franjo Tudjman, that was founded in 1990 and came to power in spring of that year. Outside Croatia, the CDU took hold in southwestern Hercegovina, where Croat ultranationalists were very strong.

Chetniks: Serb royalists, led by General Draza Mihailovic during World War II, who fought to restore the exiled Serb Karadjordjevic ruler. The Chetniks ultimately fought against Tito and the Partisans, collaborating eventually with Italy and Germany. In the 1990s the term *Chetnik* was used to designate ultra-Serbs who promoted the Greater Serbia program.

Communist/socialist: terms used to describe the character of the regime in the "second" Yugoslavia (1945–1992). Those who came to power during World War II declared themselves communists, followers of the mid-nineteenth-century philosopher Karl Marx. But when the Yugoslav communists developed an ideology of their own, after the 1948 break with the USSR, the communists' mother country, they began using the term "socialist" more regularly. The official explanation was that Yugoslavia was building socialism as a stepping-stone to communism. In reality, the terms *communist* and *socialist* were often used interchangeably by ordinary Yugoslavs and even by party members, who had long since forgotten, or had hardly known, the ideological or political reasons for using one term or the other.

Contact Group: an ad hoc association of major powers established in spring 1994 after both the Vance-Owen and Owen-Stoltenberg peace plans had been rejected. The group consisted of France, Germany, Great Britain, Russia, and the United States; their representatives operated outside the framework of existing international organizations (EU, NATO, OSCE, and UN) to work for a settlement for the former Yugoslavia.

CPY (Communist Party of Yugoslavia): a federal party in the former Yugoslavia that after 1952 was formally known as the League of Communists of Yugoslavia (LCY).

CSCE/OSCE (Conference on Security and Cooperation in Europe/Organization for Security and Cooperation in Europe): acronyms for the association of European states established at the time of the Helsinki Accords (1975). The CSCE, unwieldy in size because nearly all European states were members, attempted unsuccessfully to deal with the Yugoslav crisis. The CSCE's 50 states became the OSCE in 1995.

Dayton Accords: the peace agreement drawn up in Dayton, Ohio, in November 1995 that ended the three-and-a-half-year war in Bosnia-Hercegovina. It confirmed Bosnia's sovereignty and unity, yet provided for a two-part state: a Muslim-Croat federation with 51 percent of the territory and a Serbian Republic with 49 percent. The accords' various provisions dealt with, among other things, Bosnia's governmental structure, future elections, postwar reconstruction, and the disarming of warring armies. The peace agreement was signed by Izetbegovic, Milosevic, and Tudjman in Paris on December 14, 1995.

DOS (Democratic Opposition of Serbia): an 18-party coalition that joined forces in summer 2000 in opposition to Slobodan Milosevic's bid for a third term as Yugoslavia's president. Among the leaders of DOS were Zoran Djindjic and Vojislav Kostunica, who ran as the opposition's presidential candidate. He defeated Milosevic in the first round of voting in late September 2000.

EC/EU (European Community/European Union): acronyms for the 12 European states that united in 1992, concluding a long-planned European economic merger. After 1992 the EC (European Community) association, which has since expanded to 15 states, has been known as the European Union (EU). It is scheduled to take in 10 additional members, many of them from the former Soviet bloc, in May 2004. One former Yugoslav state, Slovenia, is one of the 10.

Ethnic cleansing: a Serbian war aim implemented first in eastern Croatia in the summer of 1991 and then rigorously applied in Bosnia-Hercegovina after fighting began there in April 1992. In Bosnia the victims were primarily Bosnian Muslims who were harassed, terrorized, raped, and murdered. Some were forced into detention camps; others were driven from their homes and became refugees. The policy of genocide was probably initiated by Belgrade, and it evoked comparisons to the Holocaust against European Jews in World War II.

FRY (Federal Republic of Yugoslavia): the "third" Yugoslavia, comprised of only two republics of the former Yugoslavia—Serbia and Montenegro. It came into being on April 27, 1992. Its leaders viewed the FRY as the legal successor to the former (socialist) Yugoslavia (SFRY); "socialist," however, was dropped from the former country's official name. In February 2003, the FRY was formally dissolved. A loosely confederated state called Serbia and Montenegro replaced it.

FYROM (Former Yugoslav Republic of Macedonia): an acronym used, at the insistence of Greece, as the official name of the new independent Macedonian state (a UN member since April 1993).

Herceg-Bosna: a self-declared Croatian state, established in southwestern Bosnia-Hercegovina in July 1992. It was headed by the Bosnian Croats, who broke with the Bosnian government, with the approval, or perhaps at the urging, of Croatia's president, Franjo Tudjman.

ICC (International Criminal Court): an international court, whose establishment was supported by 120 nations at a meeting in Rome in 1998. It became operational in early 2003 and meets, like the UN war crimes tribunal, in The Hague. The United States, under the administration of George W. Bush, refuses to participate in the court, fearing that U.S. citizens may be prosecuted by it.

IFOR (Implementation Force): a NATO-headed (U.S.-led) military force established to implement the Dayton peace in Bosnia-Hercegovina and Croatia. IFOR troops replaced UNPROFOR in the area for one year, beginning in December 1995. SFOR (Stabilization Force), a down-sized NATO force, replaced IFOR at the end of 1996.

JNA (Yugoslav National Army): the army of the former Yugoslavia (Socialist Federal Republic of Yugoslavia/SFRY), which came under Serb control in late 1991 and early 1992. Although the acronym JNA is taken from the Serbo-Croatian language, it is generally used in English-language publications.

KLA (Kosovo Liberation Army): a guerrilla army, organized by Kosovo Albanians in 1993. The organization was strong among Albanians abroad and little known inside Kosovo until 1997–1998 when it stepped-up guerrilla activity against Serb authority in Kosovo. The head of the KLA was Hashim Thaci.

Kosovo: an autonomous province within the Serbian republic that was in turn a component of the federal republic of the former Yugoslavia. Kosovo lost its autonomy to Serbia in 1989. It regained a measure of autonomy in summer 1999, after NATO's 78-day war against Yugoslavia. Although it still remains a part of Serbia, Kosovo's status is now governed by UN Resolution 1244. Its population is 90 percent Albanian.

Krajina: a rugged region that stretches from the Adriatic Sea in the west to the Hungarian border in the east, located approximately where the southern boundary of Croatia meets the northern borders of Bosnia-Hercegovina and of Serbia. Originally, the Krajina ("the frontier") constituted the divide between the Habsburg and Ottoman empires. The warrior frontiersmen who occupied these lands (Vojna Krajina, or military frontier) were engaged in past centuries by Vienna to fight the Turks.

LCY (League of Communists of Yugoslavia). *See* **CPY**

LDK (Democratic League of Kosovo): the leading Kosovo Albanian party, established in 1991. Its leader was Ibrahim Rugova, a literature professor, who advocated a pacifist policy toward the Serbs.

NATO (North Atlantic Treaty Organization): the association that acted as a Western military counterbalance to the Eastern, communist, and Moscow-dominated Warsaw Pact during the Cold War in Europe, beginning in 1948–1949. The Warsaw Pact collapsed with the fall of communism in eastern Europe in 1989. NATO's only military engagements occurred in 1994 and 1999, in Bosnia and Kosovo, respectively. Since the fall of communism, NATO has been redefining itself and expanding eastward. In 1999 the Czech Republic, Hungary, and Poland, former Warsaw Pact countries, became members. In late 2002, seven more states were invited to join, among them Slovenia.

No-fly zone: a provision of an EC and UN Security Council resolution adopted in October 1992. Intended to control the war in the former Yugoslavia, the resolution had little effect until spring 1994, when NATO bombs were used to enforce it.

OSCE. *See* **CSCE/OSCE**

Otpor (Resistance): a Serbian student movement, whose members participated in opposition to the Milosevic regime in Serbia in 2000. Boasting 70,000 members, the organization held concerts, operated a Web site, and distributed propaganda to gain support for the movement.

Pale (pronounced pa-lay): the capital of the self-declared Serbian Republic of Bosnia-Hercegovina, located some 16 kilometers from Sarajevo, the Bosnian republic's capital city.

Partisans: World War II fighters who supported Tito, the Moscow-trained communist, against the foreign occupiers of Yugoslavia (chiefly Italians and Germans). The Partisans also fought against the Ustasha (Croats) and the Chetniks (Serbs).

Rotating presidency: a feature of the executive branch of the government of the former Yugoslavia. The 1974 Yugoslav constitution established an eight-person executive, with one representative from each of the country's six republics and two autonomous provinces. In a preset order, the head—or president—of the presidency would change annually, on May 15, allowing each republic or province to preside over that body once each eight years. A crisis in the rotation process in 1991 precipitated the collapse of federal Yugoslavia.

SAR (Serbian Autonomous Region): a self-declared autonomous political entity that appeared as the former Yugoslavia started to disintegrate. Serbs in Croatia (March 1991) and Serbs in Bosnia-Hercegovina (September 1991) established SARs (one in Croatia, several in Bosnia) and worked with the Republic of Serbia to achieve Serbian national unification (irrespective of republic boundaries).

SDP (Serbian Democratic Party): a party made up of former Serbian communists who renamed themselves in 1991. Headed by Slobodan Milosevic, it extended its organization to Serbs outside the Serbian republic—for example, to Bosnia, Croatia, and Montenegro.

SFOR (Stabilization Force). *See* **IFOR**

SFRY (Socialist Federal Republic of Yugoslavia): the official name of post–World War II Yugoslavia, until its disintegration in 1992.

UNHCR (United Nations High Commission for Refugees): a standing UN body that assumed the job of processing refugees (nearly 2 million) from the war in the former Yugoslavia. The monumental assignment was directed by Sadako Ogata.

UNMIK (United Nations Mission in Kosovo): an interim force, organized in June 1999 after the NATO war with Yugoslavia, to oversee the establishment of order in Kosovo. Headed by Bernard Kouchner and governed by UN Resolution 1244.

UNPROFOR (United Nations Protection Force): a UN force established in January 1992 to monitor the truce between Croatia and Yugoslavia. Headquarters for UNPROFOR were set up in Sarajevo in spring of that year, and after war began in Bosnia-Hercegovina, UNPROFOR troops (referred to alternately as blue helmets or blue berets) also took on the task of dealing with refugees and dispensing humanitarian aid there as well. UNPROFOR had no authority to use military force.

Ustasha: Croat rightists, led by Ante Pavelic, who linked up with fascist Italy and Nazi Germany during World War II, partly in order to achieve Croatian independence. The Ustasha fought against Tito's Partisans and perpetrated racist policies against Serbs and Jews. In the 1990s the term *Ustasha* was resurrected and used by propagandists as a name for Croat nationalists.

Vojvodina: an autonomous province within the Serbian republic, which was in turn within the former Yugoslavia. Vojvodina lost its autonomy to Serbia in 1989. Its population, only 44 percent Serb (and 20 percent Hungarian), was ethnically very mixed.

Yugoslav: simply means "southern (*yugo*) Slav." In reality, it has meant various things since the early nineteenth century, when national identities began to take shape in Europe. For linguists, the term included all peoples who spoke south Slavic languages: Bulgarians, Croats, Macedonians, Serbs, and Slovenes. For politicians, the term has evolved historically. The Bulgarians were excluded even before World War I; since 1991, when the "second" Yugoslavia fell apart, the remaining southern Slavs—with the exception of the Serbs—have officially rejected (political) Yugoslavism.

Annotated Bibliography

Andreas, Peter. "Criminalized Conflict: The Clandestine Political Economy of War and Peace in the Balkans." *East European Studies,* Meeting Report 261. Washington, DC: Woodrow Wilson International Center for Scholars, October 30, 2002. A fascinating report on the origins, development, and persistence of smuggling and underground activity that characterizes the economic life of the former Yugoslavia, particularly Bosnia.

Banac, Ivo. *The National Question in Yugoslavia: Origins, History, Politics.* Ithaca, NY: Cornell University Press, 1984. A definitive scholarly work on the development of national cultures and national politics of the various south Slavic peoples, focusing especially on the two and one-half years from the creation of the Yugoslav kingdom to the introduction of the constitution of 1921.

Benderley, Jill, and Evan Kraft, eds. *Independent Slovenia: Origins, Movements, Prospects.* New York: St. Martin's Press, 1994. Eleven articles, mostly written by Slovenes. Some cover historical and economic background, while others take up topics that had a direct impact on Slovenia's democratization and independence movement in the 1980s. Particularly interesting are sections on social movements, on the politics of punk, on women and Slovene independence, and on strikes and trade unions.

Bennett, Christopher. *Yugoslavia's Bloody Collapse: Causes, Course, and Consequences.* New York: New York University Press, 1995. A well-written, highly readable account of the causes and events of Yugoslavia's disintegration. Blames Milosevic and Great Serbism for Yugoslavia's "bloody collapse." An excellent introduction for beginners and experts alike.

Bose, Sumantra. *Bosnia after Dayton: Nationalist Partition and International Intervention.* New York: Oxford University Press, 2002. Looks at post-Dayton Bosnia as a testing ground for post–Cold War interventions while international security systems redefined themselves as agents of democracy and nation building. Rejects both multinational integration and ethnic separation in favor of constitutional and electoral changes that have proven successful in Bengal (between Indians and Pakistanis). Contains an excellent, engagingly written chapter on the city of Mostar, as a case study of ethnic and political intransigence.

Boyle, Francis A., comp. *The Bosnian People Charge Genocide.* Proceedings at the International Court of Justice Concerning *Bosnia v. Serbia* on the Prevention and Punishment of the Crime of Genocide. Amherst, MA: Aletheia Press, 1996. A fascinating book about the legal proceedings (charging genocide) in the case of Bosnia and *Herzegovina v. Yugoslavia* (Serbia and Montenegro) heard at The Hague in 1993. Compiled by Francis A. Boyle, professor of international law at the University of Illinois, who represented the Bosnians and who maintains that international politics subverted the work of the International Court of Justice.

Bringa, Tone. *Being Muslim the Bosnian Way.* Princeton, NJ: Princeton University Press, 1995. An excellent work by a Norwegian anthropologist who lived for more than a year in a Bosnian village. Describes Bosnian village life, its "Muslim customs," the role of women in Muslim village society, the effects of modernization, and how what might be called "folk Islam" conflicts with city-based Muslim authority.

Burg, Steven L., and Paul S. Shoup. *The War in Bosnia-Herzegovina: Ethnic Conflict and International Intervention.* Armonk, NY, and London: M. E. Sharpe, 1999. Two prominent political scientists thoroughly and objectively detail the political and international aspects of the Bosnian war, using dozens of illustrative maps and assessing the dilemmas of intervention.

Carnegie Endowment for International Peace. *Unfinished Peace: Report of the International Commission on the Balkans.* Washington, DC: Carnegie Endowment for International Peace, 1996. The findings of a Carnegie Institute commission that did on-site investigations between September 1995 and April 1996 of the overall situation in the Balkans. Fifty-seven concluding recommendations generally urge major-power commitment in assuring economic and political stability in the region. An excellent chapter on the international response to the war in Bosnia includes a severe indictment of the major powers.

Chandler, David. *Bosnia: Faking Democracy after Dayton.* London and Sterling, VA: Pluto Press, 1999. Offers a provocative thesis that international organizations are "imposing" democratic standards on the Bosnians rather than allowing Bosnians to develop democracy themselves. Suggests also that democracy in Bosnia is less important to the international powers than is the "democratic process," which has given the international community meaning and purpose in post–Cold War Europe.

Cigar, Norman. *Genocide in Bosnia: The Policy of Ethnic Cleansing.* College Station, TX: Texas A and M University Press, 1995. An account of ethnic cleansing in the Bosnian war that describes the genocide against the Muslims, particularly by Serbs, as initiated and sustained by Belgrade as part of its Greater Serbia program. Criticized by some as being pro-Muslim.

———. *Vojislav Kostunica and Serbia's Future.* London: Saqi Books, 2002. An examination of the thought and actions of Vojislav Kostunica, who succeeded Slobodan Milosevic as president of Yugoslavia in October 2000. Prepared for the Institute of Conflict Analysis and Resolution at George Mason University, and based on interviews and journalistic reportage. Concludes that Kostunica is essentially a conservative nationalist who supports unifying ethnic Serbs and opposes Western meddling in Serbian affairs.

Cigar, Norman, and Paul Williams. *Indictment at The Hague: The Milosevic Regime and Crimes of the Balkan Wars.* New York and London: New York University Press, 2002. Makes the case for the indictment of Slobodan Milosevic for war crimes in Bosnia-Hercegovina and Croatia, by recounting the crimes and citing eyewitness accounts, thereby assigning "direct" and "command" responsibility for the various crimes. Two-thirds of the book contains supporting documentary material, including indictments against Ratko Mladic and Radovan Karadzic as well as Milosevic.

Clark, Wesley K. *Waging Modern War: Bosnia, Kosovo, and the Future of Combat.* New York: Public Affairs, 2001. An insider's look at Washington, D.C., politics and policy making by the U.S. general who was simultaneously commander of NATO in Europe and head of the U.S.'s European command from mid-July 1997 until mid-July 1999, when the U.S. Defense Department fired him, just six weeks after NATO's war with Kosovo. Offers fascinating insights into power struggles between the Pentagon and the State Department as they related to Bosnia and Kosovo.

Cohen, Lenard. *Broken Bonds: The Disintegration of Yugoslavia and Balkan Politics in Transition.* 3rd ed. Boulder, CO: Westview Press, 1997. A balanced and objective assessment of Yugoslavia's predissolution crisis by a political scientist who offers an excellent background analysis of the area's political life, republic by republic. Follows up with a detailed, almost day-to-day account of Yugoslavia's political disintegration.

————. *Serpent in the Bosom: The Rise and Fall of Slobodan Milosevic.* Boulder, CO: Westview Press, 2001. A study of the political career of Slobodan Milosevic, which is seen as inseparable from the authoritarian, illiberal political system and the sociocultural character of Serbian society. Nationalism, which Milosevic once called a "serpent in the bosom," is viewed as a tool used by the populist ruler to manipulate the populace.

Cohen, Roger. *Hearts Grown Brutal: Sagas of Sarajevo.* New York: Random House, 1998. A moving, poetically told story of Yugoslavia's creation in 1918 and its demise 73 years later, as viewed through the lives of several cross-ethnic Sarajevan families. The gripping narrative belies the author's (a *New York Times* journalist) love for Yugoslavia and its people and also his censure of the international community that contributed to that country's tragic end.

Crnobrnja, Mihailo. *The Yugoslav Drama.* 2nd ed. London: I. B. Tauris, 1996. A former diplomat (Yugoslav ambassador to the European Community until his resignation in 1991) and economist and a Serbian critic of Milosevic gives an insider's view of Yugoslavia's troubles. Focuses on the 1980s and the early war years.

Daalder, Ivo H., and Michael E. O'Hanlon. *Winning Ugly: NATO's War to Save Kosovo.* Washington, DC: Brookings Institution, 2000. A study by two Washington think-tank analysts of the 18-month period from early 1998 through mid-1999, when policy makers in the West were focused on Kosovo. Concludes that the cause was worthy and the efforts only partially successful, but that the strategy adopted, particularly by the United States, was seriously flawed. Contains a useful chronology of events as well as relevant agreements and resolutions.

Dizdarevic, Zlatko. *Sarajevo: A War Journal.* New York: Fromm, 1993. A chronicle covering the period from April 1992 to August 1993, by the editor of *Oslobodenje,* the Sarajevo newspaper that continued publishing throughout the war. Expresses bitterness over Western intellectuals who espoused the cause of Sarajevo while watching its demise comfortably from abroad. An introduction by Joseph Brodsky, the late Russian poet-in-exile and Nobel Prize winner.

Djilas, Aleksa. *The Contested Country: Yugoslav Unity and Communist Revolution, 1919–1953.* Cambridge, MA: Harvard University Press, 1991. An excellent study by a political scientist on communism's historical impact on Yugoslav unity, from the establishment of the Yugoslav Communist Party in 1919 through the mid-1950s, when Yugoslav theorists began asserting that Yugoslav unity had become a reality.

Doder, Dusko. *The Yugoslavs.* New York: Random House, 1978. A journalist's fascinating portrait of Tito's Yugoslavia and the Yugoslav people, drawn from interviews with party heads, intellectuals, dissidents, and ordinary citizens during a time when the country was experiencing rapid modernization and growing consumerism, although still under authoritarian rule.

Donia, Robert J., and John V. Fine. *Bosnia and Hercegovina: A Tradition Betrayed.* New York: Columbia University Press, 1994. An examination of the past and present in Bosnia-Hercegovina by two Bosnia specialists, a medievalist and a modern historian, focusing on Bosnia's rich tradition of diversity, pluralism, and toleration, and disputing the notion that Bosnia's history is characterized by tribal hatred and violence.

Filipovic, Zlata. *Zlata's Diary: A Child's Life in Sarajevo.* Translated by Christina Pribichevich-Zorić. New York: Viking Press, 1994. The everyday life and thoughts of a Sarajevo schoolgirl who began writing her journal at the age of 11, shortly before war began in her country. Compared by some with *The Diary of Anne Frank.*

Friedman, Francine. *The Bosnian Muslims: Denial of a Nation.* Boulder, CO: Westview Press, 1996. A detailed study by a political scientist of the origins and development of the Bosnian Muslims. Depicts the tense history of a people torn between a religious and secular identity. Poses theoretical questions for the social scientist about the ethnic or religious group and its relationship to the state.

Gjelten, Tom. *Sarajevo Daily: A City and Its Newspaper under Siege.* New York: HarperCollins, 1995. A reporter for National Public Radio who covered the former Yugoslavia from 1991 to 1994 tells the moving story of the Sarajevo daily newspaper *Oslobodjenje,* whose multiethnic staff of journalists continued publishing the paper underground and under siege.

Glenny, Misha. *The Fall of Yugoslavia: The Third Balkan War.* 3rd ed. New York: Penguin Books, 1996. One of the early books on the war in the former Yugoslavia, completed in 1992 when the war in Bosnia was just beginning. Written by the BBC's Central European correspondent, who focuses on the Serb-Croat war in the Krajina area and offers insight into the dealings of local warlords and their military operations. Assigns greater responsibility for the war in the former Yugoslavia to Croatia than do most others.

Gordy, Eric D. *The Culture of Power in Serbia: Nationalism and the Destruction of Alternatives.* University Park: Pennsylvania State University Press, 1999. An imaginative, intelligent look at Serbia's "nationalist authoritarian" regime in the 1990s that maintained control by making alternatives to its rule unavailable. Looks at political options, the media, music—the section on rock versus turbofolk music is particularly interesting—and sociability as it was eroded by economic and psychological pressures.

Gow, James. *Legitimacy and the Military: The Yugoslav Crisis.* New York: St. Martin's Press, 1992. A British military historian looks at the transformation of the Yugoslav National Army in the 1980s. Argues that attempts to recentralize and consolidate military authority at the expense of the territorial defense units, which were republican-based, helped focus national objectives, particularly in Slovenia.

———. *Triumph of the Lack of Will: International Diplomacy and the Yugoslav War.* New York: Columbia University Press, 1997. A British scholar of war studies looks at the ineptness of the world powers—Germany, France, the United Kingdom, the Russian Federation, and the United States—in dealing with the Yugoslav war, which resulted in the loss of respect for them and the international organizations (the United Nations, NATO, and the European Union) who acted in their names.

Gow, James, and Cathie Carmichael. *Slovenia and the Slovenes: A Small State in the New Europe.* Bloomington and Indianapolis: Indiana University Press, 2000. An excellent work with provocative themes by two scholars who examine Slovene culture, politics, economics, and society, as well as security concerns in the 1990s that related to the rest of Yugoslavia and led ultimately to Slovenia's courtship of the EU and NATO.

Gutman, Roy. *A Witness to Genocide.* New York: Macmillan, 1993. Startling reports of ethnic cleansing in Bosnia in summer 1992 written by *Newsday*'s foreign correspondent, who received a Pulitzer Prize for his reporting. Led the United Nations to condemn the detention camps, and helped open the centers to International Red Cross inspection.

Hall, Brian. *The Impossible Country: A Journey through the Last Days of Yugoslavia.* Boston: David T. Godine, 1994. An engaging narrative by a travel writer who spent May through mid-September 1991 in Yugoslavia as the war was beginning and the country was breaking apart. Hall, who was traveling in Croatia, Serbia, and Bosnia, records the feelings, opinions, and gradual individual adjustments to a siege mentality. Effectively refutes the stereotypes of hostile ethnic and religious communities by focusing on ordinary people and how they relate to the breakdown of the social order.

————. "Life and Letters: Rebecca West's War." *New Yorker* 72 (April 15, 1996): 74–83. Examines how Rebecca West's two-volume work *Black Lamb and Grey Falcon* became the chief resource for many seeking to understand the war in Yugoslavia. Suggests that the work is more about West's romanticism than about Yugoslavia, and therefore very misleading about the nature of the southern Slavs.

Halpern, Joel M., and David A. Kideckel. *Neighbors at War: Anthropological Perspectives on Yugoslav Ethnicity.* University Park: Pennsylvania State University, 2000. Offers perspectives and insights other than political to the Yugoslav story, with a focus on society, culture, values, and attitudes, generally from regional points of view. A collection of essays pondering how cultures emerge and develop, and, in some cases, how they decay and end.

Holbrooke, Richard. *To End a War.* New York: Random House, 1998. A riveting, blow-by-blow, day-by-day account of how the Dayton peace settlement of 1995 was hammered together in just three weeks, orchestrated by the author, an unorthodox, impatient, and sometimes self-serving U.S. diplomat. Holbrooke's views and relationships with key Balkan leaders are especially interesting.

Honig, Jan Wilhelm, and Norbert Both. *Srebrenica: A Record of a War Crime.* New York: Penguin Books, 1996. A devastating account of the ethnic cleansing of the "safe haven" of Srebrenica in July 1995. Holds the Dutch government and Dutch peacekeeping mission partially responsible.

Ignatieff, Michael. *Virtual War: Kosovo and Beyond.* New York: Henry Holt and Company, 2000. Offers two perspectives on the war in Kosovo: one is that of the insider, the son of a Canadian diplomat, who in the 1950s spent his formative years in Belgrade and maintained contacts with friends in Yugoslavia; the other is that of the Harvard Kennedy School professor of international studies, who, in examining the "virtual" nature of the war NATO fought in 1999 in Kosovo, focuses on the moral implications of modern warfare.

Jelavich, Charles, and Barbara Jelavich. *The Establishment of the Balkan National States, 1804–1920.* Seattle: University of Washington Press, 1977. A well-written historical survey of the creation of national states in the Balkans. Treats each of the Balkan national peoples individually and also against the international and diplomatic background of the nineteenth and early twentieth centuries.

Judah, Tim. *Kosovo: War and Revenge.* New Haven and London: Yale University Press, 2000. Written with the freshness of the eyewitness report, by a journalist for the *London Times* and the *Economist,* this Kosovo story focuses on the period 1995–2000, years that saw the Kosovo Albanians move from pacifism to militancy, causing the international community to commit to NATO bombing of Serbia. A real page-turner.

——. *The Serbs: History, Myth, and the Destruction of Yugoslavia.* New Haven and London: Yale University Press, 1997. A lively and balanced history of the Serbs that spans the centuries, written by a former correspondent of the *London Times* and the *Economist.* Puts the events of the 1990s, including ethnic cleansing, into historical context.

Kaplan, Robert D. *Balkan Ghosts: A Journey through History.* New York: St. Martin's Press, 1993. A journalist's best-selling book on the Balkan peoples, describing them as having dark, impenetrable souls that lead them to outbursts of inexplicable passion and violence. Criticized by academics for its playing to lovers of Dracula legends. About 75 pages are devoted to the Yugoslavs. Has been widely read by world leaders seeking to understand the horrors of the war in Yugoslavia of the 1990s.

Kaufman, Joyce P. *NATO and the Former Yugoslavia: Crisis, Conflict, and the Atlantic Alliance.* Lanham, Boulder, New York, and Oxford: Rowman and Littlefield, 2002. An excellent overview of how NATO in the 1990s redefined its philosophy and policies in the post–Cold War era—as a direct response to ongoing events and crises in Yugoslavia—from an organization that focused primarily on defense of its members to one that also saw as its mission monitoring peace and stability in the region.

Kent, Sarah. "Writing the Yugoslav Wars: English-Language Books on Bosnia (1992–1996) and the Challenges of Analyzing Contemporary History." *American Historical Review* 102, no. 4 (October 1997): 1085–1114. A thoughtful essay by a historian on recent works published on Bosnia and the war that destroyed the former Yugoslavia.

Kurspahic, Kemal. *As Long as Sarajevo Lives.* Translated by Colleen London. Stony Creek, CT: Pamphleteer's Press, 1997. An account of Sarajevo's wartime experience as viewed by the editor of the city's daily paper *Oslobodjenje.*

Lampe, John R. *Yugoslavia as History: Twice There Was a Country.* New York: Cambridge University Press, 1996. A look at a millennium of history and the peoples who occupied the territory that would become Yugoslavia—twice—in the twentieth century before succumbing to violent disintegration.

Maass, Peter. *Love Thy Neighbor: A Story of War.* New York: Alfred A. Knopf, 1996. A *Washington Post* journalist who spent 1992 and 1993 covering Bosnia tells the human side of the story. Treats victims with compassion and the perpetrators (especially the Serbs) with disgust. The world powers (and journalists, too) who stand back and observe while evils are being done are considered predatory. An enlightening study of the human response to a war situation.

Magas, Branka. *The Destruction of Yugoslavia: Tracking the Break-Up, 1980–92.* London: Verso, 1993. An intelligent and perceptive analysis of Yugoslavia's breakup by a Croatian journalist and historian whose sympathies are pro-Yugoslav and socialist, and who became alarmed by the various nationalistic manifestations of the 1980s.

Malcolm, Noel. *Bosnia: A Short History.* New York: New York University Press, 1994. A well-written, thoroughly researched narrative history about Bosnia's past. Concludes that Bosnia was essentially complex and unique, both politically and socially, and that it had a strong tradition of tolerance that has been obliterated by wartime misinformation. A must read.

———. *Kosovo: A Short History.* New York: New York University Press, 1998. An excellent introduction to the history of Kosovo from its beginnings through 1998, based on impressive research of archives and literature in seven or eight languages. Focuses on providing factual evidence about the mythical accounts of the Serb and Albanian past, generally to the detriment of assertions of Serbian folklore.

Mazower, Mark. *The Balkans: A Short History.* New York: Modern Library, 2000. An exciting, eloquently written, and brief interpretive work on Balkan history, beginning with the significance of the mountains to Balkan life and ending with the 1990s and a discussion of the nature of violence—a must read.

Meier, Viktor. *Yugoslavia: A History of Its Demise.* Translated from German by Sabrina P. Ramet. London and New York: Routledge, 1999. A European journalist and old-Yugoslavia-hand's well-regarded study of the country's collapse, which looks at the pivotal political developments of the 1980s through 1992 (prior to the Bosnian war), blaming Serbian nationalism and Slobodan Milosevic for the breakup while commending the Slovenes for acting rationally in response to challenges from Belgrade.

Mertus, Julie. *Kosovo: How Myths and Truths Started a War.* Berkeley, Los Angeles, and London: University of California Press, 1999. Completed before the NATO bombing of 1999 and based on interviews conducted between 1994 and 1996, examines key developments between 1981 and 1990 that contributed to the "truths" held by Albanians and Serbs about one another and how these so-called truths helped bring about war.

O'Ballance, Edgar. *Civil War in Bosnia, 1992–94.* New York: St. Martin's Press, 1995. Covers the actions of all national groups, reminding the reader that not only Serbs operated militias in Bosnia.

Owen, David. *Balkan Odyssey.* New York: Harcourt Brace, 1995. A long, detailed, and fascinating account of the negotiation process during the Bosnian war by one of the leading negotiators, who has been widely depicted as an appeaser. Provides insight into the motives of the Western powers (e.g., the Americans were moralistic but refused to send in troops); has valuable assessments of the Yugoslav leaders and their actions; and gives the reader a look at the profession of a late twentieth-century diplomat whose job requires demeaning oneself daily, its only compensation being hobnobbing and jet-setting with the world's political elite.

Pavlowitch, Stevan. *Tito: Yugoslavia's Great Dictator. A Reassessment.* Columbus: Ohio State University Press, 1992. A brief biography of Tito, placed in the context of greater European developments. Examines not only the international backdrop against which Tito came to power in Yugoslavia during World War II but also the European-wide developments of the early twentieth century that impelled the future Yugoslav leader to go abroad to find work, to fight Austria's foes, and to find a new ideology.

Poulton, Hugh. *Who Are the Macedonians?* Bloomington: Indiana University Press, 1995. A readable and balanced guide to the history of the Macedonian peoples (Bulgarian, Greek, Serbian, and Macedonian) and their relations with their neighbors. Presents a particularly complicated story in reasonable, organized, and lucid fashion.

Power, Samantha. *A Problem from Hell: America and the Age of Genocide.* New York: Basic Books, 2002. A widely read, influential book, hotly debated in government circles, on the issue of the moral responsibility of governments to intervene abroad against atrocities and genocide. The author, a journalist, was in Bosnia during the war.

Ramet, Sabrina P. *Balkan Babel: Politics, Culture, and Religion in Yugoslavia.* Boulder, CO: Westview Press, 1999. A collection of nine essays by a Yugoslavia expert, three on each of the general topics indicated in the book's title. Especially good essays on the area's churches—Catholic and Orthodox in particular—and very good sections on rock music, men and women, and the press.

———. *Nationalism and Federalism in Yugoslavia 1962–1991.* 2nd ed. Bloomington: Indiana University Press, 1992. A major study by a noted political scientist who analyzes the struggle between Yugoslavism and various antithetical nationalisms in the 30 years before socialist Yugoslavia's collapse in 1991. Depicts the challenges to Yugoslav unity, even in an earlier (1984) edition, as potentially fatal to the state's survival.

Rieff, David. *Slaughterhouse: Bosnia and the Failure of the West.* New York: Simon and Schuster, 1995. A writer who lived in Bosnia for extended periods between summer 1992 and fall 1994 (Rieff is the son of Susan

Sontag, who produced *Waiting for Godot* in Sarajevo during the siege) eloquently describes the plight of the Sarajevans: how the civilians came to understand that their fate was to be victims and how they reluctantly realized that the West, particularly the United States, whom they trusted and believed, would abandon them.

Rogel, Carole. *The Slovenes and Yugoslavism, 1890–1914.* New York: East European Monographs, 1977. Covers the national cultural and political awakenings of the Slovenes, while elaborating on Slovene development during the 25 years preceding World War I. Depicts the Slovene national consciousness as strongly committed to Yugoslav cooperation, especially in political matters, given that Slovenes felt that their small numbers precluded establishing a viable independent national state.

Rohde, David. *Endgame. The Betrayal and Fall of Srebrenica: Europe's Worst Massacre since World War II.* New York: Farrar, Straus and Giroux, 1997. A definitive, day-by-day account that exposes the hopeless task assigned to the Dutch peacekeepers of the doomed "safe haven." Written by a *Christian Science Monitor* journalist whose reporting on Srebrenica won him a Pulitzer Prize.

Rothschild, Joseph. *East Central Europe between the Two World Wars.* Seattle: University of Washington Press, 1974. An in-depth political history of the newly established independent states in eastern Europe. An 80-page chapter on Yugoslavia thoroughly covers the political intrigues and bumblings of the fledgling south Slavic kingdom during the 1920s and 1930s.

———. *Return to Diversity: A Political History of East Central Europe since World War II.* New York: Oxford University Press, 1989. An interpretive work on the states of eastern Europe that summarizes interwar and World War II developments before analyzing communist rule in the area. Titoism and Stalinism are treated in a separate chapter, while the collapse of communism in eastern Europe is discussed in terms of "revenge" of the repressed peoples who rejected communist uniformity in favor of national diversity.

Rusinow, Dennison. *The Yugoslav Experiment, 1948–1974.* Berkeley: University of California Press, 1978. A definitive scholarly study of socialist Yugoslavia's attempt at modernization. Covers the interplay between economic and political forces that affected Yugoslavia's development in the three decades following World War II. Concludes that the Yugoslavs by 1974 had produced a hybrid that was neither Western nor Eastern; it was some of each—laissez-faire socialism.

Samary, Catherine. *Yugoslavia Dismembered.* New York: Monthly Review Press, 1995. A brief, general, introductory work, translated from the French, on Yugoslavia's breakup and the ensuing war. Includes useful statistical data, maps, biographic sketches of leading figures, and a chronology of main events through mid-1994. Accepts a political scientist's approach that national identity is a *political* choice, and considers the *realpolitik* response of the international community as disastrous.

Sell, Louis. *Slobodan Milosevic and the Destruction of Yugoslavia.* Durham and London: Duke University Press, 2002. A basic introduction to the political life of Slobodan Milosevic and the events that followed from his embrace of the Serbian national cause. Written by a U.S. diplomat with a variety of experiences from his Yugoslav diplomatic assignments—Zagreb in the mid-1970s, Belgrade in the late 1980s, Sarajevo in 1995–1996 as adviser to Carl Bildt, the UN High Representative, and Kosovo in 2000 as director of the International Crisis Group (ICG).

Sells, Michael A. *The Bridge Betrayed: Religion and Genocide in Bosnia.* Berkeley: University of California Press, 1996. A historical perspective on genocide in Bosnia. The author argues that it was part of a Christian holy war.

Silber, Laura, and Allan Little. *Yugoslavia: Death of a Nation.* 2nd ed. New York: Penguin Books, 1997. The single most enlightening book on the breakup of Yugoslavia and the beginnings of the war, as told by the players themselves through interviews conducted by the authors, a *London Financial Times* journalist and a BBC reporter. Implicates the guilty—particularly Milosevic, but Tudjman as well—for the evils that befell Yugoslavia by using testimony from political enemies and allies alike. (The authors' filmed interviews, along with other news footage, are available as part of a television documentary.)

Singleton, Fred. *A Short History of the Yugoslav Peoples.* Cambridge, England: Cambridge University Press, 1985. An excellent brief historical survey of the people of Yugoslavia and of Yugoslavia as a state. Provides a concise introduction for one unfamiliar with the region.

Stokes, Gale. *The Walls Came Tumbling Down: The Collapse of Communism in Eastern Europe.* New York: Oxford University Press, 1993. Deals broadly with the fall of communism in eastern Europe. The chapter entitled "The Devil's Finger: The Disintegration of Yugoslavia" is perhaps the best single brief introduction to the internal forces and events that contributed to Yugoslavia's collapse.

Sudetic, Chuck. *Blood and Vengeance: One Family's Story of the War in Bosnia.* New York: W. W. Norton, 1998. A highly acclaimed book by a *New York Times* journalist who regularly reported on the war in Bosnia. Personalizes the conflict—that in the book culminates with the 1995 Srebrenica massacre—by viewing events through the lives of one rural family that is related to the author through marriage.

Tanner, Marcus. *Croatia: A Nation Forged in War.* New Haven and London: Yale University Press, 1997. An overview of the rise, fall, and rebirth of Croatia from medieval times to the present by a journalist from the *Independent* of London. A welcome scholarly survey, with an in-depth, well-documented account of the recent Croatian-Serbian war. The author treats the Croats sympathetically.

Thompson, Mark. *A Paper House: The Ending of Yugoslavia.* New York: Pantheon, 1992. Written before the Bosnian war overshadowed events in the former Yugoslavia. A narrative travelogue by a journalist who offers valuable impressions and insights into history and the lives of ordinary people, who lived in a fragile "paper" structure.

Vickers, Miranda. *The Albanians: A Modern History.* New York: Tauris Press, 1995. A history of the Albanians, rather than of Albania proper, which is a relatively new state and does not include Yugoslav Albanians. Covers the Albanians of Kosovo (a province of Serbia since 1945) in some depth, focusing on their role in and importance to that area.

———. *Between Serb and Albanian: A History of Kosovo.* New York: Columbia University Press, 1998. An excellent overview of the history of Kosovo from the twelfth century through the end of 1997, looking at both the Kosovo Serbs and the Kosovo Albanians and offering a balanced account of their lives, objectives, and interactions.

Woodward, Susan L. *Balkan Tragedy: Chaos and Dissolution after the Cold War.* Washington, DC: Brookings Institution, 1995. A detailed scholarly volume written by a political scientist and senior fellow of the Brookings Institute who for seven and a half months was adviser to Yasushi Akashi, special representative of the United Nations Secretary-General dealing with the former Yugoslavia. Portrays the Yugoslav conflict as a breakdown of political and civic order that might have had a different outcome had it not happened at the same time that the international order was also in transition.

Zimmermann, Warren. *Origins of a Catastrophe: Yugoslavia and Its Destroyers—America's Last Ambassador Tells What Happened and Why.* New York: Times Books, 1996. A well-written memoir by the last U.S. ambassador to Yugoslavia, who was present during Yugoslavia's disintegration. Valuable for its insider's view of key players, particularly Milosevic and Tudjman, and for its insight into post–Cold War U.S. foreign policy, which was depressingly inadequate, a point that the author acknowledges from the perspective of hindsight.

DOCUMENTARIES, FILMS, WEB SITES, AND SPECIAL MATERIALS

Documentaries

Bringing Down a Dictator. PBS, aired March 30, 2002, one hour. Narrated by Martin Sheen. Accompanying Web site: www.pbs.org/weta/dictator. Focuses on the Serbian student movement Otpor (Resistance) that was financed with U.S. money and directed by Americans convinced that civil revolt, rather than outside military action, would bring down Slobodan Milosevic.

Srebrenica: A Cry from the Grave. PBS, aired January 17, 2000, 90 minutes. A BBC production narrated by Bill Moyers. The story of Srebrenica, which had become a UN safe haven in 1993, and the massacre there of more than 7,000 Bosnian Muslim men. Particularly chilling is the footage of the Serb General Ratko Mladic, who tricked the Bosnians into surrendering their weapons and later celebrated with the UN Dutch troops who had done nothing to stop the slaughter.

We Are All Neighbors. 1994. Granda Television International, available from Films Incorporated. An award-winning documentary on Bosnian Muslim women.

Yugoslavia: The Death of a Nation. Based on the first edition of the book by the same name by Laura Silber and Allan Little. New York: TV Books/Penguin USA, 1996. Shown on the Discovery Channel in late 1995. Originally a five-hour presentation; a sixth one-hour segment was produced in mid-1996 to bring the narrative up through the end of the war and the Dayton peace conference. An excellent, highly praised, prizewinning documentary that contains revealing interviews with major actors in the war in the former Yugoslavia.

Films

No Man's Land. 2001 Golden Globe and Best Foreign Film Academy Award winner. Produced by Frederique Dumas-Zajdela, Marc Baschet, and Cedomir Kolar; written and directed by Danis Tanovic, 2001, 97 minutes. In Bosnian with English subtitles. An antiwar fable, billed as a comedy, with action confined to a trench occupied by three combatants, a Serb and two Bosnians, one of whom is lying on top of a bomb that will explode if he is moved. Emphasizes the absurdities of war through the representatives of the world who come to the trench: a German bomb expert, an ambitious journalist, and a UN official whose main concern is to protect the image of his organization. A startling and provocative ending.

Vukovar Poste Restante. Produced by Dank Muzdeka Mandzuka and Steven North; directed by Boro Draskovic; screenplay by Boro Draskovic and Maja Draskovic, 1994, 96 minutes. Serbian/Croatian with English subtitles. Distributor: Tara Releasing, 124 Belvedere, No. 5, San Rafael, CA 94901. A fictional antiwar story set in Vukovar, the city that was essentially destroyed by fighting in fall 1992. The hero, a Serb, and the heroine, a Croat, marry at the beginning of the film and are separated by war and growing ethnic prejudice. The film was criticized by the Croatian authorities for allegedly having a pro-Serbian bias.

Welcome to Sarajevo. Directed by Michael Winterbottom, based on the book *Natasha's Story* by Michael Nicholson, 1998, 102 minutes. The ugliness of civil war as seen through the eyes of journalists who sympathize with the victims but are powerless to help. With the adoption of an orphan girl, one journalist tries to make a difference. Based on a true story.

Yugoslavia, the Avoidable War. Directed by George Bogdanich. Hargrove Entertainment, 2002, 165 minutes. A controversial film sometimes characterized as pro-Serbian. Looks at the Yugoslav wars as a product of anti-Serb propaganda, partially encouraged by the U.S. administration because it was useful to have a black-and-white picture, with clearly defined enemies—that is, the Serbs.

Web sites

The following are useful electronic sources for research and up-dating the ongoing events in former Yugoslavia.

www.iwpr.net (Institute for War Reporting). Click on "Balkans," then specific area.

www.crisisweb.org (International Crisis Group). Click on "Balkans," then specific successor state.

www.un.org.icty (UN/International War Crimes Tribunal/Yugoslavia site).

www.titoville.com. An informative and sometimes amusing Web site for Tito aficionados. Contains bibliography, speeches, photographs, songs, and so on. A piece of Tito nostalgia.

Special Materials

Balkan Battlegrounds: A Military History of the Yugoslav Conflict, 1990–1995. Washington, DC: Central Intelligence Agency, 2002. Sales information: www.access.gpo.gov/su_docs. Volume 1 covers the history of the battles; volume 2 contains military maps.

Haviv, Ron. *Blood and Honey: A Balkan War Journal.* New York: TV Books/ Umbridge Editions, 2001. A powerful photographic collection that documents the human drama of the wars in Yugoslavia, described by one reviewer as "a pictorial guide to hell."

Yugoslav Civil Wars 1991–1999. Printed Material, Transcripts and Ephemera from the British Library Collection. New York: Norman Ross Publishing, 2002. A microfilm collection containing material about the wars, the NATO bombing of Yugoslavia, war crimes, and so on. Among the sources are printed brochures, pamphlets, maps, posters, reports from international organizations, eyewitness accounts, and personal testimonies.

Index

About the Author

CAROLE ROGEL is Associate Professor Emeritus of History at Ohio State University. She is coauthor of *Historical Dictionary of Slovenia* (1996) and author of *The Slovenes and Yugoslavism 1890–1914* (1977), as well as many articles on Slovene cultural and political Yugoslavism. Since her retirement, she has lectured and written extensively on recent developments in the former Yugoslavia.